FIJI
A Place Called Home

FIJI
A Place Called Home

Daryl Tarte

PRESS

Published by ANU Press
The Australian National University
Canberra ACT 0200, Australia
Email: anupress@anu.edu.au
This title is also available online at http://press.anu.edu.au

National Library of Australia Cataloguing-in-Publication entry

Author:	Tarte, Daryl, author.
Title:	Fiji : A Place Called Home / Daryl Tarte.
ISBN:	9781925022049 (paperback) 9781925022056 (ebook)
Subjects:	Tarte, Daryl.
	Fijian Australians--Biography.
	Fiji--Politics and government--History.
	Fiji--Social life and customs.
Dewey Number:	996.11

All rights reserved. No part of this publication may be reproduced, stored in a retrieval system or transmitted in any form or by any means, electronic, mechanical, photocopying or otherwise, without the prior permission of the publisher.

Cover design and layout by ANU Press

Cover photo: Wyndham Resort, Denarau Island, Fiji. Courtesy of Wyndham Resort, Denarau, and Meralyn Tarte.

This edition © 2014 ANU Press

Contents

Epigraph..vii
Dedication...ix
Preface..xi
Introduction..xiii
    Stewart Firth
Prologue: The Early Days.........................xvii

Part One: Taveuni: The Colonial Period

1. People Along the Road........................3
2. The Old Home....................................17
3. The Plantation...................................23
4. The Young Overseer...........................35
5. Island Life..43
6. Marriage..55
7. An Array of Characters......................65
8. Sale of the Plantation........................73
9. Farewell Taveuni...............................79

Part Two: Greater Fiji: Life In The Nation

10. Sugar...85
11. Tourism...103
12. Commerce and Industry...................111
Interlude: A Fijian Delicacy—Balolo........121
13. Diplomacy.....................................125
14. Politics and Leadership...................131
Interlude: A Conversation of Spirits........141
15. Sports..147
Interlude: China Rose...........................153
16. Clubs...157

Interlude: Rotary—Service Above Self 163
17. Religion 165
Interlude: The Veli—Fiji's Hairy Myth 171
18. The Underprivileged 177
19. Media: The Voice of the People 183
20. Rumblings of Discontent 187
Interlude: Reflections on Coups 195
21. Women: The Real Mother Lode 199
22. Islands 205
23. In Search of a Soul 217
24. Conclusion 219

'Each blade of grass has its spot on earth whence it draws its life, its strength; and so is man rooted to the land from which he draws his faith together with his life.'

Joseph Conrad, *Lord Jim*.

This book is dedicated to my family.

Preface

When we glance at a map of the world, Fiji is but a few dots in the vast Pacific Ocean. In world terms, it is very insignificant. Yet, it is considered by many to be uniquely different from other places.

My family has lived here for six generations, so I call it home.

But throughout my eight decades of life I have constantly asked myself, what makes it so special? Over the years I have regularly put pen to paper, or in modern terms, fingers to the keyboard, and tried to explain this uniqueness.

This book contains many of my observations of the profound changes that have taken place in our islands over the past 80 years and profiles some of the diverse people who give this nation its unique character.

When I use the term Fijian I am referring to the indigenous people of Fiji.

Daryl Tarte

Introduction

Stewart Firth

This book is by a European Fijian. Europeans have always been a tiny minority in Fiji: 2.1% of the population in 1881, 2% in 1936, 1.4% in 1966, and fewer since independence in 1970. Yet Europeans were central players in Fiji from the time they came in the 19th century, and they dominated the country during the colonial period, from 1874 until 1970. Europeans had advantages of technological know-how, political organisation, and military might that guaranteed their supremacy in societies that were encountering the rest of the world for the first time. Fiji was one of those societies and, in a process mirrored across the Pacific Islands, it became a British colony. Before that, European settlers had come to Fiji, especially in the 1860s, when the American Civil War disrupted cotton cultivation. As the price of cotton soared, hundreds of Europeans from the Australasian colonies headed for Fiji to make their fortunes as planters. One of them was James Valentine Tarte, the great-grandfather of the author of this book, and the founder of a family who have lived in Fiji ever since and who call Fiji home.

The modern history of Fiji is well known, but its basic outlines bear repeating. In order to give their colony an economic foundation, the British encouraged investment by the Colonial Sugar Refining Company of Sydney (CSR), which arrived in 1880 and became Fiji's leading plantation company, with estates concentrated in western Viti Levu and Vanua Levu. For labour to work on the plantations, the British turned to their vast possessions in India, bringing more than 60,000 Indians to Fiji between 1879 and 1916, and ushering in a fateful change in the demography of the colony. A mere 14% of the population in 1901, the Indians were a majority by 1946, fuelling fears among the indigenous Fijians that, unless they continued to enjoy the protection of the British, they would lose control of their own country. The British, initially concerned that the Fijians might die out, protected and preserved Fijian society by a separate system of administration that kept many Fijians living traditional lives in villages rather than becoming part of a modern workforce. The Indians, meanwhile, rose in colonial society, establishing small businesses, entering the professions, and bringing their skills to the civil service. As historian Brij V. Lal has pointed out, the circumstances of Fiji's divided colonial society led to the assertion of different and competing principles by different groups. While the Fijians called for the paramountcy of Fijian interests and the Indians called for parity, the

Europeans, who were at the apex of business and government, enjoyed and defended a position of privilege.[1] The sympathies of the Europeans, meanwhile, lay principally with the Fijians.

This, then, was the society into which Daryl Tarte was born in 1934. His family were by then substantial plantation owners on the island of Taveuni, producing copra from the 'dead straight' rows of coconut trees on their estates. They were neighbours to an extraordinary collection of planters whose idiosyncrasies and foibles he describes, and to a small group of other Europeans who worked for the government. In the manner of the time, Europeans stuck together, ostracising any among them who married Fijians, and taking their superiority for granted. Colonial society was founded upon hierarchy, something that suited Fijian preconceptions and favoured the British. As Tarte writes, whenever the Governor visited Taveuni, 'he came ashore at Somosomo and was carried on a litter by Fijian bearers. He was always dressed in his white uniform with an abundance of gold braid and plumed hat and was received with great pomp and ceremony by the Fijians.'

The country of Tarte's childhood and youth, however, was not the country of his adult years. By 1968 he was living in Suva as Secretary of the Fiji Sugar Board, and for the next three decades he was intimately involved in the sugar industry, which was not only a major source of exports but the foundation on which a whole social system of Indian settlement was built. Much of the country's politics, too, revolved around sugar and the competing claims of landowners, growers and mills. Tarte focuses on the people of the sugar industry, their achievements, peculiarities and personalities, from Swami Rudrananda, 'the saffron–robed Hindu monk, who for 50 years had been the vocal champion of cane farmers', to Lord Denning, who sided with those farmers against CSR in his arbitration of 1969.

The British were under no illusions about the chequered political prospects of an independent Fiji, given the depth of the divide between the Fijian and Indian communities. They were constantly reminded of what might happen by appeals from the people of Fiji. On the Indian side, in 1965 the political leader A. D. Patel called for 'complete independence in the not too distant future,' saying that 'without political freedom no country can be economically, socially or spiritually free.' On the Fijian side, the Great Council of Chiefs reminded the British: 'We find ourselves to be a minority people in our own land. The form of government which is being demanded by certain elements in Fiji and overseas, in the name of 'democracy', would result in our being placed under the political control of immigrant races. It was not for this that we ceded our land to your

---

1 Brij V. Lal (ed), *Fiji: British Documents on the End of Empire*, Series B, Volume 10, London, 2006, p. xl.

illustrious forebear.'[2] The Indian leaders wanted independence; the Fijian leaders wanted to preserve constitutional links between Fiji and the United Kingdom, or at the very least their own paramountcy in an independent Fiji. The Indians welcomed democracy; the Fijians feared it. In the end, the British departed on terms they hoped might secure the dominance of the Fijians, in particular of the country's first prime minister, Ratu Kamisese Mara. For Tarte, 'Independence Day on the 10th October 1970 was one of the most moving' of his life.

Mara came to bestride the politics of Fiji like a colossus. Except for a break in 1987, he was prime minister of Fiji from 1970 to 1992, and president from 1993 to 2000. Tarte is an admirer of Mara, and of the three other chiefs who led Fiji into independence: Ratu Edward Cakobau, Ratu George Cakobau and Ratu Penaia Ganilau. Their passing in the decades that followed (Mara was the last to die, in 2004) coincided with Fiji's descent into unprecedented instability, as one coup followed another, the Fiji Military Forces became the dominant political force, and tens of thousands of Fiji's best people departed its shores to seek a more secure life elsewhere.

Tarte's account of more recent, more troubled times in Fiji is a reminder that people's long-held fears for the country were, to an extent, borne out. Fiji's coups have been terrible events. Tarte describes his dismay and anger seeing the flames rising above Suva during the riots that accompanied the 2000 coup, engineered by George Speight and 'a dangerous bunch of heavily armed ignorant thugs.' He finds himself disquieted by the coup six years later, and he rightly identifies 'the migration of talented people from Fiji' as the most serious consequence of its coups.

Yet his account of life in Fiji since the 1980s also reveals that the very worst fears held for Fiji—of widespread communal violence and the wholesale destruction of society—have not been realised. Fiji's coups have been Fijian in character: forceful, sometimes chaotic, but in the end restrained. By comparison with coups in other parts of the world, they have been models of moderation. As Fiji has alternated between coups and elections, Fiji's governments have been often ineffective or repressive, but never disastrous. Looking ahead and seeking an ethos that will bind the people of his country together, Tarte calls for the values of *vakaturaga* to be the ones that guide all the people of Fiji of whatever race or belief, the values of respect, humility, kindness, tolerance and understanding.

---

2 ibid., pp. 241, 352.

Prologue: The Early Days

The Tartes had deep roots in England. Apparently the family had been part of the Huguenot's escape from France in the 16th and 17th centuries. They had first settled in southern England before spreading to London and Birmingham. It is recorded that John Tarte became Lord Mayor of London in 1614 and that Edward Tarte became Vicar of St Mary's in 1782.

My great-grandfather, James Valentine Tarte, became apprenticed to an electrical engineer but had a very adventurous spirit, so when he heard of the rich gold finds in Victoria, Australia, he decided to try his luck. It seems that he was a rather wild character, as on the trip to Australia, he found himself in trouble with the ship's Captain on a number of occasions and was put 'in irons'.

In a diary that he compiled later in life he tells of his experiences in the gold mining town of Ballarat. When gold mining failed to yield the expected results, he set up a store to supply the miners with their needs. This was so successful that he moved into trading in gold claims and made himself a small fortune.

He then met up with Adam Lindsay Gordon, who was later to become one of Australia's best known poets. At that time Gordon was into horse racing and James became a jockey. Steeplechasing was his specialty and also his downfall. On one occasion after a fall, his horse stamped on his face as it was getting up and destroyed one of his eyes. It took him a long time to recover, and during this recovery period he began to hear about land sales that had started in the Fiji Islands.

Despite the scary tales about fearsome Fijians and cannibalism, my great-grandfather decided to venture forth again. The first port of call was Suva and he claimed to have been on 'the first steamer to anchor in the harbor.' He recorded in his diary: 'We went ashore to find a few native huts and soon a crowd of natives appeared. We started to land a horse. When it was up in the air on a hoist the Fijians couldn't make out what it was. But when the horse was landed in the water, and stood up and shook itself, they took off and started to climb coconut trees.'

He tells how the next day they sailed on to Levuka which was then the capital. 'A quaint little town with two hotels.' The word in Levuka was that the best land in Fiji was on the island of Taveuni. So that is where he headed, acquiring 300 acres of choice land at a place that he called 'Woodlands'. Cotton was the popular crop of the day. After constructing a Robinson Crusoe-type house, he and the labour he was able to recruit began hacking down the thick bush. 'The weather was really against us. For 16 days it never stopped raining—heavy rain. We had to sleep on the ground and I often got up during the night to wring out my clothes.'

He eventually got established, harvested his cotton crops, bought more land from settlers who found the going too tough, and decided to bring to Fiji the lady he intended to marry. Clarissa, the lady of his choice, who was from Melbourne, would have had little idea of the primitive conditions in Fiji. James met her at the Levuka Hotel and their wedding was recorded by the British Consul as the first white wedding in Fiji. Many years later, my mother would describe her as 'very beautiful in a rather regal way—with the long tapering fingers of a pianist.' She said Clarissa liked to sing to my sister and I when we were small, and she would often rub my head and comment: 'It's such an unusual head that he will have an interesting life.' Indeed I have.

When they reached Taveuni, Clarissa was carried on a stretcher the three miles from the coast to her new home in Woodlands. Soon after her arrival, she experienced her first hurricane. According to James, 'she almost died of fright.' But it was the hurricane of 1874 that destroyed their fragile home and motivated James to buy land on the coast and build a house that no hurricane could destroy. The stone walls of this house were a metre thick and the house stands to this day, 150 years on.

It was in this house that their first child was born. James tells the story:

> Cara was having her first birth pains. It was a moonlit night and I saw figures moving around the house in a rather threatening way. I got out my revolver and went out to challenge them. I saw that their leader was a man I had punished the previous day. He came and stood before me and told me I had shamed him before his people and he was going to kill me and burn my house down. I pointed my revolver at him and told him that my wife was about to give birth and that if he would try to do anything I would shoot him. There was a tense standoff for a while so I suggested that he and his men should go and sit under a tree till dawn while I attended to my wife, then I would come out and talk to them. My son was born shortly after that and when it was daylight I carried him outside and presented him to the Fijians. Here is your new Turaga (chief) I told them. For a while they just stared at the tiny child, then they turned and walked away.

He tells another story of how he was supervising the same gang of workers as they were clearing land. When he had to return to his home, he took out his glass eye, placed it on the fork of a tree and told the men that he was leaving, but his eye would watch them and make sure they kept working.

Sugarcane and coconuts were the next crops James planted. He built a sugar mill on the estate and by the turn of the century he had a flourishing enterprise of over 7,000 acres. There were 3,000 head of cattle, as well as horses, mules and donkeys. The estate was divided into many paddocks separated by 30 miles of six-foot-high stone walls, and there were tram lines over most of the estate.

He died while on a holiday in Australia in 1919, and his body was embalmed and brought back to Taveuni. As it was being lowered into the grave, a rope broke and the coffin fell. The Fijians in attendance muttered that this boded ill for the family. I think they were wrong.

Part One

Taveuni: The Colonial Period

1. People Along the Road

When I was born in 1934, Fiji was a firmly controlled outpost of the British Empire, having been ceded to the Crown by the Chiefs of Fiji in 1874. The Governor sat at the top of the hierarchical pile. These were colonial civil servants who had served their time throughout the Empire and worked their way up the rigidly stratified structure. Despite his absolute power within Fiji, the Governor had to refer all matters to London for final decision. He ruled the islands through the Legislative and Executive Councils, the former being made up of official heads of government departments and a minority of elected members representing the three major races. It was a rather farcical arrangement, as the majority was able to pass whatever legislation they chose. The Executive Council, consisting of the Governor, a few heads of departments, and appointed European members, functioned as a cabinet.

The society was divided by race. Europeans were the small, privileged minority who had little interaction with people of other races and enjoyed privileges denied to others. For example, Europeans could drink alcohol without restriction whereas Fijian and Indian people had to obtain permits. Europeans jealously protected their elite position. Fijians grew increasingly concerned as Indians sought greater political power, and Indians looked upon Fijians as a group crippled by their customary obligations.

Here was a classic example of the British policy of divide and rule. Living as I was on the rather remote island of Taveuni, I was quite unaware of the complex issues of race and government.

For the first six years of my life I had only a vague concept of what existed outside Taveuni. My world was a lush and peaceful island 30 miles long and eight miles wide. Dad said it had the second highest mountain and was the Garden Isle of Fiji, and my sister, Jeanine, and I believed him. But as a small boy I had no concept of the meaning of Fiji except that the island was an integral part of, in fact was the most important part of the colony, whatever that meant.

My mother spoke constantly of a place called Australia, for that was where she came from, and I had to believe that it was also a beautiful place, for she spoke of it with such nostalgia and affection. That's where her mother and father and the rest of her family lived. From her description, I imagined it to be a place covered with gum trees, just as our plantation was covered with coconut trees. It was also apparently the home of real koala bears and millions of sheep. Strangely enough, Dad seemed to detest Australia. Although he had gone to one of its best public schools, Geelong Grammar, where he had been the cricket captain and apparently successful, his father had later made him stay on and work as a jackaroo on a sheep station. He hated it so much that he ran away and scrounged enough money for passage back to Fiji. He refused to read any Australian magazines that Mother received from time to time and complained bitterly when she tuned into the Radio Australia news on our wireless at nine o'clock every evening.

I was about five when I began to hear a lot about a man called Hitler. I assumed that he was an absolute monster, as news about his activity caused Mother to weep with worry about Australia being drawn into another world war. I had no conception of a war except that it apparently resulted in a great deal of death and destruction.

Dad looked upon the impending war from a somewhat different perspective. He said it would mean a greater demand for coconut oil for use in making glycerine. I understood this had something to do with the manufacture of ammunition. As our livelihood depended on the making of copra, from which coconut oil was produced, his view seemed to make sense. After all, I did not see how a war could come to Taveuni. What is more, Mother always complained about our poverty, which I couldn't understand as it seemed that we lived so much better than others on Taveuni. If we made more money because of the war, that sounded OK with me.

My world was filled with a curious collection of people about whom my parents had clear perceptions. Most of them lived on their plantations on the fertile western coast. These plantations were linked by a government road, which was administered by a Road Board on which Dad served as a member. It sounded important, but strangely enough, despite his membership on the board, Dad never ceased to complain about the dreadful state of the road. It seemed quite all right to me, as it was a lot better than our rough plantation roads. It was in fact a one-vehicle-wide track that meandered along the coast and, where this was too precipitous, up into the hills and mountains. It forded countless creeks, which periodically flooded, making passage across—what we were told were Irish crossings—quite impossible. But this flooding of the creeks only made our journey up the coast more exciting.

Dad always said the secret to maintaining the road in good order was to keep the drains open. The Road Board employed four Punjabis at the south end to do this work. These were bearded, turbaned, ageless men, always terribly polite and hard working. They lived in a small house near our plantation and departed for work at dawn each day and often walked four to six miles before starting their daily task of chipping away at the gravel road with their hoes. They filled in potholes and opened the drains until dusk when they wearily returned to their humble abode. They made wonderful potato curries and rotis, and sometimes, as a treat, Dad would pay them to make a curry for us.

It appeared to me that the Europeans had a pre-eminent position on the island. The Punjabis were quaint and different. The Fijians were looked upon as nothing but 'lazy buggers' who would never aspire to anything. The Indians were mere 'coolies' with no status, and the half-castes were looked upon as a rather pathetic group, only slightly better than the 'lazy buggers.' We of course never mixed socially with anyone but the Europeans.

At the extreme south end of the road was Vatu Wiri, where my great Uncle Rood and his wife Aunty Edie and my three cousins Adrian, Spencer, and Talei lived. I was terrified of Uncle Rood who boasted that he was born Rude, christened Rude, and had been Rude ever since. While his face had a roughness about it, he had deceptively kindly eyes. He was always drinking whisky and gin and yelling at people or abusing his labour. Dad told us awesome stories about how he used to whip the labour. Although they were our closest relatives, Dad and Mother didn't seem to enjoy going to visit them and they seldom came to our house. They lived in a spooky old place with dark interior rooms filled with old paintings and furniture. It was the house built by my great grandfather in the 19th century and I always sensed his ghostly presence.

Aunty Edie was a wispy old lady with long grey hair that was plaited and tied at the top of her head. She was thin and put on lots of airs and graces. Dad and Mother said that this was to cover up for Uncle Rood's brashness and the fact that she was only a clerk's daughter. She always laughed at Uncle Rood's excesses and loved to tell risqué stories. We were told that Uncle Rood was a great gambler and spent vast sums of money on poker and horse racing. He always seemed to be winning and bought all Aunty Edie's jewellery from his gains and sent her and Talei on a world tour. I didn't see much of the two boys, Adrian and Spencer. They went away to boarding school in New Zealand when the war broke out in 1940 and Europeans were advised by the government to send their wives and children to New Zealand. Dad and Mother resisted this advice.

Next to our house was a Morris Hedstrom store. Morris Hedstrom was the largest trading company in Fiji and one could buy absolutely anything from a cotton reel to a sack of flour at their branch. It was managed by a kindly old gentleman named Ernie Walker. We were told that he had been a Sergeant in the Black Watch and I understood this to be some kind of select group of soldiers with close links to the King of England. I remember when I was small and ran around with no shirt he would grab me and tweak my navel and say, 'I'll cut it off and sew on a button.' I was never quite sure whether he meant it. Ernie Walker lived on his own, but we were told he had a son who later won a scholarship and went away to be educated. (In fact, in later years he was to become Fiji's most senior civil servant, Minister of Finance, and Fiji's Ambassador to Japan.) We got on well together, but for some strange reason my parents seldom entertained him. I got the impression that he was regarded as a storekeeper, while we were planters, and his Black Watch connections didn't really alter the proper social order of things.

One night, very late, our telephone started ringing and Dad and Mother began talking in hushed tones. Dad went out in his car and I went back to sleep. I was told next day that poor Ernie Walker had gone up to the old Ura house, which was a spooky place that had fallen into complete disrepair, put a rifle into his mouth and blown his brains out. It seemed like a stupid thing to do, and I was never told why. However, I did hear people talking about money problems and drink and women. I felt sad about Mr Walker.

The next house north from ours belonged to my Uncle Herbert. He was another mystery man. I knew he was my father's full brother, but he was strange and we saw little of him. I later found out that he had disgraced himself and the family by falling in love with the daughter of one of our Indian copra cutters. Apparently that was about as low as you could go. Dad banished him from the plantation and later bought out his inheritance. He left the island and even changed his name. But he married the Indian woman and had a son and some lovely daughters who I met when I was much older.

While we were told that the Tarte plantations were the largest and best kept on Taveuni, there was also the Couborough Estates. These were three properties, totalling more than 20,000 acres, which had been carved out of the virgin bush by a Scotsman named A. A. Couborough. His son, who had inherited them, had gone back to England and later died, and the plantations were managed by his trustees. Old Couborough was reputed to have accumulated a vast fortune, which, as a true Scotsman, he never spent. According to Fijian 'talk,' he buried it in a cave near the old home on the Ura Estate. In fact, when Dad was much older, he spent a small fortune trying to find the loot. Dad was an inveterate and quite successful prospector, who discovered and sold a gold mine, a cooper mine, and a manganese mine. For about six months he used a gang of ten Fijians to dig up all the rocky ground around the Couborough house, but he never found a thing.

One of the Couborough Estates was Salia Levu, a property of 12,000 acres directly across the island from our plantation. It was managed by a jovial man named George Crabbe. His wife, Myrtle, was a scarlet-faced person who seemed to spend most of her days drinking gin and her nights drinking whisky. This was the only estate on the eastern side of the island and my parents used to say it was the wettest place on earth. It was apparently drenched in 250 inches of rain annually, and was known to have had 360 inches in one year: one inch for every day of the year. The only way to get to Salia Levu was by horseback along a track that wound through our plantation, then through thick bush and along the steaming hot plantation roads of Salia Levu. For us kids, it was always an exciting ride, and we would be rewarded when we got to Salia Levu with a feast of fresh prawns and crayfish from the abundant reefs. Being on the eastern side of the island, Salia Levu always felt the full force of the south-east trade winds and huge seas crashed onto the rugged coastline. It was a wild and exciting place.

Back on the western side, the next property to ours was a small one with a palatial home owned by the redoubtable Godfrey Garrick. I seldom saw him, and had a mental image of a giant-sized Father Christmas. My parents always spoke of him with great respect, for he was a lawyer and spent most of his time looking after his legal practice in Suva. Nabono was simply his country estate home. The name was derived from a Fijian term 'Na Bogi Ono' which meant six nights. We were told that the great Lauan chief Ma'afu, who came to conquer Taveuni, stayed there with his fleet for six nights before going up the coast to wage war on the Tui Cakau, the paramount chief of Taveuni.

Next to Nabono was Ura, another of the Couborough Estates. Managers seem to come and go, but I best remembered Willie Peterson. Alhough Willie was a half-caste, (the term used in those days for mixed-race people), he was for some reason considered to be a cut above the others. He giggled a lot, but was always most polite and respectful. He always addressed Europeans as Mr or Mrs, and they always called him Willie. His wife Mary was a dark-skinned half-caste, but everybody loved Mary. She was so gentle and affectionate with children, and had about six of her own.

From Ura, there was a long drive up through the heavily-wooded hills. Dad drove this section of the road with great care, blowing his horn constantly as he crawled around the tight corners. I remember one day as we were driving up the coast, as the trip to the centre was called, in his blue Chev (he would never own anything but a Chevrolet), we had an accident. As we went around a bend we collided with another car. Both of us were doing only about 15 miles per hour and I don't think the accident was anyone's fault. But the poor Indian taxi driver, whose name was Ram Autar, never had a chance. Dad exploded in rage and almost throttled the speechless and terrified Ram Autar who readily confessed that he was speeding and didn't blow his horn and that his brakes had failed. Dad made him pay for the cost of damage to his car, and I think it broke the poor fellow, for I never saw him driving his car on the road again.

After the bushland we came to the Douglas Plantations. There were many Douglasses and countless stories about them. The patriarch of the clan was Charlie, a dumpy man with a huge belly and short thin legs. He never stopped talking and, Dad said, told the most outrageous lies. His sons Reggie and Eddie were my father's age and the same shape as their father. A visit to the Douglas house was chaotic, as all the men and women tried to talk at the same time and tell different versions of the same story or incident. Their voices became louder and louder as they each sought to dominate. We kids used to sit wide-eyed and speechless, looking from one to the other as the stories unfolded.

One of Charlie's brothers, whose name was Toysy, (which seemed a strange name), was a real playboy and had apparently sired a number of illegitimate children by Fijian women. When he was drowned in the sea off our house after his boat capsized, my parents said it was just retribution for his multitude of sins.

There was also a sister who suffered from some mental disorder. We all thought she was rather pathetic and felt sorry for her. One day we were astounded to hear our parents say that she had eloped with a Fijian and was living in a cave. Later she was quietly removed to New Zealand and we never saw her again.

Adjacent to the Douglasses lived the Harness family, who, I think, my parents regarded as the only other normal family on the island. Mick and Ella were happy and friendly people. A relative owned the plantation that Mick managed and we all expected that when that relative died, Mick and Ella would inherit the place they had lived all their lives. When the old girl did pass on and left it to someone else, we were all mortified as the Harness family departed from Taveuni forever.

Mick was a tall, rugged individual who seemed to work hard. He loved his whisky and drank prodigiously at parties. When he was full he would sing and dance with great merriment. He drove an old Ford lorry and when it was time to go home, he would bundle the family onto the truck and somehow steer it along the perilously narrow roads. Ella never growled at him and I don't think they every came to grief. His son Bobby was my best friend, and his pretty, curly-haired sister Evelyn was regarded as my girlfriend and possible future spouse.

Next to the Harness family was the third Couborough Estate, Soqulu. It was managed by Wal Warden. Mr Warden was a veteran of the First World War and apparently had a piece of shrapnel embedded in his back to prove it. He and his wife Dorothy were everybody's friends. They even treated their labour as friends, and not many people approved of this attitude. He had the easiest of jobs, Dad said, because he was paid a salary and didn't have to worry about anything. Indeed, that seemed to be the case, as he never appeared to do any real work.

One of the delicacies of Taveuni was the wood pigeon, which thrived in the mountains above the coconut tree line. They fluttered about in the trees and when they rested, about 40 feet up, you could shoot them with .22 rifles. Mr Warden always seemed to be out shooting and he often boasted of bringing in

50 at a time, many of which he gave away to friends. Mother and Dad sometimes went out shooting with them, until one day when Mother was reloading her rifle and accidentally shot Mrs Warden in the foot. That was the last time she ever held a rifle.

Wal Warden's other passions were his vegetable garden and raising poultry and eggs. He made a weekly visit to Waiyevo to see the District Officer and present a gift of pigeons, vegetables, homemade butter, or eggs. As the District Officer was always a temporary resident, he had to buy all these essentials, so the gifts from Wal Warden were much appreciated. When, some years later, he was awarded an MBE (Member of the Most Excellent Order of the British Empire) by the King, the locals said it was for giving Meat, Butter, and Eggs to the District Officer.

Wal Warden was also an inveterate snoop and gossip. The main form of communication on the island was the telephone. A single, eight-gauge, wire telephone line ran from Waiyevo to the south, and another one to the north, and the exchange to link the two was at Waiyevo. The number for each of the plantation houses was a Morse code letter. Ours was one long ring and three short rings. Of course, no conversation was private as anyone could pick up their receiver and listen to what other people were saying whenever they heard a ring. This was apparently how Wal Warden picked up all his gossip. The line was a fragile connection, as it was strung from coconut tree to coconut tree, and whenever we had a hurricane and trees were blown down, the telephone went out of action. It was also used to communicate government messages to the planters. On such occasions, the code—three longs, three shorts, and three longs—was rung by the exchange and everyone was expected to pick up their receiver. This was called a 'press ring' and when everybody indicated to the exchange operator that they were ready and listening, the message was given out.

Wal Warden was a great sporting enthusiast and was particularly knowledgeable about cricket and tennis. When the cricket test matches between Australia and England were on, he remained glued to the radio and as soon as there was anything to report he would ring people on the telephone. However, he said that he never participated in games because the shrapnel was so close to his spine that if it moved he could become paralysed. I don't think my parents really believed this story and felt that he only spoke about it to give himself a kind of heroic glamour.

Next to the Wardens lived Jack Taylor. Jack was a wiry man with piercing black eyes and bushy eyebrows. He wore long khaki trousers and was never seen without his dirty felt hat. He was gruff and unfriendly and had a swarm of half-caste sons. His wife was a Fijian lady who, we were told, had once nursed him when he became seriously ill, and he married her in appreciation of the care she gave him. He was largely ostracised by the Europeans on the island for marrying a Fijian and consequently did not mix socially. I don't think this situation worried him as he was an independent minded fellow and didn't care a damn about Taveuni society.

The next stop along the road was the Roman Catholic mission at Wairiki. There were a number of Catholic Fathers, who we often saw, and a number of nuns who we seldom saw. My parents joked about a tunnel that reputedly ran between the Fathers' residences on one side of the compound and the nuns' quarters on the other. They made snide remarks about illicit meetings and indecent goings on, but to us, the nuns who we did see all looked too sterile to do any of the things that my parents hinted at. The nuns taught at a large school while the Fathers saved souls.

One of the Fathers, I remember was a bearded Frenchman, Father Cockereau. He was known to us, however, as Father Cockroach and we believed that this was his real name. He was greatly admired by Dad for his engineering skills. He diverted a stream through the mission compound, constructed a pelton wheel from odd bits and pieces, and generated enough electricity from the water to light up all the houses. He even installed lights on poles within the compound.

This was something quite new for Taveuni, and one night as Mick Harness was driving his family home from a party soon after they had been installed, Bob woke up at the precise moment they passed the Wairiki Mission and seeing the lights on the poles exclaimed, 'Look Mum, stars on sticks.' It was a phrase that we remembered for a long time.

There was another such phrase that we used constantly. Whenever we were driving home at night from a party up north, Jeanine and I would go to sleep in the back seat and sometimes wake up and ask, 'Where are we?' Invariably, Dad or Mother would reply, 'Just passing a coconut tree.' Considering the hundreds and thousands of trees on the island it wasn't much indication of our position, but we laughed about it.

Close by the mission was another small Morris Hedstrom store, run by a curious little man known simply as George. I never found out if he had another name, but to distinguish him from other Georges he was called George Wairiki, as he lived at Wairiki. He was effusively obliging and always laughing. Our parents only called in to buy goods that they could not get elsewhere, and when they did he always gave us sweets.

The hour long drive along the 15-mile south-end road terminated at Waiyevo, the government station and hub of the island. Located on high land overlooking the beautiful Somosomo Straits were the hospital, the doctor's residence, the wireless operator, the District Officer, who was also the District Commissioner, the jail, the courthouse, the post office, the road foreman's house, the Public Works Department Depot, the rest house, and the tennis club.

The resident doctor was always an Englishman, Scotsman, or Irishman on a two to three year term with the colonial service. Doctor McCawley was a doctor I remember well, for I think he once saved my life. He was a rotund Irishman who had a son by the name of Martin. Martin was a veritable Irish terrier with a violent temper. It seems that whenever he and I met at the tennis club we ended up fighting. One day when he completely lost his temper he took to me with a cane knife. I'm sure that I would have lost my head if his equally angry father had not intervened in the nick of time.

Another doctor I remember well was Doctor Verrier. His name was actually Isaacs, but he was so afraid that Hitler would win the war and persecute the Jews in Fiji that he changed it to Verrier. He was a fat bachelor who spoke with a frightfully English accent and was, my parents said, 'a little odd.' I didn't know until much later what that insinuation meant. He was artistic and one of his creations was redirecting a small stream across the sloping lawns of his garden. At certain intervals he made little concrete waterfalls with a space behind them where he placed candles. At night he would sit on his verandah and gaze wondrously at what he termed his private fairyland.

On one occasion after a cattle muster on our plantation, I was galloping home on my pony at dusk and didn't see a temporary barbed wire fence that the stockman had strung across the road. I ran into it at a full gallop. The poor horse got dreadfully tangled in the barbed wire and had to be destroyed. I came out of it, luckily, with only a badly lacerated leg, and was rushed up to the hospital to be attended by Dr Verrier. I have a vivid memory of Dr Verrier clad in a green gown with a lamp on his forehead, peering down at me lying on his operating table. As he administered the chloroform he chortled, 'Don't worry old chap, I won't cut off your leg.'

The doctor presided over a small hospital of about 20 beds for people other than Europeans. He was assisted by a native medical practitioner who had some years of training in Suva but wasn't fully qualified. He also had three or four Fijian and Indian nurses.

Separate from this building was the cottage hospital, which was exclusively for Europeans. Here a qualified European nurse gave specialised attention to the white patients.

The other key person at the government station was the District Commissioner. This post was later downgraded to District Officer. The District Officer or Commissioner was the head of the government establishment on the island and also filled the role of Magistrate. He was always an Englishman with the Colonial service and many of the District Commissioners and District Officers who came to Taveuni had served in Africa or the Caribbean before coming to Fiji. They came in all shapes and sizes, with varying attitudes toward the locals. Some had appallingly high opinions of themselves and never managed to forget that they were the sons of English aristocracy. They came and went and many made no impact upon the island or the people. But others, like Phillip Snow, who was a District Officer when I was a boy, made a life-long commitment to Fiji. Phillip Snow's great contribution was to popularise cricket, and he later took Fiji teams out into the world. He was captain of the Fiji team for some time and wrote a book about cricket in Fiji. 40 years after serving on Taveuni, while living in retirement in England, he was still involved in arranging tours of Fiji teams to England.

Then there were eccentrics like Christopher Legge. My parents told us that while serving in Africa he had contracted blackwater fever, which sounded quite horrible. Apparently his temperature, which had gone up to 115°, was cited by the British Medical Association as the highest ever recorded temperature for a man who had survived the fever. My parents said this accounted for his strange behaviour.

While serving on the bench as the Magistrate, he would often suddenly get up and walk out of the Court without so much as an excuse me to the Prosecuting Officer or defending lawyer who may have been addressing him. After a while he might return, but on some occasions the Court Clerk would have to go and search for him. They would sometimes find him walking around admiring his garden, or swimming in his pool, or perhaps sitting down reading a book. He had simply forgotten that he was hearing a case.

He was indeed an odd chap, but the people accepted him as the King's representative and gave him appropriate respect. There were times, however, when I found him hard to understand. Once, my parents were having dinner at his home when he suddenly left the table. He came back a little later to announce that the toilet was blocked. He then looked quizzically at Dad and asked, 'Do you think Daryl may have stuffed the cat down the toilet?' I was aghast at such an idea and somewhat disappointed that Dad didn't rebuke him. But I think Dad and Mother were so busy trying to stifle their amusement that they couldn't do anything else.

Another colourful character who lived at Waiyevo was Walter Zink. Walter, who operated the Wireless Station, was a black-skinned half-caste with a rough face. His duty was to man the Morse code set and receive and despatch telegrams for Taveuni people. If people wanted to order goods urgently from Suva or send a message to a friend or a business associate in Suva or Australia, they would telephone the exchange and say, 'I want to speak to the Wireless Operator, please.' When Walter came on the line, he was told, 'I want to send a cable to Suva to John Smith. J for Jack, O for Oliver, H for Henry, N for Nancy,' and so on. Of course, everyone on the island could listen in to the message being read, so if it was private and very confidential, such as a message to the bank manager, one had to drive to Waiyevo and hand it to Walter personally.

Walter Zink was also the bandleader. He had a group of five men who played steel guitar, ukulele, mandolin, and bass drum, and they appeared at every party held on the island. His repertoire was confined to the popular songs of the day, like 'Blue Birds Over the White Cliffs of Dover,' or 'You Are My Sunshine,' or 'Look for the Silver Lining.'

The main attraction at Waiyevo was the tennis club, a one-room wooden building with high shutters all around that was only opened by members on Saturdays and Sundays. It faced onto two lawn tennis courts, which was the reason why all the Europeans gathered there, clad in white and carrying big picnic baskets. They played singles, doubles, or mixed doubles all day and ate their lunches. The ball boys were provided by the Headmaster of the Bucalevu Provincial School, which was a school for sons of Fijian Chiefs and other respected Fijian families that was just north of Waiyevo. One of these ball boys would later become Governor-General of Fiji, but in those days he was regarded as just another Fijian boy. Whenever Europeans passed along the government road in their cars these boys from the Bucalevu School would stop and salute.

After tennis we usually went to the doctor's or the District Officer's place for drinks. Quite often, after being at the club all day and after having a 'few' with the doctor or District Officer, my parents would call at the Warden's or the Harness' on their way home. They would drink whisky and have boiled eggs and toast, and play card games or have singsongs around the piano before heading home. A downpour of rain was often a signal that it was time to go, as the dozens of creeks along the way could flood and leave us stranded on the road, taking us all night to get home. It was really quite a treacherous journey, but it didn't seem to stop my father from drinking quite a lot. He always got us home safely. If we did arrive at a creek that was flooded, Dad would stop on the bank and wade out into the torrent to test its strength and depth. Only if the water was below his knees would he come back to the car and decide to venture forth. If it was too high, we would all sit in the car and sometimes go to sleep until the torrent subsided.

The road north from Waiyevo was not one that we travelled very often. It was regarded by Dad, out of jealousy I think, as being a terrible ordeal. In fact it was much flatter than our south end road as it snaked its way for 18 miles around steep headlands rather than winding up into the hills. Just north from Waiyevo was the chiefly village of Somosomo. This was where the paramount chief of Cakaudrove, the Tui Cakau, lived. Whenever the Governor visited Taveuni, he came ashore at Somosomo and was carried on a litter by Fijian bearers. He was always dressed in his white uniform with an abundance of gold braid and plumed hat and was received with great pomp and ceremony by the Fijians.

This was also where the bazaars were held to raise funds for the war effort. We were constantly being asked to raise funds to assist Britain and many of the ladies knitted jerseys and socks, which were sent off to England. Dad also made charcoal out of coconut shell. This was cooked in 44-gallon drums and was apparently used for gas masks. Considerable sums of money were raised at these bazaars. Silver coins had gone out of circulation and had been replaced by notes. There were even penny notes and we children had a great time seeing how many penny notes we could accumulate. They were about three inches long and one inch wide.

At that time the Tui Cakau was treated with some respect by the European population but, despite his high station in Fijian society, was still regarded as an inferior mortal. He had the reputation of being a lazy drunkard and was despised by the planters because his extensive plantation was neglected and overgrown with weeds and bush.

Next to the Tui Cakau lived Duncan Hedstrom, his wife Rose, and their three daughters. Duncan was apparently the black sheep of the Hedstrom family, which owned the trading, shipping, and industrial empire of Morris Hedstrom. His over-indulgence in whisky had reduced him to a frail, shaky man with a bad temper. His wife and daughters were lovely people and good friends of my mother and Jeanine.

Duncan hated any form of authority and was constantly rebelling against new laws introduced by the local authority. The head of this body was the Medical Officer and it was Dr Verrier who decided it was time for planters to replace wooden shutters with glass windows. When Duncan refused to co-operate, Dr Verrier went to see him and said that unless he complied he would close down his labour quarters. Duncan became so irate that he lashed out and hit Dr Verrier on the nose, causing it to bleed profusely. Verrier calmly dabbed his nose with a silk handkerchief and pompously exclaimed, 'Dear, dear, Mr Hedstrom, you must be a very sick man.' Whereupon Duncan hit him a second time. Dr Verrier sniffed blood into his nostrils, turned his back, and walked away.

Duncan Hedstrom's neighbour was Percy McConnell, an unsociable, mean, bad-tempered Scotsman. He lived on a hill surrounded by a forest of mango trees and one could only reach the house by climbing about 200 steps. He seldom visited anybody and very rarely entertained.

Mua was the next estate north. This was a rocky plantation with low coconut yields. To overcome this problem, the owner, Mr Bull—I always thought this was a funny name—imported a new variety of coconuts called Malay Dwarfs. They were short trees that were planted 90 to the acre, compared to 55 to the acre for the Fiji Tall trees. These trees came into bearing in five years, compared to eight years for the Fiji Talls, and the yields increased significantly. Much to everyone's annoyance, Mr Bull refused to sell any of his seed nuts to other planters.

Also living on Mua were the two strange Moresby brothers. The elder brother was a recluse and we never saw him. One day he went out bush walking and simply disappeared. Search parties were sent out and they scoured the mountains for days. It was generally thought that the older Moresby must have fallen into one of the many rocky caves and either been killed or slowly died of starvation. Logan Moresby, the younger brother, was, however, well known. He was a blacksmith by trade and could fashion anything from horseshoes to precision-made scissors and emasculators. He had his forge and piles of coal in a filthy, cluttered shed, surrounded by odd pieces of discarded metal from which he made his wares. He always wore heavy black or grey flannel clothes that were covered with coal dust or grease. He had piercing black eyes and bushy eyebrows and a huge walrus moustache that he sucked on continuously. Logan was a gruff, uncommunicative man, quite intolerant of his helpers or clients as he went about his daily work fashioning metal on his anvil.

Although he had two Fijian assistants, I could never understand why they stayed with him, for he abused them dreadfully and referred to all Fijians as 'Bloody Black Bastards.'

Just north of Mua was Naselesele, the northern most tip of Taveuni. From this point on, the road started to curve around towards the east. Naselesele was the home of the Petersons and the Ensors. They were always kind to us kids, but they were people of lower status. Their white ancestors had acquired large tracks of land, but when their descendants married Fijian ladies, they bred prolifically and the holdings were cut up into smaller uneconomical holdings. The families lived modestly and had a closer kinship with the Fijians than the Europeans.

North of Naselesele was Nagasau, the home of the McKenzies. Just as my Aunty Edie was known as the Queen of the South, so Mrs McKenzie was called the Queen of the North. That is not to say that Aunty Edie accepted that Mrs McKenzie was of equal status. We all laughed at her manner of speaking, which was coarse compared to Aunty Edie. Aunty Edie often told the story of how Mrs McKenzie was entertaining ladies for afternoon tea and saying, 'Yous that want milk can milk youselves.' Mrs McKenzie had a son, Max, who spoke just as roughly. In fact, he never stopped talking. Then there was a daughter named Viti, who we were told nearly married my father. Apparently Dad was so smitten with Viti that for some months, every Friday afternoon after he had completed his work, he would ride his horse the 35 miles from Vuna to Nagasau, where he would spend the weekend courting Viti. We never did find out why the romance was broken off, but I suspect that it was at the instigation of my snobbish grandmother. Max was a jovial chap who had one thing in common with Uncle Rood, he was an inveterate gambler on the Australian horse races. There was also a half brother, which was something I couldn't understand, named Bill McKay. He had a lovely wife named Helen and lived on the last estate on the north road. He was a kindly gentleman, but for some reason I could never understand, Dad did not like, nor trust him.

2. The Old Home

We were told that our house had been built by Methodist missionaries back in the early 1800s. Its three-foot thick walls were constructed from rock and homemade coral cement. It was built on a three-acre block with a separate title and was acquired by my grandfather. Many of the missionaries and their families were buried in an adjacent graveyard, which seemed to me to be crawling with ghosts. I never went near the place on my own. Dad put in a tennis court between the graveyard and the house, and I started wielding a racquet from an early age. The rest of the three-acre compound was divided into garden, chicken yard, and the garage area. The garden was filled with colourful shrubs and flowers, which were always kept neat and tidy, and the extensive rich green lawn was mowed by hand, weekly

The missionaries were obviously determined that the house would never be destroyed by hurricane. All around the wide verandahs, huge wooden shutters hung from the top plate, and these could be lowered part way or closed completely. Likewise, all doors could be bolted and battened. When completely closed up, the house was like a fortress, and we felt completely secure when hurricanes battered us.

As kids, we loved hurricanes. We were exhilarated by the sound of the wind howling around the house and watched in awe as it wrecked the coconut trees and other buildings. Just before a hurricane struck or as it was subsiding, Dad and Mother would allow us to go down to the point at the bottom of the garden and watch the huge seas crash on to the rocky coastline. We did not understand the financial losses that followed such 'blows,' as they were called, but it was obviously a worrying time for Dad. Immediately after a hurricane, he sent the headmen out to assess the damage and collect whatever nuts had fallen from the trees, because he knew that these would be the last ones for a long time.

We were seldom alone in the house, for there were always servants about. The cook's name was Ali Asgar. A tall, thin, quietly spoken and polite Muslim, he had twinkling eyes and a quick smile. He always wore a white shirt and long khaki trousers, but never any shoes. He spoke only Hindi. In my youth I knew him only as Ali Cigar, and I thought that was really his name. Although I was but a small boy, he always showed the respect due to me as Chota Sahib (small sahib). He never scolded me or denied me any morsel of food that I might scrounge from the kitchen. The kitchen was his domain, and he didn't do any jobs in the house except when it was his Sunday on duty, every second week when he had to do the job of both the cook and the houseboy/servant boy. Mother trained him in the culinary arts and he mastered an excellent range of dishes, which he prepared for over 30 years until he died.

There was also Mahadeo, a young lad who was brought into the house to learn the ropes. He replaced another houseboy named Rupi, who was found to have leprosy and was sent to the government leper station on the island of Makogai. It came as a bit of a shock to us when we discovered that we'd had a leper in the house, but his was an isolated case.

Ali Asgar and Mahadeo started work at daybreak. They lived up at the labour lines and walked the half-mile to the house in the morning. Their first job was to light the wood stove and serve Dad his early-morning tea. We all had breakfast together at six-thirty. Morning tea was served at nine and lunch at eleven. Afternoon tea was two o'clock, drinks at five o'clock, and dinner at six-thirty. The boys were on duty throughout this period except for one hour off at lunch. Theirs was a six-day week, but they had alternate Sundays off.

Mahadeo was a short and excitable person with a tremendous enthusiasm to learn about our ways. He waited on the table and did all the odd jobs around the house. While we ate, he pulled the punkah. This was a large fabric covered frame hanging from the ceiling over the centre of the dining table. A cord was attached to the bottom centre and Mahadeo stood outside on the verandah pulling the cord back and forth, moving the punkah like a fan and creating a gentle draft over the table as we ate.

There was also Shiu Narayan, the milkman, who always looked dirty but was an extremely polite old man who spoke no English. He had to rise in the pre-dawn hours every day of the week, herd in a dozen cows, milk them, and have fresh milk in the kitchen in time for Dad's morning tea at six am. He then separated the balance of the milk in the milk separator. The cream was stored in the icebox, and after he'd cleaned the separator and milk buckets, he went out in the garden to work for the rest of the day. We ate lots of milk, butter and cream, but the Rood Tartes frowned on this. They claimed that all the cows were so riddled with tuberculosis that they would only consume bought dairy products. None of us ever got tuberculosis.

Then there was Vula, a grossly fat but happy Fijian man who did all the washing and ironing. Monday was washday, and all the week's dirty clothes were boiled up in a huge copper and scrubbed on a wooden rack before being hung on a clothes line strung across the back lawn. Once they were dry, Vula spent the rest of the week standing before a huge ironing table on the back verandah, singing and chatting to Mahadeo or dozing as he ran the heavy charcoal iron, and later a kerosene iron, over the pile of clothes. I remember one day when he actually went to sleep on his feet, leaving the iron stationary on one of Mother's best dresses. She smelt the fabric burning and came rushing out to berate Vula. When she saw that it was one of her best dresses, she burst into tears. Vula put his fat, comforting arm around her shoulders and said, 'Don't cry, Marama, it's just a piece of cloth.' Whereupon my distraught Mother howled even more and pounded him with her fists.

One of Dad's hobbies was making guava wine and he stored the bottles under the ironing table. As the wine fermented and the pressure on the crown seals increased, the tops would often fly off with a resounding pop. Quite often this occurred when Vula was on the verge of dozing off, and it provided great merriment to us kids to watch his startled reaction.

Dad had a number of other hobbies, one of which was making jigsaw puzzles for us on his fretsaw. He worked tortoise shell and made some fine ornaments and combs. He was also quite clever on the guitar and used to sing us all kinds of songs.

During my sixth and seventh years, my mornings were taken up with correspondence school. Papers were received by Mother from Suva and the correspondence teacher spoke to us on the wireless. But the real burden fell on Mother to teach me, Jeanine and my cousin Talei, who was my age. Jeanine was two-and-a-half years older than me, and a far greater handful for Mother. She was intelligent and headstrong, and there were frequent blowups, leaving Jeanine in a rage and Mother in tears. When this happened, Talei and I would run off to play until order was restored on the front verandah where school was conducted.

When school was over I would often go fishing off the rocky point at the bottom of our garden. Beneath the surface of the calm sea was a multitude of colourful fish that could easily be enticed onto a small hook by a piece of fresh meat that I got from Ali Asgar. I would spend hours sitting on the rocks catching the colourful little reef fish, which were far too small and bony to eat. My real ambition was to catch one of the large spotted rock cod that hid in their rocky lairs. I often saw them, but never managed to pull one to the surface, for they were far too big and simply gobbled up my bait and snapped my line.

Our main physical link with the outside world was a 400-ton motor vessel named Yanawai that was owned by what my parents called BPs. This was Burns Philp, a large trading company like Morris Hedstroms. The Yanawai was an all-purpose ship. She had a forward hold that was filled with merchandise for planters, like my father, and for the branches of the trading company, which was delivered on the outward journey. When she began her return journey, the empty hold was filled with sacks of copra, which were taken back to the mill in Suva. She also had six quite comfortable two-berth cabins, a ten-berth cabin, and a dining saloon and deck space.

The Yanawai made two trips per month, taking two days to reach Taveuni from Suva, and another two days sailing up the Taveuni coast discharging cargo, and then over to Buca Bay, Rabi, and Laucala. She then turned around and began retracing her route loading copra, cattle and other cargo. The real excitement about the arrival of the ship from Suva was that she brought mail. We had our own private mailbag to which only the Post Master in Suva and Dad had keys.

On boat days, I would sit on the highest part of the roof searching the horizon for tell-tale signs of the ship. It took about two-and-a-half hours from the time I spotted the tiny speck on the horizon and called out with glee that I could see her until she dropped anchor at Uncle Rood's place. When she was nearly in, we would all pile onto the lorry and drive down to Vatu Wiri to collect the mail and other things that were in the personal care of the supercargo. We then returned home, the bag was opened and mail was sorted and read while Dad waited for the ship to complete unloading at Vatu Wiri before moving up to our wharf to discharge our empty copra sacks, drums of fuel, timber, corrugated iron, barbed wire, motor parts, and other goods necessary for the operation of the plantation.

After lunch, if Dad was going out on horseback around the plantation to inspect any work, I would often ask to go with him as I had my own pony. More often I rode with the lorry driver, Ali Mohammed, as he went out to bring in the copra from the fields to the copra dryer.

To the south of our house was a long beach where Jeanine and I often played with Fijian boys and girls. In those days there were seashells in abundance and we had a unique collection. We would build sandcastles or swim in the shallow water, but swimming was much better and safer in the rock pool at the bottom of our garden.

The nights came around all too soon, but there was often fun in the evenings. In those days toads were prolific and came out on the lawns in the thousands at dusk. Dad hated them because they got into our water supply and blocked pipes. He claimed that Aunty Edie had brought them to Taveuni as pets and that she had a great deal to answer for. We would go out with wooden clubs and copra sacks and beat the poor creatures to death, put them in bags, and toss them into the sea. We did this hundreds of times without making the slightest impact on the toad population. It wasn't until years later when they had consumed all their natural food that their numbers dwindled.

Another nocturnal creature was the flying fox, which Dad also hated. He claimed that they destroyed the young coconut flower and ate pawpaws and other fruit.

These giant bats came out at dusk and settled on fruit trees. Hanging upside down, they were easy to shoot, and the Fijians took them away to eat. Their stench was so dreadful that the thought of eating them made me sick.

In those days, the house was illuminated only by benzene lights, which Mahadeo lit as soon as it became dark. They were noisy things that attracted all kind of insects and occasionally blew up. I was scared of them and kept my distance. After dinner, Dad would read his mystery novels and Mother would knit, sew clothes, or play cards or snakes and ladders with Jeanine and me. Jeanine was a real bookworm and much preferred to read her books. We would go to bed at about seven-thirty. Dad would follow at about eight-thirty, but Mother would always stay up to listen to the nine o'clock news from Australia. Her insistence on listening to the news always irritated Dad and I am sure contributed to their eventual divorce.

I slept in a single bed in a narrow side room with my head to a window that faced the missionaries' graveyard. I hated the position of the bed and often slept with my head turned around so I could see out the window. There were always strange and sinister noises in the dark and otherwise silent night.

Once we had all gone into the bedrooms, the doors to the bedroom part of the house were bolted. I was never quite sure why, because the rest of the house was left wide open and no one ever entered or stole a thing. Nevertheless, I always checked to make sure that my own door was locked. The worst nights were often after Dad had told some of his terrifying ghost stories. He had a repertoire of unexplainable experiences that put the fear of God into me.

The old missionary house was spooky enough on its own and there were weird noises up in the ceiling. The spare room at the other end of the house was the worst, as there was a manhole into the ceiling and my worst fear was that I would be made to sleep in that room.

In my room I was surrounded by books, jigsaw puzzles, wooden building blocks, my Meccano set, and numerous other toys. I had a tricycle, which I rode a great deal. On wet days I rode it up and down the long front verandah with our parrot Cocky sitting on the handlebars. Cocky was a green Mexican parrot that we had inherited from my grandmother when she left Fiji for good in 1936. He had an amazing vocabulary, which he'd aquired over his 30 year life span by listening to my grandmother, Mother, Dad, the cooks, the houseboys, and others. He was most vocal when it rained, and this was when I rode my bicycle on the verandah with Cocky singing and chatting away merrily. One of those he mimicked best was my Mother on the telephone. He would gabble away for a while, then say, 'Yes. yes, no, you don't say, no,' and burst into hysterical laughter. For some reason he detested Mother and whenever he was out of his cage, strutting around the house, he would try to ambush her by creeping up behind her and nipping her ankles. She would scream with fright as Cocky launched his assault. Sometimes he would creep up behind her as we were sitting at the dining table. Jeanine and I could see what was about to happen and would desperately try to contain our mirth. But when he sank his sharp beak into her ankles and Mother realised that we had been party to the deception we were in real trouble. Trouble meant being belted with a scrubbing brush and locked in the bathroom for an indefinite period.

3. The Plantation

The operation of the plantation gravitated around Dad. In the 1940s, the Waimeqere Plantation was just over 3,000 acres in size: 1,500 acres were planted with coconuts, there were 300 acres of grass paddocks, and 1,200 acres at the back, bordering on the Couborough Estate of Salia Levu, were under secondary growth, mainly guava. 1,000 head of cattle grazed under the coconut trees and were fattened for the market in the grass paddocks. About 100 families lived on the plantation and were completely dependent on Dad for their income, housing, water, fuel, medicine, meat, and land on which to grow their basic crops.

Dad was the owner, manager, and accountant. He had to order all the necessities to run the plantation, understand mechanics, plumbing, carpentry, and animal husbandry. He had to attend to medical needs, solve family problems, and lend the labour money when they were in need.

It was an extremely demanding task that we took for granted because things seemed to work and day to day life went on in an orderly fashion.

Although I was always in close contact with the labour, I never had any familiarity with them and saw little of their wives and children, except those who were allowed to mix with us. The children were taught to be in fear of Dad in particular, and even me, though I was a small boy. If a labourer's child was misbehaving, the mother was likely to say, 'Look out, here comes the Turaga.' Dad was always known as the Turaga Levu or the Bhara Sahib by the Indians, while Mother was the Marama or Mem Sahib. Jeanine was Chota Mem Sahib or Marama Lailai, and I was Chota Sahib or Turaga Lailai. Our common names were never used, at least not in our presence. Even when I was a mere six or seven, I was treated with respect. It was understood that one day I would be the Bhara Sahib or the Turaga Levu and would rule over them and their children.

Most of the labour were the second or third generation born on the plantation. Some had seen Dad grow up and had taught him how to ride horses or do other practical things around the plantation. I don't think any of the labour had any wish to leave, even if there was somewhere else to go. They knew that they could depend on Dad to take care of them in a crisis. He was firm and dictatorial, but he treated them fairly. In those early days, I can't ever recall anyone being fired. If they were ever late for work or failed to carry out orders, they would be severely reprimanded or sent home and told there would be no work for them that day and no pay. They never asked for an increase in wages or other benefits. When Dad could afford to pay more—when the price of copra went up or when we had a few years of high production—he increased wages. During the depression years when we were paid virtually nothing but trade goods for copra, Dad kept all the labour in work while other planters laid off workers. Our plantation was their home and they understood we would go through the good times and bad times together.

Of course they never got rich and had few material possessions. There was no school and little entertainment. But Dad did what he could. In the late 1940s he bought the old Couborough house at Ura and used all the timber to construct neat little cottages, a movie theatre, a shop, and a café. These were the first self-contained cottages on any plantation. On the other plantations, labour lived 'in lines', which were barrack type quarters where they had one small room and a detached, and sometimes shared, kitchen. They washed their clothes at a communal tap and used a common pit latrine. We still had some 'lines' but Dad upgraded them to make the rooms much larger. He built individual kitchens and bathrooms, and clean, hygienic toilets. The toilet block was quite unique. Dad had blasted down through 20 feet of solid rock to one of the many subterranean streams that flowed out to sea, and built the toilets above this stream. The labour quarters were all within a compound, which was kept nicely mowed and planted with colourful shrubs.

When the theatre was finished, he arranged for films to be sent up from Suva and shown every Wednesday and Saturday night. The labour were allowed in free of charge, while outsiders had to pay three shillings. He also brought in a Chinese shopkeeper and installed him in the shop so the labour could buy their basic needs and enjoy Chinese food, ice cream and bread.

Each family was allowed an area of land on which to plant food crops such as dalo, cassava, yam, bele and fruit. They could use up to 20 coconuts per week and had free access to other fruit trees such as breadfruit, jack fruit, and pawpaws, which were scattered all over the plantation.

Once a week the stockman killed two head of cattle. These were slaughtered under Dad's guidance and after the choice cuts, such as the fillet, sirloin, brains, tongue, kidney and rib roast, were sent to his house, the rest was divided among the labour, free of cost. If any family had a marriage or a death or some other special occasion, they only had to request a free steer or goat. Dad seldom refused.

When anyone became sick, Dad would diagnose the problem after consulting a large medical manual and he ministered whatever medicines he had on hand. If the problem was beyond his ability to cope with, he would arrange for the person to be taken to the hospital at Waiyevo at his own expense. Sick people miraculously became better when he suggested this course of action. In those days, the hospital was called the Vale ni Mate, the House of Death. It was generally considered that the hospital was where you went to die. Boils, stomach complaints, and headaches were the most common problems, but accidents did occur on the plantation.

If a man was suspected of feigning illness he was given a large dose of Epsom salts. This threw his stomach into such turmoil that few attempted this ruse to escape work.

The labour worked five days a week, except for the vata boys—who tended the copra that was being sun-dried—who rotated on a seven-day basis. Most work was finished by three pm They could then tend their food gardens, go fishing, or sleep. It was a casual, relaxed type of life and I never detected any unhappiness. Indeed, they were quite well off because Dad charged nothing for the benefits he provided. It was a type of paternal feudalism that is now despised. But in those times Dad was looked upon as a progressive employer. In fact he was accused by other planters of giving his labour too much. Certainly they were under his complete domination and had no alternative but to accept whatever he gave them, but they were free to leave at any time. They were not bound to him in any way. Some Fijians did opt to return to their villages, and when they did, Dad helped by paying their fares home.

It could never be said that we got rich at their expense. Certainly we maintained a lifestyle that must have seemed quite grand to them. We lived in the valekau (wooden house) as the main homestead on a plantation was called. We had people to wait on us. We had comfortable beds and nice clothes. But for most of his life, Dad was indebted to the bank. He had considerable assets, but that was all. Like the labour, we lived off the land, and our beef, milk, butter, cream, eggs, poultry, and self-grown crops cost little. Mother cultivated a vegetable garden where she grew lettuce, tomatoes, cabbage, carrots, beans, cauliflower and other things. We also had turkey, which the labour were not allowed to touch. We went fishing and ate prawns and crayfish. There were pigeons in abundance in the bush. To the British colonial civil servants we appeared super rich, but we were not.

I don't recall having any sense of superiority over the labour that lived on the plantation, although I did look upon them as our labour. I sensed that they somehow belonged to us and I knew that one day I would be responsible for them. They were part of our way of life and we were at the top of the pecking order. There was never any abuse or cruelty, although unquestioned obedience was expected and given. Dad was their absolute ruler. No one, not even the headman, ever questioned his judgement or any of his orders. Indeed, he never invited comment or opinions.

While producing copra was a routine, mundane activity, cattle work was exciting. We had a mixed herd of crossbred Hereford, but Dad took great pride in the Friesian herd that he began developing in the 1940s. He imported bulls from overseas and maintained that Friesians were the best all-purpose beasts, for they gave good milk and beef, and could be trained as strong, docile working bullocks for the carts.

Although we ran about 1,000 head on the plantation, there were thousands of others running wild in the back lands. During the war years, Dad undertook to supply cattle to the United States forces stationed in Suva, and to meet this demand he devised a way of trapping the cattle in the wild.

He had gates made in the fences surrounding the grass paddocks and occasionally left them open so that the wild cattle would wander in and get a taste of the succulent grass within. After a day or so, they would be driven out again. When he made a commitment to ship cattle on the Yanawai and knew the exact day that the ship would arrive he put his plans into action.

On the day before the boat arrived, the gates would be opened so that the wild cattle could come in. A number of tame milking cows would be taken up to the grass paddocks and released among the wild cattle. Then, in the dark of night, the stockman would silently go around and close the gates. At dawn they would storm out of their hiding places and drive the unsuspecting wild cattle towards the cattle race. The milking cows would be the first to head for home and the others, seeing no alternative, followed. The 15 or 20 stockmen would crack their whips and yell and whistle, and in no time the whole herd was into the race. The stockmen kept after the cattle down the three-mile race and before they knew what was happening, they would find themselves penned in a secure yard on the beach beside the wharf. This was when the tricky work started for the stockmen.

The headman had to enter the congested yard with the untamed cattle angrily milling around and somehow loop a head rope over the horns of one of them. This head rope had a slipknot and once it was over the horns it was pulled tight. He then had to quickly tie it to the end of a long rope that ran from the beach to a whaleboat that was moored 30 yards out. Once the ropes were joined he would yell 'pull,' and four or five men on the boat would drag the beast off the beach into the water and out to the boat, where it was lashed to the side by the shortened head rope. Once ten head were secured to the whaleboat, a small tugboat towed it out to the Yanawai. Canvas belly slings were lowered by the ship's winch and passed under the animal's stomach, and it was lifted aboard and lashed on deck.

3. The Plantation

Needless to say, the cattle objected vehemently to all this handling and the stockmen were often in mortal danger and were sometimes gored. The furious cattle would often break out of the pen or slip the ropes as they were being towed out to the boat, and escape. All the labour and their wives and children came to watch this spectacle and they yelled and screamed with delight at the excitement.

When the tame domestic cattle were shipped, it wasn't nearly as much fun. But even then incidents did occur. These cattle were shipped to the butchers in Suva or sometimes to the leper island of Makogai.

Round up time was also a lot of fun, for Jeanine and I were allowed to take part. We had our own ponies, which we learnt to ride at an early age. Round up usually happened twice a year. It entailed herding all the cattle into the stockyards to be sorted, branded, and castrated. The stockmen would go out at dawn and drive the cattle from the various paddocks into the cattle race, which ran from the grass paddocks to the stockyards. As each paddock was cleared, they would move to the next, until they got to the grass paddocks where Dad, Jeanine, and I, and various others would join them at daylight. All the cattle in the grass paddocks were then driven into the race. This was never easy, as they tended to hide in the shade of a huge, twisted grove of vau or wild hibiscus that dotted the paddocks. But they finally responded to the cracking of the stock whips and the yelling and whistling of the stockmen. Once they entered the race the excitement began, for they had to be kept moving lest they turn around and break out of the race. It was a thrilling, never-to-be-forgotten experience, to be part of this movement of 600 to 1,000 head of cattle charging down the race, bellowing and raising clouds of dust with the riders in hot pursuit cracking their whips.

By nine am, the cattle would be confined in the holding yards around the stockyards. They were then driven into a narrow race just wide enough for one animal. This race had sturdy posts and was lined with stout timbers. Dad stood on the platform above and called out how each beast was to be classified as it passed beneath him. Further along the race, stockmen controlled gates which allowed the cattle to exit into selected yards.

This sorting went on all day and late into the afternoon. The cows, calves and breeding herd would then be taken to their respective paddocks, and the fats to the grass paddocks. The branding and castrating would be left until the following day. This task started early in the day, before the heat set in. The young bulls were driven into the race one at a time and jammed into a tight space so they couldn't move. Dad always did the castrating himself, while one of the stockmen did the branding. The stockmen loved all the excitement and had a great deal of fun throwing the bloody testicles at each other.

Some of the old cows that were not sent back to the bush land were used as shark bait. The sea off our house was infested with sharks, and it was unsafe to swim off the shore. Dad constructed a low concrete wall across the mouth of the small, rocky inlet, which served as our swimming pool. We would often lie in this at high tide with underwater goggles on and peer out into the depths. Quite often we saw sharks gliding by. They were bold and aggressive. Quite often when we were walking along the beach or standing on the rocky headlines of our garden, we would see their sinister black fins cutting the surface. We feared and hated them and revelled in the thought of catching them. The technique Dad used was to take an old cow down to the small rocky beach near the house. It was driven into the water and shot with a .303. The throat and stomach were cut open to release the blood and guts. These would be allowed to drift out to sea. A rope would then be tied to the legs of the carcass as it drifted off the rocky headland beside the pool. The rope was then fastened to a tree in the garden.

This would be done in the evening, just before dark when sharks were more inclined to swim in closer to shore. We would sit on the cliff above the rocks and watch the guts and the trail of blood drift away. It wouldn't be long before there would be a splash and in an instance the guts would disappear beneath the surface. 'Shark, shark,' someone would yell.

But we would have to wait until dark before the big ones came close to the rocks to feast on the dead cow. Their appearance would be signaled by a huge wake of phosphorescence and the rope going as taut as a guitar string as the shark tried to drag the carcass away. We would maintain a hushed silence, for the first predators were usually a little timid. But once they got a taste of what was available, they would come in for the kill and others would follow and begin tearing at the carcass and nothing would scare them away.

We would flash our torches over the huge bodies as they lunged out of the water and rolled across the top of the carcass. Dad would stand on the rocks with his .303 and try to get a shot at a grey nose as it came out of the water. The gun would roar and a huge body would explode in the sea. More often than not, those that were injured would be preyed upon by other sharks. It was an awesome sight to see five or six sharks, 12 to 15 feet in length, gorging themselves just ten feet away from you.

Mother clung to us, terrified that one of us would slip into the water and be devoured. But there was no fear of falling in as far as I was concerned. My feet were firmly rooted to the ground.

It was also a lot of fun to put out a shark line. An enormous steel hook baited with a chunk of meat was attached to a length of chain and a long rope was tossed off the rocks. The rope was then tied to a tree. We would sit in the dark,

3. The Plantation

silently watching the stars, waiting for the bait to be taken. The first sign would be a slight movement of the rope. It would gradually tighten and as the hook bit into the shark it would get frantic and desperately try to escape. There was no hope of pulling the shark to shore and we left it to drown itself. Only when the struggle ceased would the huge beast be pulled onto the beach. In this way bronze whalers, grey nurse, and tiger sharks up to 18 feet in length were caught. We would always open up their stomachs and find a strange assortment of undigested bits and pieces. The jaws were buried until the flesh rotted and the teeth could be extracted for ornaments. The rest of the body was discarded.

Sometimes we would go the beach at Korovou for a picnic. The government road ended at Uncle Rood's plantations and a rough plantation road meandered through his land to the Fijian village of Vuna at the extreme southern end of the island. We had to leave the car or the lorry at the village and walk a short distance to the beach, which was at the base of the beautiful Vuna Lagoon. The sand was pristine white and the sea that washed upon it was clear and free of sharks. Shady trees protected us from the sun and we laid out our mats and had our picnic. The sand was ideal for building castles and we had some lovely picnics there, until the Chinese storekeeper was murdered.

Throughout the small islands and villages in those days, trade was conducted by the Chinese. At Vuna, there was a branch of the Kwong Tiy chain and the manager was a Chinaman (that's what we called them) who spoke appalling English and only slightly better Fijian. He usually found it more effective to communicate in Fijian. Kwong Tiy bought all the copra that the Fijian villagers produced and sold them tinned goods, biscuits, tea, sugar, clothing and other incidentals in exchange. Little money changed hands, as most transactions were contra-ed against the other.

Whenever we went to the beach we called at the store to buy lemonade. The conversation would often go like this:

Q. Do you have any lemonade?

A. No.

Q. Oh, you don't have any?

A. Yes.

Q. So you do have some?

A. No.

Q. (angrily) Do you have it or not?

A. Yes. I not have it.

One day Dad got word that the store had been broken into, the safe busted, and that the Chinaman was missing. He informed the police and when they arrived from Waiyevo, he went with them to the place of the alleged crime. We were agog at the news of any crime, let alone murder, for it was unheard of on the island. With the knowledge he had acquired by the extensive reading of mystery novels, Dad concluded that it was a case of murder and the whole area was searched for the corpse. It wasn't long before the police noticed an unusually large number of crabs on a particular area of the beach, where we usually had our picnics. They became suspicious and began to dig. Sure enough, the unfortunate Chinaman's body was curled up in a shallow grave. The next day, two Fijian villagers who had begun to spend money rather foolishly were arrested, questioned, charged, and taken to Suva. They were found guilty and hanged. It was a story that Dad retold and embellished many times over the years. After that we never really enjoyed going to the Vuna beach. We did, however, often go to the lookout at the southern end of the village, a spot on a high cliff overlooking the outside edge of the Vuna Reef. Huge seas rolled in and crashed onto the reef, sending spray cascading high into the air. It was an exhilarating place where we always took visitors.

Dad looked upon the Vuna villagers somewhat differently to his own labour. His labour were his servants, whereas the villagers were independent. That is not to say that he respected them. In fact, he was critical of how they used their extensive and fertile land. They could have made a lot of money out of it, he claimed, but instead they let it go to bush and wasted their days sleeping in the village. There were, however, certain village chiefs with whom he had a good relationship. Maina, his chief stockman, was a high chief from Vuna. Then there was fat Karalo, who was nicknamed Elefante by his people, as he was as big as an elephant. There was also Lui Lala, who seemed to be a cut above other Fijians. He and his family were hard working boat builders who owned a small store. Then there was Baba, (which always struck me as an unusual name for a Fijian), whose clan often did weeding contracts for Dad. Our carpenter, Waisiki, also came from Vuna.

I think one reason Dad tried to maintain good relations with the Vuna people was that his grandfather had bought a great deal of land from them, and there was always a slight feeling of guilt at having acquired it for a few shillings an acre. There was always some fear in the back of his mind that they may try to claim it back. In fact, they made a claim to the Royal Commission conducted by Sir Alan Burns in 1959.

Uncle Rood, on the other hand, despised them so much that he wouldn't have them on his land. Not that any of them ever wanted to work for Uncle Rood.

3. The Plantation

Dad did engage Baba and others from time to time to do weeding contracts. He would negotiate with Baba, saying that a certain paddock needed to have all the lantana and guava pulled out, and the two of them would ride around the paddock, inspecting the amount of work that needed to be done and agreeing a price of say £100. Baba would then bring up a gang of 40 or 50 men who would complete the job over five or six days. Dad would ride around the paddock each day to ensure they were doing the job properly. The gang would build a temporary shelter on site and sleep there. Quite often Dad would provide rations and also kill a steer for them to eat. The money earned by the gang would be used for a communal project in the village.

Dad also brought in gangs of men from other islands such as Koro, Vanua Levu, or Lau, but this cost a lot more, as he had to charter a ship to transport the men to and fro. There were always gangs of men searching for work, but Uncle Rood usually had trouble getting any to work for him. Dad told the story of how Uncle Rood had grievously offended the redoubtable Ratu Sir Lala Sukuna, who was a high chief from Lau. Whenever the Yanawai came in, Uncle Rood would sit on his verandah, which faced down the extensive sweeping lawn to the front gate, which opened onto the beach where the passengers disembarked. In those days it was forbidden for any Fijian or Indian to set food inside the house compound and no one dared to do so.

On one occasion, Uncle Rood watched as passengers disembarked from the Yanawai launch and to his amazement he saw a Fijian come up to the front gate, open it and start walking up the lawn to the house. He screamed out in anger, 'Get out of my garden you black bastard.' Of course he didn't know until much later that it was Ratu Sukuna, who took such umbrage at the insult that he gave instructions to his people in Lau that no Fijian should work for Uncle Rood. His orders were obeyed for many years.

The BBC brought us the devastating news of the bombing of Pearl Harbour and I began to learn about a horrible little bug-eyed man called Tojo. He meant no more to me than Hitler, and Hawaii seemed just as far away as London. But when the Japanese took the Philippines and Singapore and began fighting in the Solomons and New Guinea, I began to understand that they were closer to home.

The first manifestation of this was the arrival of American troops. A large garrison was stationed in Suva and Nadi, warplanes began flying overhead, and ships of war passed by our shores. Dad and Mother became worried about what would happen. But the troops seemed to be benefiting us. Many Officers came up on the Yanawai for R&R. They often came ashore and were entertained by my parents, and on their return to Suva sent us all kinds of luxuries that were available in their canteen but unavailable to us: tinned ham, chocolates, nuts, liquor, and cartons upon cartons of Lucky Strike, Camels, and Phillip Morris cigarettes.

It was about this time that Jeanine and I started smoking. We had previously tried dried banana leaves, but these were not too good as they often burst into flames and scorched our eyebrows. When the US cigarettes arrived, it was easy to steal them without Mother knowing. Our favourite retreat was Jeanine's dollhouse. Dad had made her a perfect ten square foot miniature house with all kinds of doll's furniture. We would sit in there for ages without being disturbed, smoking to our heart's content. If some of our friends happened to join us, there was the danger of smoke billowing out, and we were caught, as we sometimes were, it was the scrubbing brush and bathroom treatment.

When the Japanese captured the Gilbert and Ellice Islands, my parents said that Fiji was next and that we would have to prepare. Dad dug a huge hole in the poultry yard and covered it with coconut logs and two feet of earth. There was one doorway leading down into this rather unpleasant burrow. It was cold, wet, and smelly, and I hoped that we would never have to hide there. Its purpose was to protect us in case of air raids. The main retreat was a hideaway up in the mountains, which would take longer to reach. It was stocked with tinned food and other basic necessities. We would only go there if the Japanese landed.

One night we were terrified to hear a battle raging on distant Koro Island. We could hear the booming of big guns and exploding bombs and could see all the fireworks in the sky, despite the fact that Koro was 40 miles away. We were certain the Japanese had arrived and the next day were relieved to get a press call that it had been the American Forces exercising in preparation for a major assault. This turned out to be the Solomons where some of the bloodiest battles of the Second World War took place.

Nonetheless, it was a long time before we felt safe. Dad maintained watchmen day and night along the coast. Their task was to sit on strategic rocky points and watch for ships or submarines. Any that were seen were immediately reported to the District Officer.

I had all kinds of images of the war. The magazines we received often contained pictorial descriptions of the brave deeds of soldiers, sailors, and airmen, who were duly decorated with Victoria Crosses, Distinguished Service Orders, Distinguished Flying Crosses, Military Crosses, and Military Medals. I developed a low opinion of Italians, as it seemed quite an easy task for a single Australian or American to single-handedly capture hundreds of them in a desert wadi. General Montgomery was my favourite hero, as he seemed invincible in desert battles as he rode his tank. The stirring words of Mr

3. The Plantation

Churchill, which I couldn't understand, always excited me, as they seemed to ring with heroism. The British airmen dressed in blue who fought in the skies over London seemed like supermen. The Germans always appeared like iron robots with absolutely no feelings. I couldn't understand how a feeble little man like Hitler could command these larger-than-life barbarians. The Japanese were clearly evil murderous swine who delighted in torture, and were led by mysterious, villainous generals and admirals. Their Kamikaze pilots baffled me, and their endless numbers scared me. The Americans all seemed to take the war so lightly that I wondered how they could possible win. They seemed to be in it for the fun.

Dad was always working and worrying about things. Ours wasn't a very happy home, for Dad seemed constantly preoccupied with his problems. While attentive to our needs in so many ways, Mother never appeared happy. Of course, at the age of six or eight, I had no knowledge that their marriage was shaky. Only many years later was I told that they had only stayed together for the sake of Jeanine and me. They often argued so vehemently at the dining table that I'd burst into tears and Jeanine would leave the table in a rage.

Dad had strong likes and dislikes about food and suffered from chronic indigestion. He had regular doses of Hardy's Indigestion Powder and whenever Mother gave him food that upset him there was a row.

The best times were when we went horse-riding together. He and Mother were at peace as we trotted along the grassy plantation roads. We inspected weeding contracts, fencing repairs, the condition of the cattle, the fall of coconuts, or the work being done on the roads. The best ride was when we went up to the hills at the back of the grass paddocks. In places it was so steep that we had to dismount and lead our horses. From the top of the hill, some 2,000 feet up, there was a spectacular view across the plantation to the west and east across Salia Levu to the sea and the distant islands of Lau. To the north we looked up at Taveuni's highest mountain, the 4,040-foot Ului Qalau. To the south was the stormy South Cape. We would often sit for hours to let our horses recover as we talked about life on the plantation and Taveuni, and sometimes Dad would relate the experiences of our ancestors.

4. The Young Overseer

With the end of the war and an improvement on Dad's financial position it was decided that Jeanine and I should go to school in Australia, she to Melbourne Church of England Girls Grammar, and I to Melbourne Church of England Boys Grammar. I was to be away from January 1946 to the end of December 1953, returning to Taveuni only for Christmas holidays.

By then I was very different to the boy who had gone away to school. My world had expanded tremendously with boundless opportunities. I was good at most sports, had lots of friends, and had been in a job which held promise of being a stepping stone to a career in accounting. As an old boy of Melbourne Grammar, I had all the connections and mixed with all the right people.

But when Dad wrote and said he wanted me to come home and help him, I had little difficulty in agreeing. The fascination of life on Taveuni remained very powerful for me.

The Taveuni that I went back to was quite different from my childhood days. Mother and Jeanine were gone and in their place were Dad's de facto wife, Adi Vuki, and their daughter Susie. I could never come to terms with this relationship. Dad had built Vuki a separate house a quarter-mile away from our home. She spent the day there and only came over in the evening for dinner and bed. She was a very attractive Fijian but spoke no English. We never conversed except for greetings and I took little interest in Susie. It seemed like a betrayal of Mother and Jeanine to do so. Vuki called Dad Jimmy, which sounded a bit odd when everyone else called him Valen, but he encouraged it as it was his way of disassociating himself from the relationship with Mother.

Dad and I had a strange relationship. We were polite to each other but not really friendly. We never said good morning or good night and seldom discussed anything of importance in any depth. He gave me no specific role on the plantation except to do all the bookwork and attend to office matters. Otherwise, he told me to be his ears and eyes and see that his instructions to the Sirdars and other headmen were carried out. The only time we seemed to have a normal relationship was when other people were in the house. I knew that his greatest concern was not to overburden me with work in the way his father and Uncle Rood had treated him. I think he was terrified that he would give me too much and drive me away. So I had a very leisurely work routine and decided myself what I would do each day.

When I came back, I had no money. Dad fitted me out in khaki shirts and shorts, long socks and brown shoes, which became my standard work uniform. For a while my only form of transport was a bicycle, which I used to go between the house and the Waimeqere compound and even the two-and-a-half miles up to Ura. I could use the lorry after work. I also had a horse and was on that every morning. Later on he bought me an old US army jeep for £20 and I got all my board and lodging free. It wasn't much but I didn't want anything.

Dad had a lot on his plate when I came back in 1953 and I suppose this is why he called for me.

First, there was Waimeqere, the coconut area consisting of 1,500 acres that produced 600–800 tons of copra annually. There were the grass paddocks, known as Woodlands, 300 acres of which was for fattening cattle before shipment. Then there were the 1,200 acres of land at the back of the estate between Waimeqera and Salia Levu. While this was not used for anything, it was a very fertile and valuable piece of land and some of it was leased out to the Indian laborers who lived at the settlement at Qarawalu.

Shortly after I returned he purchased the Ardmore property of 300 acres, which was the land surrounding our homestead at Navaca. This produced 150 ton of copra annually.

He also acquired the lease of Ura, the Couborough plantation some two-and-a-half miles up the coast from us. This produced 300–400 tons of copra annually.

In addition to all this he operated the cinema theatres on the plantation and up the coast. Films were shown on Saturday and Wednesday at the Vuna hall, on Friday at Somosomo, and on Saturday at Naselesele.

In 1954 he became a boxing promoter and put on some of the best boxing contests then seen in Fiji. These were not to make money. After meeting expenses he paid all takings to the boxers, who received the highest purse ever paid in Fiji. People came from all over Taveuni and Vanua Levu to see the fights and he always put on a huge party after the event. That alone cost him a small fortune.

Then, of course, he continued with his prospecting and eventually discovered a large copper deposit at Udu Point on Vanua Levu and manganese at Nayau in Lau. He sold both these mines to the Japanese for a handsome sum, but the costs of developing the mines was such that I don't think he really made any profit.

To run these enterprises he employed about 150 men and housed all of them and their families. It was a big operation for one man.

The men who helped him run this operation were absolutely and completely loyal and obedient to his every command.

4. The Young Overseer

The head sirdar was Ram Rao. He was in his 40s and had been born on the plantation. He suffered from Parkinson's disease and his hands shook dreadfully when he was nervous or angry. As head sirdar, he had considerable status and any order coming from him was seen as coming from Dad, and God help anyone who disobeyed.

Ram Rao's job began at six am when he did the rounds of the labour quarters to make sure all the men were up and ready to begin work at seven am He then conveyed the instructions of the day to the various groups.

Firstly, there were the ten men known as vata boys, because their task was to empty the vatas or hot air dryers and make room for the daily production of green copra. This amounted to 150–200 bags, each weighing 130 pounds.

There were three methods of drying copra. The vatas were large wooden trays on steel wheels that ran on railway lines. Two or three bags of copra were spread out on each to be dried by the heat of the sun. At night, or when it rained, the trays were rolled along the lines under shelter of a big shed. It took six to seven days of good sun to reduce the moisture content to six to eight per cent. Men had to be continually turning the copra so that it got an even application of sun. Because the copra often got wet or simply because of the high humidity, sun-dried copra was often discoloured or mouldy, but if there was consistent sun it did produce the highest quality copra.

Then there were the hot air dryers. We had two types. Originally there was the steam boiler which was fired with coconut husks and timber and produced steam that was piped into a chamber in which there were a number of wire trays on which the copra was thinly spread. It was dried to six per cent moisture content in 24 hours and produced pure white copra. It was regarded as the very best. When maintenance of the boiler became too high, it was discarded and we made another type of hot air dryer. This was a square shed in which there was a wire platform on which 20–30 bags of copra could be spread out to about two feet depth. Underneath, was a steel pipe or 44-gallon drums were welded together to form a flue. A fire was built at one end in a fire box and the hot air dried the copra in 48 hours. The copra had to be turned with shovels two or three times during this period.

Then there was a third type of copra drying device, called a smoke dryer. This was the same as the hot air dryer except there was no flue underneath. A fire was built in a pit and the copra was cooked by the heat of the fire and the smoke. The smoke and the fire blackened the copra and this type of dryer was eventually banned.

The vata boys also had to go out and cut firewood for the dryers. After lunch they went out to the fields on the lorry or tractor and trailer to bring in the fresh copra, weigh it, and spread it out on the vatas or in the dryer. They finished work by three to four pm.

There was also a chota sirdar, or small sirdar, who was responsible for getting all the copra cutters out in to the fields. We were fortunate in that most of our copra cutters came from the Indian settlement of Qarawalu. This was an area of land which had been subdivided many years before and sold to Indians. They lived on these blocks and provided us with labour, which meant that we did not have to house them. The chota sirdar, Irawadir, lived at Qarawalu and went out with the copra cutters at daylight and allocated them their tasks for the day. This was done by starting at the bottom of a field and giving a man and his family two to three rows of trees to work, depending on the fall of nuts on the ground. Each man then went up these rows collecting the nuts into piles, and cutting them open. His wife and family would sit on the ground and using special knives to gouge out the fresh coconut. This would then be put into hessian bags which we supplied and stitched up. About 30 men and their families were engaged in this task. A single man would cut about three bags but a man and his wife and two or three children could cut up to about ten bags in a day. The man himself would tell Irawadir how many bags he could manage each day. Each bag had the cutters individual mark on it so that when it was taken to the dryers and weighed, Ram Rao would know what weight to credit to the particular cutter, who was paid according to its weight.

The bags were collected from the fields by bullock carts, which were made on the plantation and were pulled by six bullocks. They carried 20 bags, which were dumped at the road heads where they were collected by the vata boys on the lorry. When the bags were taken to the vatas or dryer, Ram Rao weighed all the copra and recorded the weights in his day book and later calculated the amount of money due to each cutter. They were paid 3/- per 100 pounds.

Ram Rao was also responsible for recording the work done and the payment due to the other employees, including the stockmen, carpenters, mechanics, road repair gangs, and people doing the weeding, bagging copra and any other activity on the plantation. At five pm he had to report to Dad with all the other headmen and explain exactly what had happened during the course of the day and receive instructions for the following day.

One of the others who attended the evening meeting was Bete, the head stockman. His real name was Laisiasa Tuimouta and I never knew why he was called Bete, which means priest. He certainly had no priestly qualities. Although he was Vuki's brother he treated Dad like a lord. He was in charge of his two brothers and four other men who were responsible for managing the 1,000 head of cattle and 2,000 goats. The cattle had many purposes: first to keep the grass eaten or trampled in the fields so that the copra cutters could find the nuts; second, to be sold for income; third, to provide a supply of working bullocks for the carts; and fourth, to provide meat and milk for us and the labour. The cattle had to be moved from field to field depending on the grass supply. The milking herd, the cows, the bulls, and the steers had to be kept separate. Two or three times a year there was a general muster when young bulls were castrated, old cattle that had no further use were sent out into the bushland, and all the other cattle were sorted into their respective groups.

Bete and his gang were also responsible for looking after the many miles of fences that separated the various fields and also the outside boundary fence. Dad believed in fences with live posts. The main posts were vau, the wild hibiscus, and those in between were wiriwiri. While this system ensured that the fence would last for a very long time, it meant that the growing posts had to be pruned from time to time, and with our rainfall the posts grew fast.

Friday was always killing day for Bete and his gang. They would go out on horseback and identify at least two steers which were shot and slaughtered before being brought in to the main compound by lorry where they were butchered and distributed, firstly to Dad and then to all the other labour. Dad's share was usually the brains, the tongue, the fine cuts of fillet and sirloin, and a basket of fat, which was rendered down and used for cooking purposes.

Sometimes goats were also killed for the Indians.

We ran 2,000 head of goats and they had to be treated for foot rot and stomach worms by Bete's gang. The goats spent the nights on the rocky coastline near the main compound. Each day the gates to their paddock were opened and they went out into the plantation to forage, and in the evening they came back to the coast. On the odd occasion they were savaged by dogs and these would have to be hunted down and shot. Goats were sold at that time for four to five pounds per head.

The other person at the evening meeting was Niko Sorby, the mechanic. It was not really necessary for him to be there, but because he worked at the garage, which was nearby, and finished work at about five o'clock he usually joined Ram Rao and Bete in the hope that Dad would offer him and Bete a whisky, as he usually did. Niko was a half-caste, a rough character who always looked terribly dirty. He swore continuously while he worked. He swore at the engine he was working on and at the boys who helped him. Despite this, Niko was a happy man and a genius at keeping all the vehicles and engines working. Spare parts were often hard to get but Niko had a great talent to improvise. At that time Dad had two ten-ton Chev trucks and one ten-ton Ford truck, which he had bought from the US Army when they left Fiji after the war. They were very cheap, in good order and extremely versatile, with four-wheel drive and winches. Then there was my jeep and Dad's Ford, as well as the power plants, the motor mowers and various other engines and, of course, Dad's 30-foot launch.

Another key man, who was sometimes called to the meetings, was Waisiki, the carpenter. He came from the nearby Vuna village and was referred to by my cousin Adrian, who didn't like him, as a 'psalm-singing son of a bitch who was always smiling at you but likely to stab you if you turned your back.' I always found him courteous and obliging. He was responsible for keeping all the buildings in good repair. There was the large copra shed, the vatas and the sheds covering them, the 20 or so labour homes, the labour lines, the theatre, the cafe, the shop, and of course the main homestead. He also constructed the bullock carts and made yokes for the bullocks as well as gates for the various paddocks. Waisiki was also a blacksmith and made copra knives and axes. The buildings had to be painted on a regular basis so there were two or three men always on this job. Then there was the water supply system. A two-inch galvanised pipe carried water from the source at Qarawalu, three miles inland, to the main settlement. If a break occurred, Waisiki had to repair it. He was an all purpose maintenance man.

Ena Kutti was the sirdar at Ura but it was too difficult for him to attend the evening meetings. Dad went to Ura at least twice a day and saw Ena Kutti and kept himself informed as to exactly what was happening. Ura was a straightforward operation. There were about 15 copra cutters who went out to a designated field each day to cut about 70 bags of copra. This was brought to the main roads by sledges drawn by two bullocks and then transported to the vatas or dryers by lorry. There were four vata boys.

Ena Kutti had a lot of autonomy in running Ura. He was a very orthodox Muslim, strict, angry and afraid of no one. He was the only man who showed no fear or respect for Dad. If he disagreed with anything Dad did, he told him so in no uncertain terms. I think he despised Dad for living with a Fijian woman and he constantly warned me not to do the same. He had a gaunt face with a big bushy moustache and always wore an old felt hat. He was as thin as a rake and was always in his most angry mood when he was fasting during the month of Ramadan. He yelled and abused the labour constantly but they understood him and took no umbrage.

There were no fences at Ura but hundreds of wild cattle came in from the adjoining bush areas and fed on the grass and this made it possible to find the coconuts. However, we always had to get in gangs of men to weed out the lantana and guava and wild mint, which grew all over the plantation. We were usually able to get groups of 20–50 men from neighbouring Fijian villages who wished to work in order to raise money for a church or school. We paid them a flat rate to weed a particular field and it was up to them how long they took. They usually built a rough house in the field and lived there until the job was finished. We provided water and killed a steer for them from time to time. Ena Kutti went out on his horse every day, supervising the cutters and keeping an eye on the weeding gangs. God help them if they didn't do the job properly. He would scream at them and if they laughed at this display of anger he was likely to run them down with his horse.

The theatre operation was taken care of by Mahadeo. My mother had taken him into the house in the early 1940s when he was about 12. He was a very small, starry-eyed lad, as keen as mustard, who kept close to me in order to learn European habits and language, and I learnt Hindi from him. He was very bright and when Dad began the theatre business in 1949 he gave Mahadeo the job of projector operator. Dad built the Vuna hall with material from the old Ura house where Ernie Walker had shot himself. The theatre was a substantial building that could seat 500 people. Adjacent to it was a store and a café, which he rented out to a Chinese man named Charlie Chung. There were two 16mm projectors and a slide projector. Films were rented from the MGM, Columbia and 20th Century Fox distributors in Suva, and British news was obtained from the British High Commission. With each film he also got selected shorts, but the main attraction was the serial, which always brought the people back. These were usually terrible third-rate cowboy movies starring the likes of Gene Autry, Roy Rogers or Torn Mix, but the people loved them and came back week after week to see the next episode. Films were always on Saturday and Wednesday. Dad sent his lorry to nearby estates and villages to transport any people who wanted to come and while he charged nothing for this transport, it was 3/- to enter the theatre. His own labour went in free. Revenue was also derived from slide advertising. Each showing began with the national anthem and everybody stood. Dad sat in the same seat each time and had two buttons at his fingertips. One was to signal Mahadeo in the projector box above when to start or stop or if the sound or picture quality was poor. The other flashed on a red light at the bottom of the screen if there was too much noise in the theatre.

During the day the theatre was used as a school for the labourers' children and on Sunday it became a church.

It was Mahadeo's job to make sure that everything ran smoothly and he did quite a good job. But Dad was totally intolerant of the slightest mistake and he gave Mahadeo a terrible time. I think he threatened to dismiss Mahadeo a thousand times, but of course both knew that this would never happen. Mahadeo had become indispensable to him. Dad later gave Mahadeo the opportunity of bringing in Hindi pictures, which he screened on Sunday, and he allowed Mahadeo to keep the takings for himself. Mahadeo also set up a small general store at his house and bought and sold yaqona and dalo. He was a real entrepreneur.

5. Island Life

This was the operation that I came back to in 1953 at the age of 19. I moved into the spare room in the old house and it seemed as spooky as ever. I was never happy there. I bolted the doors at night but there was that damn manhole in the ceiling above my bed where there were strange sounds.

My day began at six am when Angana served me breakfast. It was always pawpaw, poached or scrambled eggs, toast and tea. I then walked up to the goat yard, opened the gates and let the goats out. I inspected them for any signs of disease or injury and sometimes did a head count. I then went on to the vatas and was there by seven o'clock to see that all the men had started on time, and discussed with Ram Roo which copra was dry enough to be taken to the copra shed that day. I stayed with the boys for a while and always maintained a friendly relationship with them. I was Turaga Lailai or Chota Sahib and was always given absolute respect and obedience, and seldom found it necessary to exert my authority. I then went on to Ura and checked on the start of the operations there. Once or twice a week I would have a horse saddled and waiting for me at Ura and I would go into the Ura fields to check on the work. On other days I would do the same at Waimaqera. Most days I would be out on horse back until 11 am despite the weather. Taveuni was an extremely wet place and I never managed to keep dry until I obtained one of the famous Australian Driza-Bone coats which were the best ever made.

At Waimaqera, I had a big grey gelding which had a good turn of speed, but one had to be careful about galloping around a copra plantation. It was safe enough on the grassy plantation roads but when you got off the roads, in amongst the trees, the rider had to have total control over the horse to ensure there were no mixed signals as to which side of a tree you wanted to go. I would check on the work of the copra cutters, the bullock boys and Bete's gang. Sometimes, if the dryer boys were going out to the bush to cut firewood, I would join them and help select the tree to fell and I would take my turn on the 12-foot crosscut saw. It was tough, backbreaking work and I couldn't keep up with the powerful Fijians but I did win their respect by sweating with them, and they always did a good days work when I was with them. Otherwise they tended to ease up and take much longer than necessary to cut their task of one lorry load.

Lunch was at 11 am, and I had this with Dad. It was usually curry or cold meat leftovers from the previous evening, fish or salad. I read for a while and then went into the office to spend a couple of hours doing all the necessary bookwork. Afternoon tea was at two p.m, which I also had with Dad. I then went to Ura or Waimaqera to check on the copra coming in and the completion of work at about four pm I was then free to go fishing in my 14-foot boat with its 10 horsepower Johnson or go spear fishing with one of the labourers.

When the evening meeting was over, Dad would order Angana to bring the drinks. A bottle of whisky, soda siphon, glasses and ice were brought on a silver tray. We poured our own whisky while Angana put in the soda and ice. We usually had two drinks before dinner except if we had visitors.

Angana had taught Dad how to ride a horse when he was a lad. He came to work in the house in 1950 when he was 60. He was effusively humble, polite and eager to please, but Dad gave him a terrible time. He would sit in his chair on the porch where there was a button on the wall, which rang a bell in the kitchen. Whenever he wanted something, be it a glass of water or an Aspro, he would press the button and if Angana did not respond immediately Dad would yell at the top of his voice. Angana would come running and gasp, 'Ha Sahib.' If he was a moment later than Dad expected, Dad would yell at him, 'Where the hell have you been?' He abused him continually no matter what he did and I never heard Dad compliment him once. Stranger still, I never heard Angana complain. He seemed to accept that this was the way of things.

When Dad was ready for dinner, he would call out to Angana—who would be dressed in his white jacket, green cummerbund and topi—to serve dinner. There was always a four-course dinner with soup, a savoury, a roast and dessert. Between courses, Angana would stand in the corner of the room and watch us eat. As soon as our plate was empty, he would bring the tray of vegetables and offer a second helping. If it was a warm night, he would stand on the verandah and pull the punkah. When we had finished he would take the plates away and bring in the next course. If he began taking the plates away before everybody had finished, he was scolded terribly by Dad.

After dinner I read for a while and was in bed by nine pm.

While this was my general routine, there were variations to it. For example, if a ship was coming in to load copra, the whole programme changed. The dry copra was stored in the huge copra shed. The night before the ship was due, contracts were let to groups of men to bag the copra. This entailed hanging hessian bags on wooden 'horses', shovelling the copra into the bags, ramming it with wooden poles and stitching the bag. Each weighed 140–150 pounds. Gangs were paid five pounds per 100 bags. Depending on the interval between ships arriving, there could be 500–1,000 bags to load.

When the ship arrived, the whole labour force was used to load the copra. The men carried the 150-pound bags on their shoulders to lorries in front of the copra shed where they were transported to the wharf. Whaleboats from the ship came to the wharf and the bags were tossed onto slings in the whale boats. Little launches then hauled the whaleboats out to the ship where the slings of copra were winched aboard. Each whaleboat carried 50 bags. During this operation, Dad drove the men at a frantic pace, and he took great pride in boasting that he could load a ship faster than anyone else on the island. Each sack had to be counted by Ramrau and the ship's super-cargo and when they agreed on the number I completed a bill of lading with a letter to the copra millers in Suva. When it arrived in Suva, the copra was graded into first, second, or reject grade. We were paid according to the price set by the Copra Board for each grade. If Dad didn't get first grade he would appeal and he usually succeeded.

Another variation to my routine was to go by horseback to inspect the water supply sourced at Ura or Waimaqera. I particularly enjoyed the ride up into the hills 2,000 feet above Ura. The water source had to be cleaned and if cattle had broken through the surrounding fence, I had to summon Bete to repair it.

It was a peaceful and beautiful place up on the shoulder of the mountain looking down across the whole expanse of the south end of Taveuni and out across the straits to Vanua Levu. I did most of my thinking up here in this lovely place. Since returning to Taveuni in 1953, I had begun to think a lot about my life.

Sometimes I would take my .22 rifle with me and, when I had completed the inspection, I would go off into the bush and hunt for wood pigeons. It was an easy walk through the bush as there was little secondary growth. The birds rested on branches of trees where they fed on berries and they were quite easy targets. I always felt a certain mystery about walking around these mountain slopes. I had a powerful feeling that there was something there for me, but it wasn't until years later that I discovered its significance.

Despite my easy lifestyle, I desperately missed the friends I had left in Melbourne. I was a naturally gregarious person and my social life on Taveuni was restricted. I sometimes regretted my decision to return, but in sober moments I understood that my destiny was to take over the Tarte land and carry on tradition.

My only friend and ally at that time was my cousin Adrian. He was about eight years older than me and had been toughened by working with Uncle Rood. After leaving school in New Zealand he joined the Civil Service and for a while was aide-de-camp to the Governor. He worked for Uncle Rood for a few years, until they had a real bust up and Adrian demanded his share of Vatuwiri so he could go out on his own. He was a hard worker with some good ideas on plantation management.

Adrian wasn't able to put his plans into effect until he had his own land because Uncle Rood would certainly not change from his own way of doing things. He brought in tractors and trailers. He started controlling weeds with weedicides, he repastured his land so he could run a higher number of cattle per acre, and when he had sufficient cattle he opened a butchery. We discussed these innovations at length over many whiskies and I tried to get Dad to see the wisdom of adopting them. Eventually he did make some concessions.

In the evenings I would often go to Adrian's place for a drink and we invariably polished off a bottle of Scotch. If there was anyone else there, such as a commercial traveller or a government official, we would play the game of Cardinal Huff. This was a certain formula to get drunk quickly. I was obliged to get home in time for dinner with Dad and if I was late and he had waited for me, I was given the cold shoulder. If l was a little drunk, Angana would watch in glee as I struggled with my food. But God help him if Dad saw him smiling.

Saturday was payday. Ram Rao came down to the office at seven am with his day book and read out the details while I entered them all in the main ledger and made the calculations of pay due and pay deductions. There were always many of these. Fijians had to pay a Provincial Tax for being away from their villages and Dad paid this on their behalf and deducted it from their wages. But mostly he agreed to advance on wages for many of the obligations they seemed to have and these too were deducted from their wages.

After totalling up the wages for the week, I gave Ram Rao the cash, which I had obtained from the Morris Hedstrom or Burns Philp stores up at Waiyevo, or I gave him a cheque to cash at Charlie Chung's store. The labour would spend their wages at Charlie's store during the week and at the end of the week he gave the cash to me in exchange for a cheque, which he then sent to his bank in Suva. It was basically the same cash going round and round.

Ram Rao took the cash back to his house and at noon the labour came to see him to collect their wages.

After Ram Rao left, I had a stream of men calling to see me to obtain loans or ask for assistance in their personal problems. Dad had readily passed all these kinds of matters over to me to deal with. In considering their requests, I had to remain sensitive to the fact that if I said no, they had nowhere else to turn. But if I was too lenient, I would be swamped by others. There remained the expectation that Dad would take care of them until they died and, when he passed on, I would do the same.

My Saturday afternoons and Sundays were free.

Invariably, Adrian and I would go diving or fishing in his 18-foot boat on Saturday afternoon. Saturday night was always dinner at Dad's with Adrian, Spencer and Talei, and maybe the Douglasses from up the coast or any commercial people or government officials who happened to be visiting. They arrived at five pm and we drank until dinner was served at six-thirty pm We always had a roast dinner, either turkey or beef. Then we went to the movies.

On Sunday I went to Waiyevo to the tennis club. I enjoyed tennis and threw myself into the game and the club's administration, and was soon made Secretary. One of my first tasks was to try and change the Constitution to allow Fijians and Indians to join. There was an outcry, and if I hadn't been a Tarte, I think I would have been thrown out. But after some gentle persuasion they agreed to allow ten Fijians to come in as a trial, but definitely no Indians.

I had become friendly with the expatriate doctors, the District Officers, the Morris Hedstrom and Burns Philp Managers, and some of the other plantation managers, and often went to their homes for Sunday dinner. I eventually persuaded the members to put in a small bar and sell drinks. It proved to be a disastrous idea, for many of the half-castes drank heavily and when they got drunk they became abusive. I remember one part-European, (that's what we started to call them), Frank Peterson from Naselesele, who would sell his weekly production of copra to the Morris Hedstrom store on a Friday and take half of his payment in cash and the rest in rum or beer. He would drink until it was gone and remain on the dry until the following Friday, when he sold another supply of copra. He was a really hard case, and very unpleasant when drunk.

The social arrangements on Taveuni had changed since my pre-school days in the early 1940s.

The state of Indians had not changed much, but some had purchased copra plantations or ran reasonably good stores and taxis and spoke good English. They had been to the schools that had sprung up in the last decade or so. Fijians were still regarded as 'lazy buggers' and the fact that most of the Fijian-owned land was overgrown with weeds was, we believed, evidence of this. But in the mid-1950s a Fijian took over as District Officer and another as Medical Officer. This forced the locals to re-appraise their attitudes and give these men the respect that was due to the office, if not to their person.

Many of the old planter families had died or sold out. There remained only the Tartes, Douglasses, the Halsteads, and the McKenzies. Managers had moved onto many of the other plantations or foreigners had bought them. These new people had no racial prejudices. The part-Europeans who were descendants of old families began to assume a higher profile and so a social levelling process was in place. But the Europeans remained at the top of the pecking order and even when people like Dad or Adrian took on a Fijian lady, she was given no status or recognition. There were plenty of snide remarks about such black–white relationships. The Douglas family used to boast of being descendants of the Black Douglasses of Scotland, but Eddie Douglas had sired so many illegitimate children from Fijian ladies that the term Black Douglas took on a different meaning and they were the butt of many jokes.

The 1950s were the last of the best years for the copra industry. Most of the plantations had been planted during the second half of the 19th century, and the trees were well past their best years of production. There was an urgent need to replant but few had the necessary confidence in the future of copra and coconut oil to invest in the long and costly task of cutting down the old trees and replanting. The Fiji Tall species, which most plantations had, did not bear until six or seven years and didn't reach maturity until 15. There was another variety, known as the Malay Dwarf, and Dad did plant up some 50 acres of these in an area where most of the old trees had fallen down. But although this variety would produce one ton of copra to the acre, it did not stand up well to hurricanes. When our Fiji Tall trees had been at their peak we were getting a half ton of copra to the acre, but in the 1950s this was down to less than a quarter ton per acre.

Our plantation was still one of the best in Fiji. The trees were planted in dead straight rows.

Underneath was rich pasture where healthy cattle grazed. Well-formed roads criss-crossed the paddocks, and the labour compound was an attractive little settlement.

All copra was sold to Island Industries Ltd, a subsidiary of Carpenters. They produced the coconut oil which was sold to the United Kingdom under a British Ministry of Food contract that was due to expire in 1959. Under this, Fiji received a guaranteed price, which was highly remunerative, but all knew that when the contract expired it would not be renewed and we would be exposed to the volatile world market.

There was increased pressure from the millers and the Copra Board to produce better quality copra and this necessitated higher drying standards, which cost money.

Then there were the social pressures to provide better housing, work conditions and pay for the labour, as well as the ever-present threat of hurricanes, which hit from time to time with disastrous consequences.

Despite all this, the copra planter lived well in the 1950s and early 1960s. This was partly due to the fact that the planters owned most of the rich flat land on Taveuni and could produce most of their needs from the land. Beef, goats, poultry, turkeys, milk, butter, cream, fresh water, fish, prawns, crayfish and all kinds of vegetables were virtually free. They had servants to do all their chores and cheap labour to work the plantations. Communication with the outside world improved considerably during the 1950s when the new airline, Fiji Airways, began flying on a regular basis to Matei airstrip at the northern end of Taveuni. They used the three engine De Havilland Rapides that seated about seven people and flew to Taveuni twice a week. This enabled us to get our mail and more urgent goods from Suva on a more regular basis, although at a higher cost. Yet, there was the difficulty of getting the goods from Matei to our southern end of the island. So Dad put in his own airstrip on Ura. As soon as it was up to Civil Aviation standards. Fiji Airways began flying in to Ura.

Charlie Chung opened a post office at his store on Waimaqera, so some of our mail came in by air although we still received our regular mailbag on the inter-island shipping service every two weeks.

This shipping service also brought us another service which we had lacked: banking.

Seeing the need to service its clients, the Bank of New South Wales placed an officer aboard the inter-island ship, which travelled to Levuka, Savusavu, Taveuni and the northern islands of Rabi, Qamea and Laucala. This officer would disembark when the ship first arrived at Vatuwiri. He would be met by his regular taxi and would work his way up the island calling at the plantation houses and providing any banking services that were required.

On the return trip, the officer would again come down the island and call in at each of the homes and do whatever he could to assist. He was often called upon to buy things for the planters in Suva or take messages. I remember once giving him my old shoes to take to a boot maker in Suva for repairs.

The telephone system had not improved. Although the eight-gauge fencing wire had been replaced by a small coaxial cable, it was still strung on the coconut trees and broke whenever there was a hurricane and the trees blew down. The single line to the south end was replaced by about four lines and at Waimaqera we were on a line with our cousins at Vatuwiri and the Vuna village. The main stores on Taveuni, like Morris Hedstrom and Burns Philp, began to stock a greater range of goods, but we still had to carry a considerable stock on our own plantation, such as new copra knives and axes, files, cane knives, twines, marking dye, nails, timber, sacks, fuel and parts for the motor vehicles, grease, oil, fencing wire, tools, pipe fittings, paint and office needs. Those that could be obtained from Morris Hedstroms or Burns Philp were delivered once a week when the delivery lorry made a trip down south. Similarly, all household goods that we could not produce on the plantation were ordered through Morris Hedstrom and Burns Philp and delivered once a week.

Dad maintained the Ura airstrip at his own expense. It had a grass surface and had to be mowed at least once a week by a man with an ordinary mower. It was an immense and boring task for the poor chap. Dad also built and maintained the terminal building and for a while even hired and paid for the officer serving the terminal.

Another of his community efforts was to give land for a school on Ardmore. The Vuna Hall had become too small and unsuitable and there was an ever increasing number of children from Waimaqera, Ura, Qarawalu and Vatuwiri in need of a school. A four-classroom block with bathrooms and toilets and teachers quarters was built. As well as giving the land he contributed to the cost of the school. While this was a charitable and noble thing for Dad to do, Adrian frowned upon it, saying that education would only lead to trouble because the labourers' children would get ideas about improving their lot and cause them to be frustrated with their way of life.

During the 1950s the winds of change were blowing across the political landscape of many colonies as the United Nations Special Committee on Decolonization pressed Britain to grant independence.

On Taveuni we were rather aghast at this, as we could not conceive of the British leaving Fiji and handing over control to the Fijians and Indians. We were aware of what had happened in Kenya and were extremely fearful of the United Nation's attitude triggering uprisings in Fiji which could threaten our own lives and the sanctity of our land. We made vows that, as ownership of the land was our sacred right, we would defend it with our lives.

In 1959, the Burns Commission was constituted. The Chiefs of Vuna went before it and said that the Tartes had acquired their land with knives and axes and, as they now wanted the land back, they would return the knives and axes. This incited fresh concern and anger towards the Tui Vuna.

We had frequent visits by men from the British Foreign Office who came to study Fiji and report back to their masters in London. Whenever they came to Taveuni, we were invited to the District Officer's home for a cocktail party and were expected to bow and scrape to them. Most of them were pompous asses who had preconceived notions of what we were like and what was best for us.

More often than not the District Officer would ask Dad to have them for dinner. He was by then the most senior and respected planter on the island, Uncle Rood having died in 1955. Some years before, Dad had been offered a Knighthood for the Tarte's services to Fiji but had rejected it because Uncle Rood was his senior. They had never offered it to Uncle Rood nor made a second offer to Dad.

Naturally, Dad entertained these men in regal fashion and it cost him a great deal but they took it all for granted and I don't think they heeded any of the views that he expressed.

I vividly remember one such official, whose name was Donald Durks. He was a weedy, pasty-faced, introverted man, with few redeeming features. Spencer was by then into shark fishing. The idea was to anchor a dead steer on the reef and wait for the sharks to come in and feed off it. We would then go out in his 20-foot boat and just watch them feed, or harpoon one and drag it ashore. I think that the District Officer at that time rather mischievously asked Spencer to take Donald Durks out shark fishing. When we got to the bait, at least ten of the 12-foot monsters were feeding on the carcass and poor Donald Durks watched and quivered in fear. He really was in a state of shock and never uttered a word the whole time. That was the day I slipped on the deck and went overboard. I swear I was back in the boat so quickly that I never got my feet wet.

In 1955, my back began giving me trouble again. I had developed Scheuermann's disease at the age of 17 and spent nine months in a metal brace. It was a spinal disorder that needed specialised treatment. But Dad was a firm believer in Fijian medicine and always had a 'witch doctor' on hand. At the time of my back flare up, he was 'consulting' a man named Masuwini who came from the northern island of Qamea and had a reputation for being able to cure anything. I tried to explain to Dad that my back problem was not something that would respond to any mumbo jumbo medicine, but he kept insisting that I at least give Masuwini a try. In the end, just to please him, I did.

Each day at dawn I had to rise and put my head over a basin of water in which certain bark and leaves were soaking and inhale the fumes for half an hour. Then I had to lie in a bath also filled with leaves and bark for another half an hour. Finally, Masuwini rubbed me down with oil then sent me down to the sea to swim for half an hour. It seemed like a fruitless exercise but I went through it for seven days. Of course, my back was no better so I went to Suva to see a doctor who took some X-rays and recommended that I go to see my specialist in Melbourne. I did this, but the osteopath said there was little he could do as the vertebrae in my spine were permanently damaged. I was quite despondent, but slowly over the next six months the pain subsided, eventually disappearing, never to re-occur.

The experience taught me never to dismiss unilaterally any natural medicine. Maybe it was Masuwini who cured my problem.

I spent three months in Melbourne on that trip, most of the time working with an interesting old man on a new concept for making copra. He was introduced to me by my Uncle, John Wilson, who owned a large electrical manufacturing business.

Old Ashford's idea was to husk the coconut with a device that he had developed, then to carry the whole nuts by conveyor belt through a tunnel heated to a high temperature by electrical power. This power would be achieved using a generator driven by a suction gas engine that would be fuelled by the husks and shell of the coconut. At the end of the conveyor journey the nuts would be cracked open and the whole kernel would pop out fully dried and in perfect condition. In theory it sounded great, and Ashford came back to Taveuni with me to work out the practical problems of the process. He did all his drawings and calculations, then went back to Australia and promptly died. So nothing came of this great idea.

Another project I worked on for some time was one that was aimed at enabling us to derive revenue from the husks and the shell of the coconut. The husk is the raw material for all kinds of coir products, such as rope and mats. I corresponded with a number of manufacturers of the coir processing machinery, mainly from Germany. There were large coir industries in Ceylon, India and the Philippines. It was a well-established process, but the difference between these places and Fiji was that, in Fiji, coconuts were not brought into a central depot, and to enable the project to work we would have to change the whole plantation management process. The cost of the machinery proved to be exorbitant, the quality of the Fiji coir poor, and the problems associated with introducing the process became insurmountable.

There was also a demand for ground up coconut shell as filler in thermosetting plastics. I negotiated for some time with Monsanto, one of the world's largest chemical companies, on the details. Grinding the shell was no problem but achieving the right quality was extremely difficult, as it would have been necessary to husk the nut expertly and clean it thoroughly before grinding the shell. Once again the process proved far too costly and so another good idea failed.

I threw myself into these kinds of projects because I could see that we had to derive a greater income from the coconut to remain viable in the long term. We were wasting valuable resources that were used in other coconut producing countries. Furthermore, I became bored with the unchallenging routine of my work on the plantation. It was a great lifestyle that I knew millions would envy, but it was unfulfilling and because of Dad's dominant role I had little power of authority.

The boredom led me to drink more with Adrian and to go on more fishing trips with him to the remote islands and reefs north of Taveuni. To satisfy my sexual needs I started an affair with a girl from Vuna village. The first night I met her, I brought her back to Waimaqera and made love to her in my room before taking her back to the village late at night. Of course Dad heard the jeep come and go and obviously heard the noise of a second person in the house. The next day he made it clear to me that I was not permitted to bring another Fijian girl into the house as it would be an insult to Vuki, who was a high chief in her own right. I found this logic difficult to understand but had no option but to accede to his wishes. So I made love to her in other places.

Apparently the Fijians from the village took umbrage to people like us having affairs with their young girls, and one evening when I took the girl back to the village, I had a scary experience. I usually drove into the village compound and let her off then went home. On this particular night I drove into the village, switched off the engine and chatted to her for a while. It was a dark night and I suddenly found that the jeep was surrounded by Fijian men. The girl was pulled out of the jeep and ran off, and the men surrounding the jeep said to me in no uncertain terms that I was not to come to the village again or to have anything to do with their women. I was angry and terrified and decided to get out of the place as quickly as possible. I switched on the ignition and tried to start the engine but to my consternation the starter failed to work. The jeep could be crank started with a handle. This handle was in the back of the jeep, so I leaned over, grabbed it, and stepped out of the vehicle. I must have looked quite menacing, standing there with a big, iron crank handle in my hands, for the Fijians stepped back. Realising I had a slight advantage, I said to them in an angry tone that I would do whatever I bloody well liked. I then went around to the front of the jeep, put the handle in place, gave it a swing and to my immense relief the engine caught. I threw the handle into the back of the jeep, stepped inside and took off in a roar. Only when I was clear of the village did I realise that I was shaking like a leaf with a empty feeling in my gut. Henceforth, whenever I dropped the girl off, I did so well clear of the village.

Soon after that, I met a girl from Laucala. It happened soon after Dad began staging boxing contests at Waimaqera. We constructed a proper covered boxing ring just beside the Vuna Hall and built a fence around it to contain 500 people. The then heavyweight champion of Fiji was Atunaisa Camaibau from Somosomo, and we got him to help us put together contests of one 10-rounder, two 8-rounders, and four three-rounders. We were able to attract the best boxers from around Fiji as Dad promised them purses they had only dreamed of. We advertised the event and on the day of the contest launches came from all over Vanua Levu and buses brought people from the length and breadth of

Taveuni. We had a packed house of 500 people and were able to pay the two main contestants £500 each. Dad took nothing but the bare essentials to cover expenses.

After the event he had a big party at his house and fed and gave drinks to all the notables who came to the contest, including Europeans, part-Europeans, Fijians, and some Indians. The whole thing meant that he was out of pocket a tremendous amount, but he took satisfaction from the fact that he gave pleasure to all those who witnessed the contest. He gave money to the boxers themselves and entertainment to the people who lived on our plantation and the surrounds. There was no funny business in the judging of the fights. The event proved so successful that we staged them every three months. There was a lot of work involved in it for me personally and we later formed the Taveuni Boxing Association, with many championships of Fiji being held at the Waimaqera Boxing Stadium.

6. Marriage

It was at one of these evenings that I met my new friend. I had a warm relationship with her before she went back to New Zealand, where she was training to be a teacher.

My association with her brought me to the realisation that if I was to make a decent life for myself on Taveuni, I would have to find a wife, otherwise I would end up having an endless string of local girls and be like Eddie Douglas, who at the age of 50 was divorced, single and still chasing girls.

Adrian and his brother Spencer, who had returned to Taveuni after serving in the Malaysian Campaign, also came to this realisation and decided to go to Australia to find wives. I gave them a list of all the girls I had known in Melbourne and ranked them with one, two or three stars. As it turned out, Spencer found no one, but Adrian met the sister of a former girlfriend of mine and invited her and her father to Fiji for an inspection of his lifestyle. He eventually married her but it was a disaster and they were divorced not long after.

Good fortune smiled on me. When Adrian purchased a new tractor from Suva Motors, the man who he dealt with was one Merv Dellar. I met him at Adrian's and he was also able to persuade Dad to purchase a new tractor. Merv was a warm, jolly man and we all got on very well together. Shortly after we bought the tractor, Dad and I had to go to Suva, and I met Merv's daughter, Jacque. This was the beginning of a dramatic change in my life.

After Jacque and I were married, we moved into the old Ura house where Ena Kutti had been living for many years. It was in a terrible mess and needed considerable renovation. Nana Tarte, Dad's mother, agreed that the Estate of H. V. Tarte should pay for all the work and furnish the house, so we ended up quite comfortable. We put in a 3kVA power plant and a new wood stove and kerosene fridge. I got Ram Charan, a young Indian boy from out of the copra cutting gang, and told him he was to be cook, and Jacque began teaching him his culinary arts. I also got Subramani, another young Indian boy, into the house as houseboy and garden boy. This left Jacque free to enjoy her life with me. She did all her own sewing and often came out to the plantation with me. We visited quite a lot and went up the coast to Morris Hedstroms or Burns Philp at least once a week to do all our shopping. We also went for picnics and quite often went boating with Adrian or Spencer.

My routine on the plantation didn't change much, but my salary was increased to £40 per month.

It didn't seem much but there wasn't a great deal to pay for, as most of our food needs were produced on the plantation, and power, water, running expenses for the jeep and my Ford car, and the cost of the house staff were provided free. We seemed to be quite well off.

As an aside, we would buy all our green vegetables from a Chinese gardener who only spoke Chinese and very bad Fijian. Jacque spoke neither Fijian nor Hindi, so when the Chinese vendor came with his van once a week she did her negotiating through Ram Charan, the Indian cook, who spoke to the Chinese in Fijian and translated to Jacque in English.

By the 1960s, people on the island had changed quite considerably since the 1940s. Aunty Edie, Spencer and Talei lived at Vatuwiri and Adrian lived on his own estate at Wainiyaku. I thought Aunty Edie was quite a kindly old thing but she led a very lonely life. For some years while Adrian was married to Prue we saw quite a lot of them, but that marriage was not destined to last.

Over at Salia Levu there were three families managing the big property. Willie Low was a Chinese who made wonderful Chinese food. Navilalai Qali was the illegitimate son of Percy McConnell, but had been brought up by his Fijian mother in the village and spoke no English. He drank prodigiously but, I suppose, because he also worked very hard in the fields, he lived for 85 years. Then there was Lorne Peterson, who was a mechanic by trade and often got so excited that he couldn't get his words out. By then there was a road to Salia Levu, so we often went across the island for a drive on a weekend and had a sumptuous meal of prawns or crayfish when we got there. Salia Levu Estate had deteriorated considerably and was covered in all kinds of weeds and its production had fallen from a peak of 1,200 tons to about 300 tons.

Back on the western side, the Morris Hedstrom store where Ernie Walker had once lived, was closed.

Nabono, where Godfrey Garrick had once had his country estate, was now owned by the Shankaran brothers. There were three of them, sons of a small storekeeper who had sacrificed all for their education. They were very decent people but the social barriers remained and they did not mix with the Europeans.

Eddie Douglas lived at Naqilai where his father had lived. Eddie had a debauched life of drinking and womanising but he built a new house and had a fine ketch, a very modern copra dryer, and a small bulldozer which he leased out. It seemed to us that he had found the right formula for life but his womanising eventually got the better of him and he went into so much debt that he lost everything. Yet he lived to be a very old man.

His brother Reggie and his wife Phyllis and their children lived at Qacavulu where the Harnesses had once been. Reggie and Phyllis were extremely rotund people with skinny legs. Reggie told the most outrageous stories about his fishing exploits and was one of those who listened constantly on the party telephone lines and he seemed to know everything that went on on the island. Most of Reggie's property had gone back to bush but he supplemented his income from a small timber mill. He had a lot of very good timber growing at the back of his property.

Just north of the Douglasses was Soqulu where Wal Warden had once been the manager. This estate had also deteriorated substantially and only a caretaker lived in the old house.

Old Jack Taylor who lived at Udukacu had long since died but his four sons by the Fijian lady he married remained and lived on the estate. The estate had also deteriorated and they had a subsistence living from what remained of their property.

The Catholic Fathers and Brothers were still at Wairiki and were very much involved in the life of the island. They took part in the affairs of the copra planters and indulged in sporting activities and the country club. Some of the Fathers were pretty solid drinkers and often called into our place when they were down south and had a few drinks with us. I found them to be very worldly men.

At Waiyevo the District Officer was a Fijian. Peni Naqasima was a nice enough chap and got on well with most of the people, but he could not control his finances and ran up enormous debts at the country club, leaving these behind when he was posted elsewhere. The doctor was an enormous Fijian man named Manulevu, which means 'big insect,' and he was indeed enormous. He was a very warm and friendly person. The road foreman at the time was George Swann. George was one of twins who had been born at dawn of the first day of the 20th century and their parents had received a cable from the King. As Fiji is right on the international dateline, it's possible they were the first twins born into the world in that century. Incidentally, the international dateline crossed the government road at Waiyevo and a sign had been put up that it was the only road in the world crossing the 180th meridian. For convenience, the dateline had been diverted around Fiji so as not to disturb the routine on the island.

The Burns Philp store was managed by Max Olson. Max was a descendant of one of the Bounty mutineers who had settled on Norfolk Island. He was a big fellow who had once played rugby for Fiji. He was married to a part-European girl named Nina. Nina was a bit of a player and once Max caught her with a Fijian man. Max tied him up and shaved one side of his head, his eyebrows and his moustache. I think he also gave him a beating.

Just north at Somosomo, the Morris Hedstrom store was managed by Keith Marshall. Keith had been born in India and had a very colonial attitude to everything, but we became very friendly with him and his wife Phil who remained our close friends for many years. Keith was a very intolerant and single-minded person who managed to offend most people on Taveuni. He loved a party and drink and it's a miracle that the two didn't cause a disaster. He would always drive on the wrong side of the Taveuni roads as he claimed that to do so would avoid the terrible corrugations on the roads. His long-suffering wife Phil put up stoically with his idiosyncrasies. Driving home one night his car stalled and he had to get out to attend to it. He opened the door and stepped out into a six-foot deep drain filled with water. Phil, who could sometimes be quite gullible, looked out the door at Keith struggling in the slush and exclaimed angrily, 'Keith what are you doing down there?' Poor Keith was almost drowning.

Just north of Somosomo lived the Tui Cakau, the Paramount Chief of Cakaudrove. He was not particularly well educated and did not exert much beneficial influence. However, he was respected for his position by most of the Europeans and part-Europeans. He owned a considerable amount of very good land but it had been totally neglected and gone back to bush, and for this he was despised by the copra planters.

Further north at Vatulaga the Miller Family lived on the property that had once been owned by Duncan Hedstrom. Mr Miller suffered dreadfully from Parkinson's disease and it was embarrassing to sit before him and watch the way he shook dreadfully.

Just north of Vatulaga was Mua Estate, which was managed on behalf of the Duncan Estate by Hubert Witts. Hubert and his wife Isabell were dinky di Australians with whom we had a lot in common. One of these common interests was poker, and quite often we would drive all the way from Ura to Mua for dinner and a game of poker. Sometimes they and others would come down to Ura and play poker with us. The fact that it was an hour and a half drive over treacherous roads is an indication of our enthusiasm for company.

Driving on the Taveuni roads at night after a few drinks was quite a hazardous business, as the roads were steep and narrow and frequently there were wild cattle roaming at night. It's surprising there were not more accidents. Adrian always carried a revolver with him and if any wild cattle got in his way he simply shot them.

6. Marriage

The Peterson family and the Ensors still lived at Naselesele and Max McKenzie remained on Nagasau. Max was an avid racing fan and spent much of his time and money following the horses in Australia and New Zealand. He was well known for the enormous bunch of keys that he carried on a chain around his belt.

Around on the north eastern side of the island, the Vunivasa property had been taken over by the daughter of the original owner. She had married an American serviceman who retired as a US Air Force colonel to come and manage the property. Colonel Kolb was a typical American who went about changing everything on the property with incredible enthusiasm. We all felt he was able to spend as he did because he could live off his American Air Force pension and spend the revenue he derived from copra on the property. But he was totally intolerant of the slow pace of doing things in Fiji and the incompetence of the bureaucracy. He fought it for many years but eventually it beat him and he went back to America. While they lived at the Vunivasa property we enjoyed James and Mackie Kolb's company as they were so enthusiastic about everything. We would often drive up to see them on a weekend or they would come down to see us.

By the end of the 1960s the age of the wealthy Taveuni planter had passed. To a degree European elitism remained but only because Europeans were owners or employers. The master–slave relationship gave way to an employer–employee relationship. The planters were subject to the laws relating to the provision of proper housing and hygiene, and the payment of tax and the provident fund. Labour inspectors came around to check the books. There were even attempts to start labour unions.

We did not enjoy great prosperity or live in luxury. It only seemed to outsiders that we did because whenever they visited we served them Black Label Whisky and roast turkey, prawns or crayfish. They saw our big old houses with servants and punkahs but they didn't realise that these things cost very little.

In reality, most planters owed money to the banks and couldn't afford any real luxuries. The price of copra hovered at about £70 per ton and the cost of production increased each year. The levels of production continued to fall as the trees grew older. Then there was the ever-present threat of hurricanes, which hit every now and again resulting in a drop in production in that year and the years that followed. It's hard to believe but even on a place as wet as Taveuni we also had droughts.

We continued looking for alternative means of supplementing our income from copra, cattle and goats. Dad made a couple of trips to Hawaii in the 1960s and one of the ideas he came back with was to plant Macadamia nuts. He spent a great deal of time and energy exploring this possibility but eventually he had to drop it because the climatic conditions were not right for Macadamia nuts in Fiji.

Others, including the well-known American film star Raymond Burr of the Perry Mason TV series, also tried Macadamia Nuts and lost a considerable amount of money.

Dad then got involved with an American company who were trying to sell machinery to produce coconut syrup and coconut flour.

But the cost of machinery and our distance from the US market killed that idea.

Dad continued with his prospecting on Vanua Levu and established a copper mine at Udu which he sold to the Japanese. But this was a one-off windfall and the costs of development were quite considerable.

We then got involved in selling husked coconuts to Hawaii and developed this market over a two-year period. But the quality of our nuts proved inferior and, once again, a good idea proved to be uneconomical.

I began planting dalo and yaqona on my own. I went in for pigs and fed them coconuts and via, a wild root crop, and for some years I managed to get a good return.

Dalo was easy to grow and fetched a good price, and the sale of yaqona over a number of years provided me with the finance to eventually move to Suva in 1968.

My relationship with Dad continued to deteriorate. He depended entirely on me to run the office but sidelined me as far as work on the plantation was concerned. I grew to resent the faith he placed in his headmen and his failure to seek my views and opinions on matters concerning the plantation.

However he didn't hesitate to ask me to do any of his dirty work. We all knew that Vuki was having affairs behind his back and I would have nothing to do with her. Once, before one of his trips to Hawaii with Susie and Vuki, he asked me to fire one of the men she had been playing around with. I enjoyed doing this. On another occasion he asked me to fire Waisiki, his carpenter of 30 years. He was fed up with Waisiki's laziness but couldn't bring himself to give him the axe. Then there was the time that Qaruwalu Indians were known to be stealing coconuts from the back of the plantation. He told me to find out who it was and get rid of them. I set up many traps and eventually caught one of the men red-handed and gave him a beating. The man was too terrified to respond, which is probably just as well as I am not a particularly big person. He went to jail.

I began spending more and more of my time looking after my own interests. I started to buy dalo from producers all over the island and sell it to Suva. As a middleman I made my cut and did quite well out of it. I also took over the lease of a 200-acre plantation between the Douglasses property and Soqulu but this proved to be a poor investment and when I established that I was not going to make a decent return, I sold out.

I used to go on quite a few extended fishing trips with Adrian and Spencer. These lasted from five to seven days and it meant leaving Jacque and the children on their own at home. It was great fun for me but I began to understand the selfishness of it and once told them that I would not go out on a regular basis, but perhaps once or twice a year. By this time Talei had married and left the island and was living in Australia, and Spencer and Aunty Edie lived in the Vatuwiri house. Spencer had pulled down the old place and built a new home which was very comfortable.

Taveuni was an ideal environment in which to raise a family. Jacque went to Suva to have both her babies at the Morrison Maternity Unit and she couldn't speak highly enough about the care and attention she received. But back on Taveuni we were on our own, without any help or guidance as to how to raise babies or children. We had been given a copy of a book by Doctor Spock, the well-known American authority on childcare, and we used this book as a bible to deal with all the matters that arose. Jacque didn't nurse the children for long and soon had them on bottle milk. When it came to hard food we ordered a gross of tins of baby food at a time from Suva. I brought in one of the Fijian labourer's daughter, Talica, to help Jacque and she did all the hard work of washing nappies and looking after the children during the day. We had a fixed routine right through the children's growing up stage. It was designed to fit in with my routine on the plantation. As they got older, Talica would feed and bathe them, care for them during the day and have them bathed and spic and span to spend time with Jacque and I from five pm onwards. That is not to say that we didn't spend time with them during the day. As soon as they were capable of doing so they would come out with me in the jeep as I did my rounds of the plantation, and I had them on horseback by the time they were 4 years old. Of course there were often trips to see Aunty Edie or Spencer or Adrian when we were on speaking terms, and visits to Dad at Waimaqera.

From a very early age we taught them to read with word cards and spent time in the evening playing various games. At a fixed time they went to bed and there was no question about this. It was an orderly and disciplined routine but there was also plenty of room for self-expression. We had a cat, three dogs, a baby pig and a magpie, and they all had the run of the house and were part of the family. I arranged for an Indian lorry driver's son and daughter to come to the house each day to play with Richard and Sandra. They were a little older but they got on well together, and Richard and Sandra learnt from them just as they learnt from Richard and Sandra.

At one stage a Fiji Air Heron aircraft crash-landed on the Ura strip. The mechanics came up from Suva and stripped it of all useful parts but left the body behind. I cut this up into a smaller frame and put it together again so that it could fit into our back yard and be used as a playhouse.

When Richard was four, Jacque began teaching him correspondence school. The papers were sent up from Suva and the teacher spoke to him each day on the radio. It was an ordeal for both of them but they somehow managed and I believe Richard ended up having a good grounding in the basics.

About this time Susie was also being taught by a private tutor who Dad had recruited from Australia with Jeanine's help. Miss Althia Purdy must have thought her appointment was going to be quite exotic, but the reality was much harsher. Dad built a school room near the tennis courts and for a while he had a part-European teacher, Joe Osborne, who taught Susie and some of her cousins, but when Susie reached the point where she needed more than Joe could offer, Dad got in Miss Purdy. He was very possessive about Susie and firmly discouraged her and Miss Purdy from visiting us. I think he feared that we might influence them in some way against him. He was terrified of losing her and did everything to suppress any ambitions that she might have. Consequently, Miss Purdy was very restricted in where she could go and what she could do. She became very frustrated and eventually left. It was rather sad for I felt the need to do something for Susie but could not make any headway.

At this time I was influential in bringing the Taveuni and Savusavu people together. There had always been a strong class gap between the communities. The Savusavu people were all part-Europeans while the Taveuni people were historically regarded as rich and influential Europeans. Even the Taveuni part-Europeans were regarded as somewhat elitist. I persuaded the Taveuni Country Club and the Savusavu Planters Club to agree to hold regular shooting and tennis competitions.

For a number of years, the Taveuni people would go to Savusavu once a year and the Savusavu people would come to Taveuni a few months later. The events proved to be unique. About 30 of us would board Eddie Douglas's ketch early on a Friday morning and sail across to Buca Bay, then take a bus to Savusavu. We would be billeted out with various families. On the Saturday morning there would be a shooting competition with .22 rifles. There were team and individual events for both men and women. There were some very good marksmen from both sides and the trophy went back and forth. I had taught Jacque to shoot and she became an expert. On one occasion I won the men's event and Jacque won the women's. She also beat all the other men except me.

On Saturday night we had a rip-roaring party with everybody getting terribly drunk and dancing to the early hours. There were some sore heads next day but those of us who were in the tennis teams had to shape up. There was a Davis Cup format with teams playing two singles matches each and one double match. It was a very competitive arrangement. In the afternoon we travelled home. Those who hadn't played tennis continued to drink all day Sunday and quite often many of them vomited all the way home across the Somosomo Straits. Eddie was often no less drunk than the others but he was a natural seaman and somehow managed to get the ship in motion, raise the sails and get us safely across the straits.

In the early 1960s, the government introduced a coconut replanting scheme. The idea was to raise copra production from 40,000 tons per annum to 60,000 tons per annum. Under this scheme, planters were paid a sum of money for clearing new land, replanting and regularly weeding young plants, and cutting down old trees. It was aimed primarily at Fijians whose land was terribly overgrown and unproductive. It proved to be a great money spinner for them, for they collected cash for thinning out their groves, weeding, replanting and then maintaining the young trees for a few years. But when the subsidy payments ceased, they lost interest, the young trees died and the land went back to bush.

A few planters like Dad did take advantage of this scheme and while some did benefit and increased their production, many failed. Dad decided to plant 200 acres of Woodlands with the Malay Dwarf variety. I tried to convince him that the Dwarfs would not do well at the elevation of 1,200 feet, but he would not accept the fact. He planted and collected his subsidy scheme payments and after about three years the Dwarfs got bud rot and died. It proved to be a total failure. The scheme itself was a disaster and production in Fiji continued to fall to about 20,000 tons in 1975 and by the end of the century it was down to 8,000 tons.

7. An Array of Characters

A fascinating array of characters continued to pass through Taveuni. Dad, the inveterate prospector, continued with his efforts to find El Dorado. He had men out prospecting all over Viti Levu and Vanua Levu. The word was out that if anybody found any unusual rock they should take it to J. V. Tarte and he would give them a reward. He became very friendly with the Director of Mines, Karl Fleischman. I think that Dad and Karl came to some kind of arrangement that if Karl fed Dad information of new finds he would exploit it and if it turned into anything they would share the spoils. Karl gave Dad many such tips that came through his office and these were followed up but few came to anything.

One such tip was that there was uranium on the island of Waya in the Yasawas. Dad purchased a Geiger counter from overseas and proceeded to set up an expedition to go to Waya to search for uranium.

He chartered Trevor Withers's Blue Lagoon cruise ship and made arrangements for himself and Karl Fleischman and some of his prospecting hands to go to Waya. At the last minute, Dad fell ill and he pleaded with me to go with Karl. I'm not sure what the motive was but I had a feeling that he just wanted me to keep an eye on Karl. In any event we boarded the Blue Lagoon cruise ship at Lautoka and went out to Waya Island where we spent the next week clambering over the island with the wretched Geiger counter. It was a very steep, rugged island, and I was pleased that I was young and fit and able to cope with it. Karl struggled to keep up with the boys and me. We found no signs of uranium on Waya but did locate a small lode of copper which was quite rich. But it was only an isolated pocket. Karl was a very intense little Jew and I always got the impression that he had some ulterior motives. I must confess I never really trusted him.

Then there was Brian McCook. Brian was a pilot with Fiji Airways and at one stage became very friendly with my cousin Talei. There were even suggestions that they may get married, but I think the Rood Tartes felt that Brian, as a lowly airline pilot, was somewhat below them and the marriage was discouraged. However, Brian then became friendly with Dad and somehow Dad must have inveigled him into carrying his Geiger counter on the plane as he flew low over the islands of Viti Levu and Vanua Levu. On one trip he was apparently flying very low on a solo flight from Nausori to Nadi. No one really knew what happened and the inquiry itself never revealed the true cause of the crash but Brian came down in the inland of Viti Levu. He was very badly injured and had to be carried out of the bush on a stretcher and spent a long time in hospital. As soon as he could be moved, Dad had him taken to Taveuni, where he stayed till he was fully recovered. Dad then helped him set up his own airline, which operated within Fiji for a few years. But it was not a success and he left Fiji to fly for a missionary group in Papua New Guinea.

Governor Art Ewing, formally of American Samoa, arrived to stay with Aunty Edie and Spencer following a request from Fiji's great fishing authority, Rob Wright. Rob said Art had been engaged by Life magazine to write a number of articles on game fishing in Fiji.

Art turned up with his 'secretary' and ended up staying for six months. He was a dashing, handsome, likeable and extremely gregarious man with what appeared to be an impeccable background as a former state governor and scion of a wealthy Ohio family who owned a large steel plant. He and Elaine became part of the family. As a devoted fisherman he was a man after our own hearts and we welcomed the opportunity of acquiring some of his reputed skills and began taking him out fishing every day.

But Art was also a gin and tonic addict who began drinking as we headed out to the fishing grounds with the rising sun and continued all day. His ability to consume gin and tonics and remain sober became legendary. Initially we tried to keep up with him but it became too much so Adrian, Spencer and I began taking it in turns to take him out.

He purported to be writing his Life Magazine articles with Elaine but we soon woke up to the fact that she was a lot more than just a secretary. Aunty Edie tried to keep up appearances by insisting that they sleep in separate rooms. We never saw evidence of any articles.

We spent many days at sea and caught countless fish. But the billfish eluded us. Finally the day came when Art and I were out in the middle of the Somosomo Straits in driving rain, a howling south easterly wind and high seas. We had been drinking all day and I was well on the way to getting sloshed when a marlin took the lure and Art got a billfish aboard.

Visibility was no more than a few yards and I had no compass, but I headed the boat into the wind as I knew that Taveuni was somewhere in that direction. We came to the coast and I headed south towards Vuna. By the time we arrived the gin was finished and we were rolling drunk. I nudged the boat against the jetty but fell against the oyster-encrusted pier and slashed my hand to the bone. I swear that I never felt a thing.

We caught a few more billfish and I believe that Art played a significant part in putting Fiji fishing on the international map. But after six months of fishing, drinking and entertaining Art and Easy (as she came to be called) we were fed up and used all kinds of excuses to avoid taking him out. Even so, it took a long time for him to get the message that he'd outstayed his welcome.

He left to spend his days in the Seychelles Islands in the Indian Ocean and in Majorca in the Mediterranean before living for a while in Sydney and finally he bought a home at Pacific Harbour where he lived until he died.

Another great character was Charlie Evans. Charlie was an Australian engineer, designer, mechanic and inventor rolled into one who came to visit the Douglas family and stayed for life.

At this time Dad was searching for a way to dry copra more efficiently and he and Charlie concocted the idea of a solar copra dryer. The concept was to build a huge solar panel that was geared to follow the sun across the sky. Heat accumulated in a chamber beneath the glass from which it was drawn into a massive concrete box filled with rock in which the heat would, in theory, be stored. At one end of this was a furnace and heat from this would also be drawn into the rock pile. Fans then sucked the stored heat from the rocks and delivered it into a chamber in which copra was laid out on trays much like the old steam dryer.

It sounded like a great idea, so Charlie was engaged to put it all together. He was to spend nearly a year and thousands of dollars building this innovative dryer. It worked up to a point and was used for a number of years. But we really didn't get enough sun on Taveuni and it took a long time to dry the copra.

Charlie also set up a garage with all the latest technical equipment, which he persuaded the Tartes and Douglasses to finance. He was certainly a good mechanic and the vehicles and engines that he serviced got the full treatment. But he charged accordingly and people gradually drifted back to their own backyard mechanics, like Niko. He got less and less work and ended up living with the Douglas family till he died.

As we were regarded as an important part of the Anglican fold in Fiji we had regular visits from bishops, priests and deacons.

One of the successors to Bishop Kempthorne, who married Jacque and I, was Bishop Vokler. He was a very large, pompous man with an enormously high opinion of the importance of his earthly duties. He often stayed with us on his visits and he had the ability to make us feel very privileged to be hosting his august being.

He considered it unacceptable that we should hold church services in the Country Club and insisted that a church be built on the island. I was opposed to the idea of spending a great deal of money, which we would have to raise, on a building that would be seldom used and nothing more than a monument to his ego. The scheme failed and I don't think he ever forgave me. He eventually left the church and went back into the seclusion of a monastery.

Another very odd churchman was the Very Reverend Whonsbon-Ashton, who presided over the Anglican Church in Fiji at Levuka. We on Taveuni were part of his fold. Like Vokler, he was full of his own importance and considered himself to be a historian of some repute. He had the odd habit of sniffing vigorously as he spoke and it was very hard to understand him as he raved on about boring historical events.

Then there was poor Reverend Maurice Basden who came to us badly shell shocked after the Second World War. He had the unfortunate habit of losing control and feverishly scratching the back of his head with both hands and mewing like a cat. It could happen at dinner or while he was in the pulpit and was terribly disconcerting to say the least. He was a very intellectual, well-meaning man and I don't think he really knew he was acting strangely. He always looked untidy and would arrive at our place with a suitcase full of dirty clothes. Jacque had them cleaned and ironed and did her best to tidy him up. He also loved classical music and would roam around our garden humming loudly to himself.

One day a big bearded 'native' dressed in short pants, a faded floral shirt and no shoes appeared at our front door and said he was our new vicar. This first meeting with Reverend Viliame Hala'apiapi, a Tongan, came as a real shock as I had become accustomed to eccentric Englishmen being my conduit to God. Despite his rough appearance, Reverend Bill proved to be a fine and sincere man who I worked with for many years, long after I had left Taveuni.

When Adrian went out on his own, he had to have his land surveyed in order to get proper title. He engaged the services of a Mr Ed Simm, a retired Government surveyor, who had set up his own practice. Mr Simm, as we called him, was over 70 when he took on Adrian's job. Short, nuggety and as fit as a flea, he was as precise a surveyor as you could ever get. But he did everything at an incredibly slow pace. It would take him 15 minutes to consume a bowl of soup and what he did in the bathroom was anyone's guess. At the end of each day when he returned to the house he would unravel his complete survey chain and meticulously dry and oil it. This would take him over an hour.

I was seeing a lot of Adrian at that time and spent many evenings at his house drinking and discussing how to cure the ills of Taveuni. Mr Simm was a teetotaler and drank only juice. He never said much. While he was with Adrian, his brother-in-law came to stay and insisted that we call him Sonny. I was 21 and Adrian about 29 while Sonny was 81. It really felt odd.

7. An Array of Characters

After he had done Adrian's job, Dad engaged Mr Simm to survey the back land, which Dad planned to sell. So Mr Simm moved to Waimeqera. Each day I would drive him by jeep to the site of his work. As we travelled over very rough bush tracks, Mr Simm sat beside me nursing his precious theodolite like it was a new baby. If I hit a bad bump and his theodolite got a bit of a shock he would almost weep.

I can never forgive myself for a dirty trick that Adrian and I played on him one evening. We were getting quite full while he sat there sipping his orange juice making sober statements. We decided to spike his juice with vodka. I am sure he didn't know what was happening and next day out in the bush must have been confusing and painful for him.

Charlie Chung, who Dad brought in to run the shop, was an amazing man. When he came to Waimaqera he had just arrived from China and knew little about Fiji. But he soon had a store, café, bakery and wholesale business going. He brought a wife out from China and they had three children. He ventured into buying dalo and yaqona and reselling the produce in Suva. The family worked 15 hours a day for years. One day Charlie went to Dad and said he was going to Canada, and off he went. He settled in Vancouver and every year he sent us Christmas cards. One year when Jacque and I were returning from England, we gave him a call from our hotel in Vancouver. He came to pick us up in a new Chrysler and took us to his restaurant, then to his hotel, and finally to his lovely home. His children were going to university and he was a wealthy and happy man. He gave all the credit for his success to Dad who charged him a pittance in rent all those years.

There were, naturally enough, tragedies on the island. Once after a party at Waiyevo, Spencer was driving his landrover with a number of people in it, including Reg Douglas's daughter. In taking a corner, he rolled the vehicle and the poor girl was crushed beneath it and died. The Douglas family was distraught and when Reg recovered from the initial shock all he wanted to do was get hold of Spencer and shoot him. Spencer was equally upset and wanted to do the decent thing by going to her funeral.

We decided this would not be a good idea and did not allow him to go. He was subsequently charged with dangerous driving, a charge that could have resulted in not just a fine but jail. The District Officer at the time, Dennis Williams, decided in his wisdom to get one of the jail cells ready for Spencer and had it cleaned out and a comfortable bed and furniture put in. When Spencer and Adrian and I heard about this we were annoyed and Adrian threatened to take action against Dennis Williams. Spencer engaged Sir Maurice Scott, the then leading lawyer in Fiji, to come to Taveuni to defend him and I think everybody on the island attended the Waiyevo Court House when the case was heard.

Spencer was fined $200 and banned from driving for 12 months. He and the Douglas family never had anything to do with each other again and Dennis Williams became a family enemy.

Prior to this, Dennis and Adrian and I had been quite friendly. Dennis had been in the Royal Navy before joining the Colonial Service and was quite a worldly fellow. On one occasion, the government requested him to carry out a survey of Ravilevu, the land on the rugged eastern coast of Taveuni, which the Tarte brothers had tried to lease in 1914. Dennis mounted an expedition with himself, the Agricultural Officer, a Forestry Officer and Adrian and I, plus, of course, boys to carry all our goods.

We climbed to the lake behind Somosomo and set off south at an elevation of 1,500 feet, but in order to get an appreciation of the land, zigzagged down to the seacoast, then up to 2,000 feet and down to the coast again. One of the features of this coast is a tremendous amount of rainfall and some 40 constantly flowing rivers. The river valleys are quite shallow at a higher elevation but down by the coast they were very steep with gorges some 200 feet deep. It took us five days to complete the expedition and unfortunately we were not able to find any animal life such as wild pigs nor any pigeons and very few prawns in the creeks and rivers. We had hoped to live off the land and so carried only a limited amount of food. By the fourth day we had run out of food, but the whisky lasted us until the end. We made shelters each night but generally we were wet all day and wet all night. It was not a pleasant expedition and the report indicated to the government that the land was suitable for nothing.

We were always getting visits from government officials or commercial people from Suva and, as the Tartes were the most notable family on the island, they always wanted to see us. Dad very seldom said no and always made time for visitors. But Adrian and Spencer became so fed up that they openly snubbed them and refused to have them into their homes unless they felt they could benefit from the visit.

Dad was a very gregarious person and also a great raconteur with a wealth of stories to relate, which he enjoyed telling to visitors. One of his specialties was the supernatural.

One such story was based on events that supposedly occurred shortly after Dad had moved into the Waimeqera house from his father's house at Vatu Wiri. He was sleeping one night in his room with all the doors locked when he suddenly woke up to find his father's cook, Kunjali, standing beside his bed with bloodshot eyes and frothing at the mouth. He had never trusted Kunjali and had often pleaded with his father to dismiss him but Herbert would have none of it, as he believed Kunjali to be a loyal and faithful servant. Dad sat up in bed and felt cold all over as he looked at Kunjali's menacing face. He said, 'Kunjali what are you doing here?' and Kunjali raised a knife as though to strike him. Dad leapt out of bed and Kunjali disappeared. Dad got out his torch and looked around the room, but there was no sign of him. He inspected all the rooms but could find no sign of Kunjali and when he checked the doors he found that they were bolted from the inside. The next day he went to his father's house and challenged Kunjali about coming to his room, but Kunjali denied all knowledge. Shortly after, Kunjali left.

When Dad was living with his father and mother, his evening task after playing bridge was to go over to the engine house and switch off the power plant, which was located close to the family cemetery where his grandfather had been buried. Dad claimed that one night, just as he'd switched off the engine, he was chilled by a sound in the graveyard.

Old James Valentine Tarte had a habit of sighing deeply, and saying, 'Oh dear, oh dear, oh dear,' and it was this sound that Dad heard. He turned around and looked towards the graveyard and saw a shimmering mass over James's grave. He went as cold as ice and when he had recovered he turned and ran back to the house.

When Dad was a young man and was courting Viti McKenzie, he used to ride from Vuna to Nagasau at the north on a Friday evening after work. He said that one afternoon as he was approaching the Ura bushland, his horse suddenly froze. It neighed in terror, stood up on its hind legs and tried to turn around to bolt home. Dad held the horse in check and did his best to quiet him and then realised that standing in front of them on the road was a huge white dog which looked to him like a wolf. He said the horse snorted and shivered and eventually got the better of him and turned and bolted. He couldn't restrain it and eventually let it go and didn't attempt the journey again that day.

On one of his trips to Hawaii he met a well known American fortune teller and not only went to see her a number of times but corresponded with her on a regular basis until the end of his life. He put great store in her predictions but few of them ever came to reality. Most of the predictions were vague and he had to put his own interpretation on them. One of these vague predictions was that there was gold within his grasp. He interpreted this to mean old A. A. Couborough's treasure that was reputed to be buried somewhere on Ura. This motivated him to spend thousands of dollars digging up the rock around old Couborough's house.

He found nothing.

Dad was a real sucker when it came to easy money or lending money. Fijians all over the island knew that if they approached him in a proper manner and presented their case in a polite and humble way he would give them what they wanted. They, and particularly Vuki's family, bled him dry. Whenever they needed money, they went to see him and he gave it to them. If they needed a bull for a feast, he would give it to them. He couldn't say no.

8. Sale of the Plantation

By the mid-1960s I was becoming increasingly disillusioned with life on Taveuni. Jacque and I had strained relationships with the Vatu Wiri Tartes and Dad, and there were few other people on the island with whom we shared common interests. Added to this was the need for further education of the children. Richard was reaching the stage where he would have to go to boarding school in either Australia or Suva. I had him booked into Melbourne Grammar School at the time of his birth, but he was still too young for this and I could not afford it.

Then there was the ever-increasing deterioration in my relationship with Dad. He was not moving towards any shared responsibility and I became more involved with my own activities. While these were financially rewarding, they were not leading anywhere and were quite unfulfilling.

The Trustees of the Couborough Estate decided that the Ura lease should be terminated and the property sold. We challenged their right to do this, as we believed we were covered under an Agricultural and Landlord Tenant Act that would have given us a 30-year lease. But they maintained that it was a Tenancy at Will and we eventually had to take the matter before the Agricultural Tribunal. The Trustees endeavoured to take over the property, which led to a confrontation. Dad posted guards along the government road and at various places around the property to ensure that they didn't establish any degree of occupation on the land, according was the advice given to us by MacFarlane, who had been Dad's lifelong lawyer.

In 1968 we had our day in court and McFarlane represented us while Sir John Falvey represented the Couborough Estate. I was quite friendly with the Tribunal and had a number of informal chats with him and he indicated that we seemed to have a reasonably strong case. However, the decision went against us and Dad and I were quite convinced that McFarlane and Falvey had struck a deal. So our lease on Ura was to be terminated which meant I would be without a home. However, the Trustees offered me the position of manager and assured me of good future prospects.

It was tempting, but at the age of 34, I began to develop a strong belief that I was wasting my life on Taveuni. I was at the peak of my physical and mental capabilities but was not developing them. I was leading a comfortable life but it was a self centred one in which I was making no contribution to society or Fiji generally. I desperately wanted to broaden my horizons by getting out and doing something useful; by seeing the world; by making contact with people; and by getting involved in the affairs of Fiji. I could not see any of this happening while Dad remained in control of the plantation and he showed no sign of relinquishing any authority.

All this led to a build up in frustration that resulted in deterioration in the relationship between Jacque and I. She was desperately concerned about the education of the children, lonely and feeling unfulfilled. Eventually she went to Brisbane for three months. I missed her and the children terribly and when she came back we were so close to each other that I thought things would be better. But then the stress set in again. We had regular rows over petty matters that led to tears and harsh words.

One day I went up to the Ura spring on one of my periodic inspections. After cleaning the spring I sat down on the mountainside overlooking the spectacular view of the south end of Taveuni and the beautiful straits across to Vanua Levu, and thought about my situation. I was never a religious person but in this moment of deep depression I turned to God and prayed with all my heart for guidance. I spoke aloud to him and poured out my feelings. I looked up at the forest-covered mountains towering above me. They were capped by a brilliantly white cumulus cloud that floated in an azure sky. I think I half expected a Godhead to appear out of that sublimely beautiful setting and make some pronouncement about my future. But of course nothing happened and I clambered into my jeep feeling a deep sense of rejection.

That evening after my bath, I poured myself a Scotch and went out to sit with Jacque who was working at her sewing machine. In no time, a row erupted and I lost my temper and flung my glass against the wall where it shattered into a thousand pieces. I stormed out of the house, got into the jeep and headed out with no destination in mind. I went south and eventually ended up at Dad's place. By then a determination had crystallised in my mind. I went in to see Dad and told him I was leaving Taveuni. I said I would go to Suva, look for a job and try it for five years. When he asked who would do the office work, I said I would fly up to Taveuni one weekend in each month to do it.

He was stunned and immediately said he had been about to hand over some of the authority of the plantation to me. I realised it was an act of desperation and told him it was too late and that I was going.

Jacque was equally stunned and terribly concerned about how this would affect our future. It was a radical thing to do. I was acutely aware that I was turning my back on a family heritage and that my action could have far reaching implications. When Adrian heard about it he came to me and said it was like a death in the family.

8. Sale of the Plantation

I was resolute and went into Suva to look for a job. When Ratu Sir Penaia Ganilau heard about it, he spoke to the Chairman of the Sugar Board who was looking for a Secretary to the Sugar Board and Sugar Advisory Council.

The Chairman, Sir Charles Marsack, told Ratu Penaia that if he was recommending me then he would take me. So I got the job and a house and I moved the whole family to Suva.

It was not an easy adjustment. I had been used to an exciting outdoor life and when on my first day at work I realised that I had confined myself to a third story office for the rest of my life, I had some very serious thoughts about the wisdom of my decision.

Judge Marsack was a crusty 80-year-old jurist who told me on my first day that he didn't suffer fools lightly. He was a grumpy man with a permanent scowl. A New Zealand veteran of both world wars who had served as Chief Justice of Samoa, and written a book about the chiefly system in those islands, he had come to Fiji to serve on the Court of Appeal, which he did in addition to his work as Chairman of the Fiji Sugar Board. The bombardments that he'd been through during the First World War had left a permanent mark and he would jump in fright at the sound of a car horn or any other loud noise. He had a terror of planes and would never fly. Whenever we had reason to travel to Lautoka we would go in the chauffer-driven car. It was during these five-hour trips that I was to learn a great deal about the great and horrific battles that he had endured in France. He had kept daily diaries that gave detailed accounts. Whenever it was necessary for us to go to the sugar district on the island of Vanua Levu, we would wait till an overseas sugar ship came into Suva and would board that for the overnight trip to Labasa where it would load export sugar and return. We were given the owners cabin, which was luxuriously fitted out, and enjoyed a very pleasant voyage.

At this stage I had no intention of leaving Taveuni for good and I did fulfill my promise to Dad to fly up to Taveuni one weekend each month to do all the office work. The arrangement worked well and Dad and I began to establish a new and better relationship. In addition to my duties with the Sugar Board, I took on the added responsibilities of Secretary to the Coconut Board and Coconut Advisory Council, so I remained well in touch with the affairs of the coconut industry.

By the late 1970s I could see that the writing was on the wall for the coconut industry. Dad and I had some lengthy discussions about what we should do and it was eventually agreed that we should sell Waimaqera but keep the 300 acres of Ardmore that surrounded the house. By this time I was fully committed to my work and life in Suva and while I was fully aware of the historic implications of selling the land that had been in the family for over a hundred years, it seemed the logical and right thing to do. Dad could no longer manage on his own. The profit margin on the plantation was hopelessly inadequate and by then I had decided that I would not go back to Taveuni.

If we had foreknowledge of the trauma we were about to go through in selling the place, perhaps we would not have done so.

The first buyer to appear on the scene was Peter Kurth, a businessman from Sydney. Kurth was an extremely plausible and gregarious person and we had little trouble in striking a deal with him for a mutually agreeable price. He had great ideas of developing Taveuni into a tourist mecca. He planned to put in an international airport, carry out a sub-division, develop a port, and put up a hotel. It was a grand plan and Dad was thrilled by the prospect of the place coming alive again. We entered into an arrangement with Kurth whereby he would pay a certain amount and the balance on a regular basis. For a while he honoured this agreement and payments came in but then he began to default. We made demands of him and very painfully we extracted payment from him. But eventually the payments stopped altogether and we had to make legal demands, which he failed to meet. Eventually we had to go to court and repossess the property. Naturally we kept all the payments he'd made but our legal costs were also very high.

We then entered into a sale and purchase agreement with Robert Hunter. Hunter was an American real estate developer who had married a local girl and had a business in Fiji. He was another very plausible rogue who had a beautiful smile, and bright blue eyes. He could look you in the eye and smile confidently and tell you a blatant lie even when he knew that you knew he was lying. For a while things went well with Hunter but then he too began to default and again we had to go through the whole rigmarole of repossessing the property.

We began advertising in Australia and the United States and an old school friend of mine came over to negotiate with us, but this too fell through. An American by the name of Torrence began negotiations and we worked towards trying to find an agreeable arrangement. When this didn't materialise he began acting as an agent in America and we entered into discussions with a number of prospective buyers. On one of my return trips from the United Kingdom, I called in to Salt Lake City and had discussions with some of the buyers there. They were very keen and it looked as though something might happen but eventually it all fell through.

Noel McFarlane introduced us to a Hungarian named Sir Leslie Nagy who was resident in Australia. We had lengthy discussions with him and eventually reached an understanding and signed an agreement under which we would retain some interest in the development that he would carry out. He had some impressive plans and McFarlane vouched for the man. However, after signing the agreement he returned to Australia and we never heard from him again.

So it was back to square one. It was at this stage that I decided to once again get involved in the property. By this time Susie had married Brian Leonard from Sydney. He had gone to visit Taveuni and after meeting Dad had been invited to stay with him at Waimaqera. He was a very personable, outgoing chap, full of great ideas and enthusiasm and Dad obviously saw the prospects of a match with Susie. He encouraged it and they were married.

Brian was full of energy and soon put his ideas into practice. This began with the building of a house and experimenting with different crops. One of those that eventually took root was peanuts.

I watched his endeavours and became encouraged with the results, for the peanuts appeared to grow well. There was certainly a market in Fiji and we had the land waiting to be developed. What we didn't have was knowledge about the cultivation of peanuts. Nevertheless, I encouraged Brian to continue with his work and to get assistance from the Ministry of Agriculture who were forthcoming in their advice and guidance. Brian had a background in the dairy industry so was conversant with the processing of products in a factory.

Once the crop was harvested he began processing the peanuts and packaging them for direct sale to shops. But he had no real resources to take it further.

It was at this stage that I decided to put in place a plan for Brian and I to take over the plantation. My concept was to make a family arrangement whereby Brian and I would form a company in which I would be the major shareholder. The company would buy the plantation from Dad and pay him an annual sum, which would support his needs until he died. Ardmore would go to Susie and Vuki, and Mother's unit in Australia would go to Jeanine. In this way, Jeanine, Susie and I would all get a fair share of Dad's estate, and mother and Vuki would be provided for. I managed to get all parties to agree, the documents were finalised, and the Taveuni Toasted Peanut Company came into being.

We arranged an overdraft from the Bank of New Zealand, brought in machinery, built a factory at Waimaqera and went into production. Brian rapidly expanded our line into dalo chips and packaged yaqona, and we began planting up a huge area of yaqona. Brian was very skilled and made most of the processing equipment himself and never stopped experimenting with ways of making greater use of the coconut. All of this cost money and yielded few results. I continued to go to Taveuni every month to keep an eye on the work. Unfortunately Brian had little concept of cost containment and efficient management and often embarked on expensive projects for which he did not have my consent. He churned out the raw and processed peanuts, the packaged dalo chips and the yaqona and I arranged the distribution in Suva. We seemed to be moving towards a successful venture. Then problems developed in the cultivation of the peanuts. It seemed that Taveuni was too wet, which led to the growth of a virus in the peanuts with toxic effects. Many of the raw peanuts were sold to a peanut butter manufacturer in Suva who began complaining about the high toxic level. To set all this right cost more money and our overdraft at the bank continued to rise.

I had set a limit on the overdraft beyond which I was not prepared to go, as I had to ensure that Dad had sufficient means to live on for the rest of his life. As we climbed closer towards that level, I realised that in order to make the project work I would have to assume direct control over the operation and make Brian the production manager. This would have meant going back to Taveuni to live and neither Jacque nor I were prepared to do this. Regretfully, therefore, I had to close down the whole operation. Dad, who had been watching developments with mounting concern said he would resume copra production while we again tried to find a buyer.

Not long after this, Ratu Sir Penaia Ganilau expressed interest in trying to get our labourers and former landowners at Vuna to form a co-operative, borrow money from the Fiji Development Bank, and buy back the land. His endeavours finally bore fruit and so we entered into a sale and purchase agreement with the co-operative and we were paid out fully by the bank. It was a sad moment as we severed our ownership of land that had been in the family for over 130 years. I battled at length with my own conscience as to whether I had the right to part with this land when I had children who might one day find Taveuni to be a haven in an ever troubled world. But the reality was that we could not afford to keep the land and also support Dad and his family, and Mother in Australia. The one most affected by the decision to close down Taveuni Toasted Peanuts was Brian, who really never forgave me for the decision. But I had stood up for him with all his problems with Dad and Adrian, who developed a bitter hatred towards him, and I had no problem with my own conscience as far as he was concerned. He had proved to be an ideas man with no commercial strength and as far as I was concerned he would have to fend for himself. After all, Susie still had Ardmore, which should have been able to provide them with a living.

The sad thing was that the co-operative was a disaster. The members tried to run the property as a co-operative rather than give the members individual titles with the responsibility to run their own farms and pay back the bank. It was a recipe for disaster and no repayments were made. Only years later did the bank subdivide the land and issue separate titles thus giving individuals the responsibility of the land and their share of debt. But in the final analysis very little of the original debt and the accrued interest was ever paid back.

9. Farewell Taveuni

As we moved into the 1980s, Taveuni became more of a backwater to the rest of the nation. Only Adrian and Spencer clung to the lifestyles that had made the Tartes different. In a way, they were a complete enigma in the late-20th century. Adrian for his part was always innovative and progressive in his utilisation of the land resources and he continued to run a diverse and profitable plantation. Spencer struggled on with copra and cattle but the bottom fell out of those markets. They ruled their employees with a rod of iron and maintained an incongruous lifestyle with their houses and servants and boats and an aloofness from the other people of Taveuni. Of the Douglasses, only Eddie remained, withered and weak, but perky and jovial despite his abject poverty.

The progeny of most of the other planter families were indistinguishable from Fijians in that they were all dark skinned. Most followed the Fijian culture rather than their ancestor's European lifestyle. The government institutions, and the stores and plantations that had been sold to local people were all run by Fijians and Indians. They had taken over the Country Club from which they had once been banned. Much of the land at Naselesele had been subdivided and bought by foreigners who settled there in their retirement or used them as holiday locations. Quite a few small tourist operations opened up for backpackers and scuba divers. Colonel Kolb sold his Vunivasa estate to other foreigners who tried a variety of crops, most of which failed. The infrastructure, roads, telephones, water and electricity remained hopelessly inadequate, as the government saw no priority to spending money on an island that no longer generated much revenue. This is somewhat surprising given that Ratu Sir Penaia Ganilau was the Tui Cakau and Governor-General and one of the most influential people in Fiji.

The Morris Hedstrom–Carpenter Group, who owned a considerable amount of land in the centre of the island, went in for cocoa and coffee on a large scale but these schemes eventually failed. Another, who bought Max McKenzie's land at Nacogai, went in for macadamia nuts in a large way but this too failed. The only viable crops on Taveuni proved to be yaqona and dalo and growers who ventured into these crops made a reasonable profit. Yet most of the rich fertile land reverted to scrub and became unproductive. Taveuni was still called the Garden Isle but sadly it was a badly neglected garden whose beauty was due to the lushness of the growth of the indigenous plants.

In April 1981, Susie rang to say that Dad was very low. I immediately made plans to go to Taveuni and as soon as I got there I knew that the end was not far off. I arranged with Jacque to get a coffin ready and to be prepared to bring it up as soon as I gave the word. In the meantime, Vuki's relations and Susie and I comforted him as best we could. He could only get relief when he sat up, so we took turns in holding his head as he sat upright in his chair. He didn't have the strength to hold his head up. As usual, the phones were out of order and it was some time before I could get in touch with Jeanine and explain the situation. By the time I did get her, it was too late and I knew she couldn't get over in time for the burial.

By this time, Brian had become a marijuana addict. He grew it in secret places all over the plantation and smoked and ate it. Most of the time he was out of his mind. On the night before Dad passed on, he came over to the house and stood on the verandah outside Dad's room crying out in a nonsensical way. He went on and on and refused to be silent or go away. I could see that he was completely out of his mind and when every effort to silence him failed I got Vuki's brothers to stuff a rag into his mouth, bind his hands and feet and take him out in the garden.

Dad died early on Saturday morning. Jacque came up with the coffin and we had him lie in state on his porch which was beautifully decorated with mats and masi. Fijians and part-European groups came all day to present regu regu. This was received by Mika, Vuki's eldest brother. Dad had apparently told Vuki that he did not wish to be buried in the family cemetery at Vatuwiri and that he wanted to lie closer to his home. So we had the men dig a hole in solid rock at the bottom of the garden. It was very difficult and it was noon before the hole was ready. A funeral service was conducted by the Anglican Vicar who came over from Savusavu. The Methodist Minister also conducted a service, as he had been asked to do so by Vuki. Finally, the Roman Catholic priest requested the opportunity to conduct a service in appreciation for all the help Dad had given to the Catholic parishioners on Taveuni. At the graveyard I gave the eulogy, as I felt I was the only one present who could speak fully on his life. It was emotionally difficult, for despite the problems we had had I did admire him for the fullness of his life and the many decent aspects of his character. He had given Jeanine and I a good start in life and for this I was grateful. Mahadeo spoke on behalf of the Indians and a chief from Vuna spoke for the Fijians.

There was a genuine sense of grief around the grave but, as Jacque said later, many of them were grieving not so much out of a sense of loss of someone they loved and respected but because the great benefactor was gone. There would be no more handouts of cash or cattle or other gifts. They were distressed because they could bleed him no more. I had released Brian early on the Saturday morning. He went back to his house and I thought no more about him. But he didn't show up at all that day and it wasn't until the following morning that I was told he had gone out in his car and disappeared. I felt obliged to find out what had happened to him but it was not until later in the day that word came in that his car was parked right up at the back of Waimaqera beyond Qaruwalu. I got a search party together and we went up to Qaruwalu and spent many hours trying to trace him. We found a track and followed this up the mountainside and eventually found some discarded clothes. Further on we discovered a discarded bible and finally, after another hour of climbing up the mountain, we found him stark naked crying out in a maniacal way. He was not aggressive so we brought him down to the vehicles and took him back to his house. Susie refused to have anything to do with him so I just left him in his house.

Later that day I was told that he was trying to cut the half-inch galvanised water pipe with a cane knife. I went over to the house and there he was, stark naked, hacking at this galvanised pipe. It occurred to me that he was trying to cut off the water and that he may try to set the house on fire. I approached him and tried to reason with him. He went into the house and came back with a can of petrol. He poured it onto the gateposts and set the benzene alight. I stood cautiously in the yard and watched this. Then he came over to where I was standing and poured petrol in a circle around me and set it alight. He had a cane knife in his hand all this time and I thought it best not to intimidate him in any way, so I waited and allowed the petrol to burn itself out. In the meantime he went back to hacking at the galvanised pipe. I realised that there was nothing more I could do for him so I went back to the house and called the police. When I explained the circumstances to them, they decided to take him up to the hospital, so he was bundled into the police wagon and taken away.

The next day I went up to the hospital where he was being held. There were two doctors present and I had lengthy discussions with them both. One doctor wanted to have him committed to the mental hospital in Suva while the other refused to do so. Unless two doctors certify a person he cannot be committed. So he was held there for a number of days until he stabilised. He was then brought back to the house and behaved in a reasonably rational way. In the meantime, I went through the house and found his stash of marijuana and burnt it.

I'd also spent the time going through the documents in the office. There in the dirty, musty old office environment were documents that had been accumulating for over 60 years. I worked for days sorting them out. Some were in good condition while others had been eaten by insects. I selected those to be discarded and burnt them. I put the others into boxes and took them back to Suva.

Jeanine had arrived a day after the funeral and I went to Matei to pick her up and drive her to the old home. On the way, I told her everything that had happened and it was quite a relief to get it out of my system. Jeanine was naturally saddened that she couldn't have been there at the end, or even at the funeral, but as we wandered around the grounds of the old house where we had grown up, we rekindled many of the memories of those early years and came to an appreciation of all they had meant to us. We both knew that this was the end of a long association with our home and it was a deeply emotional time for us.

One evening, I arranged for all the labour to come to the house and they gathered on mats on the grounds. We drank yaqona and I tried to express to them my appreciation for the loyalty they had given to Dad during his lifetime. These were people who had been born on the place, the descendants of employers of my great-grandfather. It was as much theirs as ours and I felt a closeness to them that was akin to that felt by a family. I told them that although I no longer lived there, a part of me would always be there and that they and the time I had spent with them and their families would always be a part of me.

A few days later, Jeanine flew back to Melbourne and after I had finally cleared out the office and said my goodbyes, I too headed up the coast to the airport at Matei.

It was a bright sunny day as the plane flew down the spectacular western coast of Taveuni, and I gazed down on all the homes and settlements that had been part of my life. I was overwhelmed with memories and emotion. By the time we passed over Ura where Jacque and Richard and Sandra had shared our lives, tears were rolling down my cheeks. Then there was the magnificent spread of Waimaqera's rich flats where row upon row of coconut trees stretched from the sea to the mountains, trees that had been planted by old James Valentine, Herbert Valentine, and Dad, and the elegant old homestead and its beautiful gardens that had been built by the missionaries so long ago. I thought of the pain and anguish, the love and fulfilment, the parties, the pleasures and the bitterness that had been part of it all.

We passed over Vatuwiri and I looked down upon the cemetery where so many Tarte bones lay. Then we were over the south cape and Taveuni began to fade into the distance.

My chest heaved with emotion and I wept unashamedly as I said goodbye to a place, a way of life, and a time in history that could never be recaptured.

Part Two

Greater Fiji: Life In The Nation

10. Sugar

For well over 100 years, the growing of sugar cane and the production of sugar has been the main economic activity in Fiji, with over a quarter of the population dependent on its wellbeing.

When I began work as Secretary of the Fiji Sugar Board in 1968, the sugar industry had reached a crossroads. For decades it had been the backbone of the Fiji economy, being the greatest foreign export earner and the largest employer. There were some 15,000 cane farmers delivering their cane to a single miller with four sugar mills. The millers employed some 4,000 labourers and the cane farmers engaged about 15,000 cane cutters in the harvesting season. Each farmer worked an average of ten acres of mainly leasehold land. Although the farmers were independent, they felt, and in fact were, dominated by the milling organisation.

The mills were owned by the giant Australian company CSR (Colonial Sugar Refining company) and while they must be given credit for developing the industry, their objective was to make profits for shareholders in Australia. The farmers believed they were being exploited and for years their political leaders had waged an aggressive campaign to gain a greater share of the sugar proceeds. This was determined by a contract between the millers and the farmers which also set out all aspects of the relationship, from growing and harvesting cane, to transport to the mills, crushing and export of sugar.

When negotiations between the growers' leaders and the millers broke down in 1968, the Chief Justice of Fiji appointed an arbitrator to determine the terms of the new contract.

Following exhaustive efforts, he was successful in appointing Lord Denning, who was the Master of the Rolls in the United Kingdom. When Denning began his hearings in August 1969, Judge Marsack, the Board Chairman, instructed me to attend as an observer. The hearing was conducted in a Catholic Parish Hall in the sugar city of Lautoka. This was a ground level building with wooden shutters around it that could seat about 500.

Denning sat on a raised platform at one end. Though an illustrious aura surrounded him, Denning was a frail little man with sharp features, very white skin, and a quiet voice. Despite his diminutive size and frail appearance, one sensed he was a strong man and there was an implication in his manner that said, 'Don't fool with me or waste my time.' Two advisors had been appointed to assist him in his task. The millers' representative was the then head of CSR in Fiji, Stuart Hermes. He was a big, gruff man with little sense of humour. He had come to Fiji from Australia as a young man and had worked his way up from the bottom of a very stratified organisation. As head of the organisation, he wielded enormous power. His staff cowered before him, farmers treated him like a god, and even the colonial civil servants feared him. If CSR wanted the government to do anything, they usually did it.

The other advisor representing the growers was a most unlikely leader. Swami Rudrananda was a Hindu monk who had come to Fiji from India in 1939 to help in the education of Hindus. He quickly empathised with the poverty stricken cane farmers and began to champion their rights. Always garbed in a saffron robe, he seldom wore shoes and often sat cross-legged on a chair in the boardroom, picking his toes. He spoke in a squeaky, high-pitched voice that belied the strength of his character, which was evident in the fiery black eyes that seemed to ignite when his anger flared, as it often did. Swami aroused both violent opposition and a devoted following. In a Sugar Advisory Council meeting on one occasion, when a fellow cane grower's representative condemned Swami for some statement he made, a loyal supporter rose and punched the critic. Hermes and Judge Marsack loathed him. A devoted follower once gave him a Rolls Royce car. It was put in Swami's garage and never used.

In a half circle around the hall facing Denning were the main players who were to present their cases. Representing the Growers were a team of five Indian lawyers. Leading the group was A. D. Patel, a brilliant young lawyer who had been sent to Fiji by Mahatma Ghandi to protect the interests of Indians. He rose to political prominence and became the leader of the opposition in the Legislative Council. He was a spellbinding speaker who captivated his listeners by beginning in a soft, slow manner and gradually raising the tempo and volume of his voice until he had his audience in the palm of his hands. Suave and always well groomed, polite and courteous, Patel was a formidable person.

Next to him was his brother, another lawyer, but the antithesis of A. D. While R. D. Patel had a great many cane grower clients, he was regarded as a buffoon. On one occasion, as he was making a presentation to Denning he waved his arms around wildly making a point and knocked a jug of water flying across the table, saturating all the papers on the table.

The third lawyer was S. M. Koya, a Muslim and heir apparent to A. D. Patel as leader of the Indians in Fiji. Koya has been described as an 'emotional chest-thumping orator full of fire and passion.' Described by another as 'an actor and a nuisance,' Koya had a violent temper that gave him a bully image. Dark, thick set and humourless, it was somewhat surprising that he should become a popular leader. But Koya was a successful legal advocate. He won his cases and knew how to excite public emotions.

10. Sugar

The fourth member of the Indian cane growers' team was another lawyer, K. C. Ramrakha, a methodical and courteous man, who won his support through brilliant debate.

I sat at a table on my own between this group and the CSR team. The company had only two lawyers up front. They were R. G. Kermode, a partner in the most respected firm of lawyers, and his assistant, Barrie Sweetman. Both of them were able and respected legal representatives but we all knew they were simply the mouthpieces for the enormous support team that CSR had brought over from Australia. One of those was the most senior official in Australia, Gordon Jackson. He usually sat inconspicuously in the third or fourth row, listening intently, absorbing everything but never showing emotion. He was a cold and calculating man with steel coloured eyes and a steely temperament.

On the other end of the arch around Denning were the Fijian growers' representatives. Their team was lead by a young Australian lawyer who was beginning to make his mark in Australian legal circles. Gerald Brennan was later to become a Chief Justice in Australia and his skills were clearly evident as he presented his argument to Denning. He was supported by an Indian lawyer, M. T. Khan, who was given the derogatory sobriquet of M. T. Can. The third member of the team was Aminiasi Katonivualiku, who would in later years disgrace himself by being found guilty of fraud.

Denning was to take evidence from hundreds of witnesses over 21 days of hearing. Each had a different style. CSR had a battery of technical men who gave clinical statements that were hard to dispute. The farmers witnesses told heartwrenching stories of hardship and misery which were all due, they claimed, to the greed and insensitiveness of the CSR management. One star was a senior CSR field executive. He was grilled for over a day by all the lawyers because he was known to be knowledgeable and fair. He was asked hundreds of questions, but before he answered any question he would pick up a glass of water that was on a stool beside his seat and have a drink. As soon as the glass was empty, a clerk would fill it up, and as soon as the jug was empty it would be filled. There was great speculation and amusement around the hall about how many glasses of water he could consume. Interest in his evidence almost seemed secondary. Each day the inside of the hall was packed, with an equal number of farmers outside leaning in through the windows. There was rapt attention as the farmers tried to assess the weight of evidence. They watched Denning eagerly looking for signs that he was favouring their case. But he was the embodiment of dignity and impartiality.

Each Friday I would return to Suva and give my report to Judge Marsack. I knew little about the sugar industry when I joined, and it was like having a crash course, for the inquiry covered every aspect of the industry. On Monday

I would return by plane to Nadi and then by taxi to Lautoka. One Monday morning, my taxi driver, in his haste to get me to the hearing on time, thought he could beat a train across a level crossing. He was mistaken and the train slammed into my side of the taxi, splitting open my head. I went to a doctor and had it stitched up and arrived at the hearing with my head swathed in bandages. Denning was most concerned.

Lord Denning had a reputation of favouring the underdog so it came as little surprise that when his final award was handed down in 1970 he said, 'If I have erred at all, I think it will be because I have been too favourable to the growers … but I would remind them [the millers] that they have had a good innings—a first rate innings—for the sugar industry in Fiji … they have done well … events have tipped the scale in their favor.'

His award was so favourable to growers that the CSR gave notice that they could not operate under the terms of the contract that he had drawn up, and that they wished to sell their interests in the Fiji sugar industry. The government negotiated a purchase, a local company was set up, over 200 CSR staff withdrew, and the industry was completely localised and changed forever.

Judge Marsack was another casualty of the award. Denning had criticised him over his policy of certifying the proceeds of sugar and this was unacceptable to Marsack. He resigned in fury and for the rest of his life bore a bitter grudge against Denning for tarnishing his reputation.

The Prime Minister, Ratu Sir Kamisese Mara, whose function it was to appoint the Chairman of the Sugar Board, was successful in bringing back to Fiji one of the most outstanding British civil servants to ever work here. Sir Ian Thompson first arrived in Fiji in the early 1940s as a young District Officer. He immediately joined the Fiji Military Forces and served with distinction in the Solomon's campaign. This was the beginning of a lifelong affinity with the Fijian people. He spoke Fijian better than most Fijians and served in most districts throughout the islands. Fijians and Indians alike trusted and respected him. He worked closely with the most distinguished Fijian Chief and leader, Ratu Sir Lala Sukuna, as Deputy Lands Commissioner and a great deal of Sukuna's mana rubbed off onto him. He succeeded Sukuna as Lands Commissioner and for a time was Acting Governor before being posted to the British Virgin Islands as Governor. When this appointment to the Virgin Islands was announced, the people of Fiji sent a petition to the British Government asking that Thompson not be transferred. When Mara asked him to return to Fiji to take up the position of Chairman of the Sugar Board, he resigned from the Colonial Service and returned to Fiji in 1971.

10. Sugar

It was my good fortune to spend the next 13 years working with Sir Ian and this was certainly one of the most rewarding periods of my life.

Part of our work involved settling industrial disputes in the industry. During Marsack's time, this centered around the settlement of the union's annual log of claims. There were three unions: the Staff Association, with 250 members, the General Workers Union, which had about 2,500 members, and the Tradesmen's Union, which had about 500 members. The process with the General Workers Union was that the Company and the Union met and negotiated, with the Chairman and the Secretary of the Sugar Board present as observers. About 20 of the Union executive and four or five company men met and held talks, usually for two days. They dressed in suits and discussion was calm and polite. The long time President of the Union was an Indian lawyer named Manikam Pillay. Manikam was a dapper little man and always showed the greatest respect to those present. He seldom spoke during negotiations, except when deadlock over an issue seemed imminent. At that point he would suggest a compromise, which was usually acceptable. His skill always resulted in a settlement over claims.

The Staff Association was a more militant, intelligent and determined group. There was no Manikam Pillay amongst them and on one occasion the two groups, the Chairman and I sat silently for two hours when a deadlock was reached. During this period, no one was prepared to say a word. Finally, the Chairman lost patience, rose and left, and talks broke down.

The Tradesmen's Union was made up mainly of part-Europeans, as they were then called. Their members were skilled mechanics who ran the machinery in the mills. The leaders were humble and polite, except when they drank too much. This was their Achilles heel and was manipulated by the company. The talks with them always began in the morning and usually broke down by lunchtime. The company provided lunch and drinks, and when talks resumed in the afternoon, the Union's representatives were mellow and ready to sign any agreement. The risk in this process was that sometimes the Union men had too much to drink and a passionate, often illogical plea was made for a greater share of the cake, or someone would lose their temper. It must be said that the Company, knowing the Union's weak negotiating position, always tried to be fair with them.

When I first joined the sugar industry, the secretaries of the General Workers Union were usually rather polite and cooperative men. They had to be, because the company was so dominant that the only way to extract any additional benefits for the workers was to work in harmony with management. But circumstances changed when the Fiji Government became the major shareholder in the milling organisation, and the secretaries became more militant. One to really shake the tree was Apisai Tora. Perhaps one of the most colorful and enigmatic Fijian union and political leaders, he made headlines for over 50 years. Trade Unionism was his platform and in 1959 he was leader of a strike that led to the first civil riots in Suva. He flirted with communism and Islam and changed his name to Mohammed Tora. Jailed for arson and sedition, he also served for some years as a minister in the Alliance Government. While proclaiming his Fijian nationalism, he called for the expulsion of Indians from Fiji, yet he later joined forces with the Indian dominated National Federation Party.

At the time he was elected as General Secretary of the Union, his counterpart in the company was an unusual industrial manager, Gautam Ram Swarup. The son of a cane farmer, Swarup was typical of a brand of Indian who had grown up in a multi-racial rural environment, done well at school, gone on to study accountancy, furthered his studies in Australia, returned to take up a position as a chartered accountant, and saw himself not as an Indian, but as a Fiji citizen. He and Tora, although intrinsincally different, found a great deal of common ground. They achieved settlement on issues that surprised many. Both were pragmatic men, and Gautam mixed forthrightness with a keen brand of Fiji humour. He teased and ridiculed Tora in a way that others could not and was not offended by Tora's bluntness and aggressive manner.

While they were both in office, the three of us were sent to visit Barbados, Jamaica, Trinidad and Guyana to study industrial relations in those sugar-producing countries. Tora had previously visited Cuba and had met Castro, and was very keen to make a diversion to Cuba to renew acquaintances. We had a hard time persuading him otherwise. In fact, throughout the trip we had a hard time keeping him politically correct. He wanted to get into the factories and stir up the workers and this upset the local managers. He was also a great philanderer. The trip was useful for us in a reverse kind of way. The Caribbean sugar industries were in such a deplorable condition that the main benefit of our trip was to learn what not to do. We returned with some valuable lessons and Tora was to admit that his union members were not so badly off.

When Rabuka mounted his coup in 1987, Tora was out of the union but was a strong Taukei (Indigenous) rights leader. Gautam was then Deputy General Manager of the Fiji Sugar Corporation. It was a very difficult time and the sugar industry struggled to keep going. Many Indian cane farmers refused to cut their cane. There were threats of sabotage in the factories. Armed soldiers set up camps and roadblocks all over the country. There were outbreaks of violence and the economy shuddered to a halt as investors withdrew their patronage. Gautam told me how, one day, as he was working in his office, a certain failed politician who had managed to be drafted into the military, stormed into his office. He was a grossly overweight part-European who, dressed in an ill-fitting military uniform, looked like a comic character. This idiotic 'soldier' drew a pistol from his holster, slammed it down on Gautam's desk and declared, 'I am now going to watch over the sugar industry.'

On another occasion during this crisis, as I was sitting with Gautam in his office he said to me, 'I am going through an identity crisis. For the first time in my life I am being forced to think of myself as an Indian.' I understood his dilemma, for although I was officially labeled 'European' and had grown up in an elite environment, I detested the classification and refused to fill in forms that required me to state my race. I had no links to Europe, and, like Gautam, I never thought of myself in ethnic terms. I was a person from Fiji, a Fiji Islander, if you like. Fiji was my home. It was where my roots were sunk.

Because it was so politically advantageous to have some influence in the sugar industry, many failed politicians tried to restore their political reputations by getting a foothold. Chirag Ali Shah had been a staunch member of the National Federation Party before he lost his seat, just before elections for a new General Secretary of the Union. He stood and won simply because he had the gift of oration, even though he knew nothing about trade unionism or industrial relations. But he was a kindly man and I spent more time with him in his garden than in his factories. He had a real gift for raising bougainvilleas and his garden on the dry side of Western Viti Levu was a blaze of color. He never told me all his secrets, except that bougainvilleas need to be put under stress in a dry environment. Unfortunately I lived in the wet Eastern side of the island and I could never get them to flower like Chirag's.

During my first year in the industry, the power was absolutely in the hands of management, but by the time I left, the balance had swung just as emphatically to the unions. During the last years of my service, by which time I was working as the Industrial Commissioner with the Sugar Industry Tribunal Office, the union was controlled by a highly skilled and experienced trade unionist named Felix Anthony. Felix had been a union leader in the aviation industry and was accustomed to talking very loudly to overcome the noise of aircraft engines. I didn't know this at first, so was rather stunned at our first confrontation when I found him yelling at me and the company officials as though we were in a street brawl. Felix was young, energetic, and very intelligent. He had good debating skills and understood the complexities of the milling operations. In many respects, he had greater skills than the industrial managers in the company and he out-maneuvered them time and again. I had many long and tedious battles with Felix and, because of my concern that he was succeeding in swinging the pendulum too far towards the unions, I suggested to him that I could assist in getting him a scholarship to go overseas and study law. I really thought he would make a very good lawyer. But Felix had the bit between his teeth and was determined to maximise improvements in workers' conditions. He too began to balance his demands to ensure that the company could survive. Even the company began to see merit in his campaign. Just before I left office, I presided over a signing session with Felix and the other three General Secretaries and the company. We signed 25 agreements that were designed to ensure the long-term relationship between the employees and the company.

Felix was to become the pre-eminent trade unionist in the country when he took over from deposed Prime Minister Mahendra Chaudhry as General Secretary of the Fiji Trade Union Congress. He was an outspoken and fearless critic of the perpetrators of the 2000 coup while remaining head of the General Workers Union.

Another example of how things had changed between 1968, when I joined the industry, and 1999 when I left, occurred when a new manager was appointed to the large Lautoka sugar mill. When I first joined, the outgoing Secretary of the Sugar Board was a man name Rob Sulch. His reputation with the farmers had been tarnished to the point that the National Federation party newspaper *Pacific Review* called him Mr Slush. I knew this was a price to pay for being in a high profile, politicised industry. Before he left, Rob took me round to meet all the main players of the industry.

The manager of the Lautoka mill was Murray Aitkin, an Australian who had spent all his life in Fiji and an archetype of the CSR mill manager. Within his mill, in his locality and township of Lautoka, and among cane farmers, he was regarded as the supreme being. This kind of adulation gave him an enormous ego and sense of superiority. When I was first escorted into his enormous office, he remained seated behind his large wooden desk and throughout the time that Rob and I spent with him, despite the fact that I was the scion of one of the most influential copra planter families, he managed to make me feel like an insect to be trampled on.

When I went to pay my respects to the newly appointed Fijian manager of the Lautoka mill 30 years later, the contrast could not have been greater. Abele had worked his way up through the complex staff structure and the board believed that he had the skills to head up what was then one of the largest sugar mills in the Southern Hemisphere. He had many of the characteristic Fijian qualities that cause them to stand out above other races of people, including respect and humility. He manifested both of these when I went into his office for the first time after his appointment. He rose quickly from behind the same desk that Murray Aitkin used, came around to greet me, went briefly down on one knee, took one of my hands in both of his, and murmured, 'Sa bula Saka' (Hello Sir), before he switched into English and invited me to be seated. This act of humility was not demeaning in any way, nor did it make me feel at all superior. It was simply the Fijian way, and it was such a refreshing contrast to the attitude of Murray Aitkin.

There is a certain irony in the fact that, over the past 50 years, it hasn't been only the big businessmen, civil servants, politicians, traders and manufacturers who have sustained Fiji's economic growth. The impetus has come from the humble cane farmer, who by extremely hard work and commitment increased cane production from two million tons to four-and-a-half million tons over 30 years. I spent a great deal of time over that period visiting many of the 20,000 farmers, dealing with their problems and listening to their views. Seventy-five per cent of the farmers were Indians, and the remainder Fijians. The Indians were mainly descendents of those who came to Fiji as indentured labourers to work for the CSR. They subsequently became tenant farmers on small ten-acre blocks of leasehold land. Even as recently as 1968, when I started in the industry, the farmer's life was hard. Most of the homes were made of corrugated iron or bamboo.

They contained the bare necessities of life, drew water from wells, and few had electricity or cars. The price of cane was about $6 per ton. There wasn't much margin for profit.

But these simple folk had a vision: to work hard, save, educate their children, and improve the quality of their lives. I watched that vision realised by many over the years. By the turn of the century there were solid concrete homes all over the cane areas and many farmers had cars, tractors and lorries. There were TV aerials on most rooftops. Farmers' sons and daughters were the doctors, lawyers, teachers, dentists and political leaders of Fiji. They had sons and daughters in professional positions living in Australia, New Zealand and the USA. It helped that the price of cane had risen to $60 per ton, but costs had gone up proportionately, and they had to cope with the constant ravages of drought, floods and hurricanes.

Typical of the fighting spirit of farmers was Bechu Prasad. In 1984, at the age of 83, he could have expected a quiet and comfortable retirement. But in a few moments of cyclonic winds, his house, which he had built himself, was demolished. The treasured possessions and mementoes that remind an old man of his youth were scattered across the battered cane fields. But his concern was not for himself, despite the fact that he had to live in a tent. He went out to help government officials distribute food rations and assist other less resilient people restore their homes and their lives.

Bechu Prasad was the son of a mill employee who acquired some land and began farming. He had little education but developed a powerful work and community ethic. Even at 83 he still went out at dawn to work the fields. He was fit and agile. His eyes were alert and sparkling with humour. A large white moustache covered his mouth. His speech was coherent and constructive. He wore a battered felt hat. Before his house was destroyed by the hurricane, he proudly displayed on its walls the Coronation Medal, the Certificate of Honour, appointment of Justice of the Peace, and the insignia of the Order of the British Empire. He was a committee member of the local school and Indian Advisory Council.

Another old-timer was Ram Kissum, a cane farmer at Rakiraki, on the north eastern part of Viti Levu. Like many others, he was the son of an indentured labourer. Years of lonely toil, years spent guiding his bullocks as they hauled his plough across the land, years spent planning and experimenting to balance inputs and outputs of the soil, turned him into a pensive and thoughtful man. He told me how he used to get up at four am and milk the cows and start work on the farm. He'd rest only a couple of times during the day and finished at eight o'clock at night. This would go on for six to seven days a week, depending on the weather. He hadn't acquired many possessions after 50 years of farming but he told me proudly that while he had one son helping him on the farm, another lived in Vancouver, another in Sydney, two were headmasters of local schools, another was studying at Madras University, one daughter was married to a school teacher and another to a farmer. He would frequently say, 'I haven't wasted my life.'

Often the most contented men and women are those who are considered 'average.' Not those of genius level nor idiots; not millionaires nor paupers; not owners of vast estates nor pockets of poor land; not residents of mighty mansions nor of hovels; not overzealous workers nor loafers. These 'average' people have enough to live on without having to struggle and are not plagued by the social stress that often accompanies great wealth or poverty. They are usually happy. They are part of the great multitude who contribute tremendously to all aspects of life but are not easily recognised, for they don't stand out above others.

Abdul Gafoor was typical of the 'average' cane farmer. He had an upright stance, a firm handshake and clear twinkling eyes. His face was fringed with a well-trimmed grey beard and he was seldom without his fez. The son of an indentured labourer, he started work at an early age, and found a quiet and fertile valley deep in the hills far from the Labasa sugar mill. He acquired a lease and began the backbreaking task of felling the virgin bush, working till late at night to turn it into a cane farm. It took him a long time but that valley is now covered with lush fields of emerald cane. The low land is terraced and planted in rice. Coconut trees surround the solid concrete home. An all-weather road meanders through the hills to the main access. He has a lorry to cart his cane. He was surrounded by a family who, like him, are devout Muslims. Despite never

10. Sugar

having been to school he learnt to read the Koran and has been on his pilgrimage to Mecca. There was nothing really outstanding about Abdul Gafoor. He kept out of politics and never tried to command the spotlight. His life was his cane farm and his family. He was the solid core of the sugar industry.

Indian people from the subcontinent have had a centuries old tradition of farming land. Those who came to Fiji brought their skills with them and adjusted easily to the intensive nature of cane farming. Fijians, on the other hand, have only in recent times been introduced to the difficulties of intensive agriculture. They have been accustomed to planting small plots of taro, cassava, yams or yaqona. Cane farming requires hard work and discipline to the timely needs of planting, cultivation, fertilising and harvesting. Many Fijian farmers who started farms adjacent to successful Indians and learnt from them have been successful. But those who have been out on their own have not done so well.

George Cavalevu made his name as a rugby player. He was a brilliant winger who captained the Fiji team that trounced the mighty Maoris in 1951. The next year, he was the star of the team that toured Australia and he has always been rated as one of the greats of Fiji rugby. After rugby, he tried a number of vocations but never settled down till he had the offer of leasing 1,300 acres of land in the Ba valley. The qualities that made him a superb sportsman obviously acquitted him to be a good cane farmer. He quickly raised production to 500 tons, and ran 200 head of cattle, 50 pigs and 200 goats, as well as planting taro, cassava and yam. George became an example to other Fijians, demonstrating that they could succeed as cane farmers. But disaster struck him in the form of a devastating hurricane that wrecked his farm. During the height of the storm, as he was trying to salvage some of his possessions, he was knocked to the ground and a four-inch nail was driven through his knee. It was some time before he could be taken to the hospital where he was to spend many painful months. The leg was saved but it was left permanently stiff. George rebuilt his farm and became an eloquent spokesman for farmers. Some years later, I led a team of sugar industry men on a tour to study the industries in Mauritius, Kenya and India. George was part of that team and on all our flights we had to be sure he had an aisle seat for his stiff leg.

Another member of that team was Atunaisa Maitoga. Atu had been a captain in the military before joining the District Administration. He went into politics and won a seat by beating his own chief. Although he had fought hard to win, the moment of his success left him with a dilemma, so he apologised to his chief for beating him. Atu was a ramrod straight man who always dressed in a coat and tie despite the weather, and conducted himself with extreme dignity. After his victory he was a candidate for the role of Deputy Prime Minister, but this never eventuated.

While in Kenya, George, Atu and I walked along the shores of Lake Victoria, took off our shoes and waded into the tepid water. We did this for a particular reason. According to Fijian legend, the Fijian people came from Kenya and what is now Tanzania. There are many placenames and words that are the same in all three places. As George and Atu stood in the water of Lake Victoria they wondered if perhaps some ancestors in ancient times had done the same. It was a defining moment for them both.

Two hours drive along the Kings Road from Suva is the village of Matawailevu, whose name means 'the source of the big river.' The village is perched on the corner of a high ridge. As the road winds round a sharp bend, stretched out below is a small valley nestling in the bosom of the surrounding hills. This is the valley of Tova, which in English means 'the flat land.' It was also the home of one of Fiji's most progressive cane farmers, Eparama Tarovia.

I told Eparama Tarovia that I would find my way to his home but he said, 'No, this is your first visit so I will meet you on the main road and show you the way.' This is the kind of gesture one would expect from a man who shows a refreshing blend of traditionalism and independence. His respect for Fijian custom was abundantly clear. Yaqona was served as soon as I arrived. Tabua (whale's teeth) hung from the walls beside photos of the esteemed leaders, Ratu Sir Lala Sukuna, Ratu Sir Kamisese Mara and the Governor General. On another wall was a tableau of the last supper, a gift from his son, who was serving with the United Nations forces in Lebanon.

He was an avid believer in all Fijian customs and traditions—customs that are often a burden to Fijians and which can inhibit their commercial progress. But in his case, these customs have supplemented and enriched his life. Traditionalist as he was, he abandoned village communal life to take up farming on his 87-acre farm, which became one of the showplaces of his district. He went to a Methodist school before going on to study agriculture. There is not much that he doesn't know about farming. Unlike many other Fijian farmers he did not learn from Indian neighbours, he taught them.

The government had recognised his achievements and appointed him to numerous committees and boards. The Fijian administration recognised him by appointing him to the Provincial Council. His family looked upon him with adulation and respect and the Queen made him a Member of the Order of the British Empire.

After spending some time looking all over his farm, he invited me back to his house for lunch. His family had prepared a magnificent spread. There was enough for 20 people. 'I must apologise for this humble meal,' he said in the typical Fijian manner of belittling their magnificent hospitality.

10. Sugar

The cane farming community and those associated with cane farming make up about one quarter of the voters of Fiji. It is little wonder then that they have been so politicised. Every budding politician tried to win their favor in order to get elected to parliament. The Indian parties' political strength has always been in the cane fields, and the poor farmers have been manipulated and pushed from pillar to post to satisfy the whims of ambitious politicians. Leaders have risen and fallen depending on the success of the promises they have made.

A leader of the Fijians in the Nadi district was Napolioni Dawai, the Tui Nadi. He was a non-conformist who paid homage to no one. He was condemned by many, feared by others, avoided by those who abhorred his brash, rude manners, and envied by those who saw him getting richer and richer. He attended the prestigious Queen Victoria School, an exclusively Fijians school, and joined the Fijian Affairs Office before serving in many different government departments where he was always found to be a misfit. He then joined the military and went to serve in Malaya, but when he was overlooked to attend an officer training course he left the army and became a magistrate. Then came the tourism boom and Ratu Napolioni successfully negotiated land leases for many of the large hotel developments in the west. In his own words, 'I know how to handle these overseas developers and screw out the best conditions. I am abrupt and rude in a joking kind of way. I don't beat about the bush or mince words.' His own landowner unit became a shareholder in the prestigious hotels on Denarau Island and operated a fleet of taxis from the hotels.

It was easy to be cowed by Ratu Napolioni. He was an enormous man with a rather ferocious face and a loud gravelly voice. He projected an arrogant, supremely confident image and was never daunted by a situation nor a person's reputation. He became a friend of Marlon Brando and visited him in Los Angeles. 'You and I are alike,' he once told Brando, 'we keep many wives.' Naturally, Dawai entered politics and became a senator. He was later elected to the House by the Alliance Party but he was never a party man and always followed his own agenda.

On one occasion, I took a five man, multi-racial group of sugar industry leaders to the first World Cane Farmers Conference in Guadalajara, Mexico. Two of the members were Swami Rudrananda and Ratu Napolioni. We sat down in the front row of a hall with some 800 delegates from the sugar world and made many interjections during discussion. Possibly because we were so multi-racial and objectively critical, or perhaps because of the impression that Ratu Napolioni and Swamiji made, the Chairman asked if I would propose the main resolution to come out of the meeting. At one stage. Swamiji wanted to make a statement and the Chairman invited him to go on stage and speak from the main podium. This entailed climbing a flight of ten steep steps, which was quite beyond the frail old Swami. Undaunted, Ratu Napolioni rose and gathered up the saffron clad old man in his arms, carried him up the steps, and gently placed him before the podium. The delegates loved this show of devotion and applauded loudly. Dawai stood like a sentinel, arms akimbo, beside the Swami, as he delivered his statement. When he finished, he again gathered up the old man in his arms and carried him back to his seat.

On our return trip to Fiji, Air New Zealand kindly upgraded us all to first class. We were delighted but, regrettably, Ratu Napolioni took advantage of the gesture and became drunk and abusive to the crew and other passengers. It was my unfortunate duty to write a letter of apology to Air New Zealand when we returned to Suva.

Research scientists, particularly plant breeders, are often quiet backroom people of whom little is seen or heard. They tend to dabble quietly in their laboratories, peering into microscopes, testing, researching and meticulously recording their results. Perhaps a paper emerges from their work and mankind benefits in some small way from their tireless but largely unheralded endeavours.

Such a model does not fit former Fiji Sugar Corporation's Research manager, Krishna Murti, a man who was certainly more highly lauded internationally than at home. Few Fiji people outside the sugar industry will have heard his name. Fewer still are aware of his significant achievements. But wherever one travels in the cane sugar world, be it Japan or Mauritius, India or Taiwan, Cuba or South Africa, the common denominator is always the same: Krishna Murti. He is internationally regarded as among the foremost cane breeders and his research papers are studied by scientists everywhere.

What brought Krishna Murti this fame?

Fundamentally it was because he was an extremely capable scientist. His first ambition was to study medicine, but he finally settled on marine biology and zoology and gained a gold medal at the University of Annamalai in Madras.

In 1960, when he returned to Fiji, he could not find employment and was told he was over-educated. Eventually he had to settle for a job as a humble chemist with the CSR at Lautoka Mill.

Fortunately, he came to the notice of Joe Daniels, himself an internationally regarded cane breeder, who was the Director of Agricultural Research.

These two began working together on a project to make wild canes flower out of season so that they could be crossed with noble canes to produce new genetic lines. They succeeded in developing a set of hybrids and this technique gave them a lead on cane breeders in other parts of the world.

The real problem faced by cane breeders was keeping pace with the expansionist policies of the industry. How could they breed new varieties fast enough?

Krishna Murti accepted this challenge and as a result achieved a scientific breakthrough that was to bring him international recognition.

He realised that the traditional method of breeding, by crossing male and female flowers and inducing new characteristics into the progeny, was far too slow. It took eight to ten years to develop a new variety in this way. Instead, he called upon his knowledge of medicine and cell biology to develop a revolutionary new technique of plant tissue culture. He placed slices of cane tissue in artificial mediums, to induce a callus formation, in which new plants regenerated very rapidly. In this way, he was able to introduce new characteristics and speed up the process of variety breeding. He presented his paper on this technique in 1974 and it immediately attracted attention from all around the world.

In Fiji he was able to develop a new commercial variety of cane known as Ono in the incredibly short span of five years. Many other varieties suitable for all types of land have since been developed.

But the benefits of this knowledge to Fiji have been more than just new varieties. Because of his reputation on the international scene, the doors of research institutes in cane-producing countries were opened to him. Exchange programmes on variety testing for diseases and pests were established between Fiji, India, Taiwan, Philippines, India, Bangladesh and Hawaii. He was invited to establish tissue culture labs in a number of countries and is regularly invited to speak at international forums.

In 1985, a partial industrial restructure took place with the scrapping of the Sugar Board and Sugar Advisory council. In their place a Sugar Commission, a Sugar Tribunal and, most importantly, a Sugar Cane Growers Council was set up. The latter was to give the growers more influence in the affairs of the industry. With this re-organisation, I became the Industrial Commissioner and the man chosen to be the Chairman of the Commission was Gerald Barrack.

Gerald served his apprenticeship in commerce. Extremely hard working and ambitious, with a talent for finances, Gerald became head of a number of prominent companies before he was asked to be the first head of the Commission by Prime Minister Ratu Mara. In this capacity, he was also chair of the sugar marketing company and the fertilizer organisation.

It accordingly fell on Gerald's shoulders to drive the restructure. Throughout the early years of the new century, he battled on gamely. The stakeholders were fully aware of the critical urgency for action, yet the politicians continued to play their divisive games.

The expiry of native land leases and the failure to renew them to the sitting tenants, as well as the coups of 1987 and 2000, had serious impacts on the sugar industry. Many skilled and experienced staff officers in the Fiji Sugar Corporation decided to migrate overseas and it was extremely difficult to find replacements. Likewise, many of the new generation of farmers left to join relatives already overseas and it was left to the old people to run the farms. The number of cane farmers dropped from 22,000 to 13,000. Efficiency in the mills deteriorated because of the lack of funds to carry out capital improvements. The costs of production rose. Production of cane fell from four million tons to under two million tons. Sugar output fell from 500,000 tons to 160,000 tons.

Experts from India were brought in to fix the mills, but they seemed to do more harm than good.

The industry structure that had been set up was dismantled and much of the drive for the industry was returned to the Fiji Sugar Corporation. Valiant efforts were made by the Corporation and government to turn things around and diversify the industry. But the reality was that the days of the industry as the economic backbone of Fiji had ended. The baton had been decisively passed to tourism.

But the sugar industry cannot be dismissed so lightly. It is embedded in the folklore of the country. I recall reflecting on a major sugar industry conference held in Nadi in 1980. The keynote speaker was the Prime Minister, Ratu Mara.

Tall and grey haired, Ratu Mara limped down the aisle with a somewhat uneasy smile fixed on his strong but tired face. Beside him was the independent Chairman Sir Ian Thompson, soon to be acting Governor General. These two men, one the nation's leader, the other the nation's sugar industry leader, holding jobs more prone than any other to public criticism, were two of the most popular and admired men in the country.

The Prime Minister gave an address that opened the 1980 Sugar Industry Conference.

But as he and other speakers discussed the future of sugar, as the conference unfolded, as the miller's executive chatted informally with the cane farmer, the trade unionist with the cabinet minister, as the vice chairman of the world's largest sugar broking house talked about sugar marketing prospects, as the chief executive of the sugar mill company talked blithely about a crop of four-and-a-half million tons of cane, what thoughts were passing through the minds of the delegates?

Perhaps Eric Jones, who would have to sell 500,000 tons of sugar that year, was reflecting on the growth of exports, way back to 1874, when a grand total of ten tons was shipped out.

10. Sugar

What about Krishna Mudaliar of Rakiraki? Did he remember when the indenture system ended and the Penang Mill had to close down in 1923 and 1924?

When the general manager of the Native Land Trust Board spoke about land, no doubt many farmers recalled with pride that great occasion back in the 1920s when the Colonial Sugar Refining Company began the tenant farm system and they became independent farmers in their own right, and were able to say, 'This farm belongs to me.'

Perhaps Viliame Rakoroi also remembered when his mataqali land reverted to him and he was able to join the sugar industry. Conversely James Shankar Singh may have remembered with bitterness the day when land that he had been farming reverted to Fijian reserve.

When George Moody-Stuart spoke about total Fiji hourly crushing capacity reaching 995 tons by 1982, did Arthur Ede, the last of the CSR engineering executives in Fiji, smile and recall that, in 1880, Penang Mill crushed a capacity of five tons of sugar per day?

When Akuila Savu spoke about the prospect for ethanol from cane juice, and Renton Righelato, research director of Tate & Lyle, expounded on sugar as a raw material for baker's yeast, citric acid, vinegar and detergent, did Krishna Murti reflect nostalgically on his student days when research meant breeding new cane varieties?

When Prem Chand Seth, the outspoken representative of the lorry owners, erupted with criticism about the transport system, did he compare efficiency with the 1890s when river punts were used to deliver cane to Rarawai Mill?

What was running through the alert but aged mind of Swami Rudrananda, the saffron–robed Hindu monk, who for 50 years had been the vocal champion of cane farmers? Was he remembering his involvement in the strikes of 1943, the conflict over the cane contract in 1959, the arbitration by Lord Silsoe, and disagreement over acceptance of his contract, or perhaps his battles with the CSR, the Denning arbitration in 1969, and the departure of CSR?

Then there was Rasheed Ali, the dynamic young executive, soon to be head of the Fiji Sugar Corporation absorbing everything like a sponge. Did he feel somewhat awed at the prospect of assuming control of the vast milling organisation? Was he aware of the ghosts of the many CSR men who had preceded him?

What was the Prime Minister thinking about as he sat unobtrusively at the back of the hall, after giving his address? Was he wondering what would happen to his nation if industrial strife tore the industry asunder? Was he conscious that the votes of the 100,000 people that the conference delegates represented could vote him in or out of office? Was he praying that tourism would grow so that the country would be less reliant on the capricious sugar industry?

What did the sugar broker from London think when he heard a farmer accuse the sugar company of continuing the CSR attitude of subjugating the farmers? Did he have doubts about our ability to supply the promised quota of sugar? Indeed, what did the humble farmer from Tavua think about having the opportunity of being able to question the vice-chairman of one of the world's greatest sugar broking houses?

What was passing through the minds of trade union representatives in the hall when the President of the Sugar and General Workers Union introduced his traditional rival, the head of the Fijian Sugar Corporation? Were they astounded at his complimentary remarks?

But the big question in the minds of most people then and now was: how long could the sugar industry continue to sustain the economic growth and prosperity of Fiji.

11. Tourism

Colonialism changed Fiji forever. So did the growth of commerce and industry—like sugar. But from the middle of the 20th century, it has been tourism that has changed the face of Fiji.

The main reasons that people come to Fiji are to experience the natural beauty of the islands and the sea, and to be charmed by the Fijian people. Yet in the 19th century, when Europeans first came to its shores, the Fijians were regarded as some of the most brutish and bloodthirsty cannibals on earth.

Many of the islands are exquisitely lovely and the Fijian people have a unique way of making visitors feel welcome. The men are physically attractive with beaming smiles and the women are warm and courteous. These are all essential ingredients for the development of tourism but they were not realised until the middle of the 20th century.

It was then that Hugh Ragg, a scion of an old pioneer family, began building a chain of hotels around Viti Levu. His son David had lived for some years on Taveuni managing a copra plantation near our own. He and my family were close friends and both owned Model-T Fords, which they drove rather wildly on the island's one-lane gravel roads. On one occasion they crashed into each other on a corner and my sister Jeanine went flying through the front window. They were not going very fast and she wasn't hurt, but it did cause some family tension.

David joined his father in the hotel enterprise, which they gradually expanded from small country establishments in the main sugar towns to the first real tourist resort at Korolevu Beach. Situated on a beautiful bay on the Viti Levu south coast, it was an instant success. For the first time, Fijian culture was put on display for visitors. They had the opportunity to see the famous Beqa firewalkers and go deep-sea fishing. When Jacque and I were married in 1957 we spent our honeymoon in one of their Fijian bures on the beach and our long and happy marriage has always been linked to Korolevu. Sadly, the enigmatic Apisai Tora, who I have referred to elsewhere, took out his spite on the hotel after a union dispute and burnt many of the bures. It was later rebuilt and continued to prosper until a dispute within the Ragg family led to its closure and sale, and it never re-opened.

During the 1940s and 1950s, the airline Pan American was flying through Fiji to Australia. As there was an overnight stopover at Nadi, some of the airline's pilots got together and constructed the Mocambo Hotel at the airport. It was such a success that they decided to consolidate their interests in Fiji tourism by acquiring a lease over lovely Yanuca Island, just off the Sigatoka coast and building The Fijian, which for many years remained the premium resort in Fiji. It provided every facility, from game fishing to golf, bowls and water skiing, and became the model for many others that followed. The architect and project manager was a dour Irishman named Paddy Doyle who stayed on as the manager of the resort for most of his life. His personality was synonymous with the place and it was never the same after he left to set up his own small resort. Perhaps the happiest day of Paddy's life was when he went to Buckingham Palace in full morning dress to receive an honour from the Queen for his contribution to Fiji tourism. The resort was later bought by the giant Malaysian hotel chain Shangri La.

Another of the great characters of Fiji tourism was Dick Smith (not to be confused with the Australian electrician).

Dick's family had a prosperous business in Sydney but he had decided to forsake the city for the islands. He acquired a Second World War Fairmile and sailed to Fiji. The Fairmile was a narrow gutted, speedy, torpedo boat that rolled dreadfully in heavy seas, but it was an exciting addition to the Fiji marine scene. Dick wanted to start an island resort and someone advised him to have a look at Taveuni. We were living on the island at the time and gave him a lot of slanted advice, hoping he would start something in our area. But it didn't suit his dream, which he eventually found in the Mamanuca Group off Nadi. At first there was Castaway Island, and later Dick's Place, which became Muscat Cove on Malolo Lailai.

This was freehold land which he shared with another developer who established Plantation Island at the other end. Dick started with a few bures, then some multi-roomed villas. Its lovely sheltered bay became a haven for overseas yachts so he put in a yacht marina. Then came time-shares and a subdivision of part of the island for the homeowners. Dick created something special on Malolo Lailai and we went there often to enjoy his hospitality and to walk on the idyllic beaches surrounding the island. It was from a hill on the island that my family and I watched the dawn of the new millennium.

Another Dick who played a significant part in developing tourism was Dick Warner. Dick was a New Zealander who came to Fiji as a school teacher before joining up with Harvey and Iris Hunt in forming the first travel agency, Hunts Travel Service. Dick was a small man with tremendous energy and an astute feel for tourism. He knew that tourists wanted to stay on a small island so he developed Treasure Island off Nadi with Dan Costello. This was a little island surrounded by sand and sea. Just beside Treasure Island, Dan started up what became the most popular budget resort for young people, Beachcomber. Dan became the face of Fiji tourism. A larger than life effervescent man who wore a heavy beard and carried far too much weight, he was always laughing, joking and enjoying life to the fullest. Dan came from an old pioneer family. His uncle discovered the Emperor Gold Mine, which has always been the richest in Fiji. Another uncle was Mine Host at one of Suva's best known hotels, The Garrick. Before going into tourism, Dan ran a successful butchery, and while I was living on Taveuni running pigs and cattle, he would often charter a small ship and come up to Taveuni to buy a shipload of livestock.

Tourism has made a huge difference, not just to the Fiji economy, but to the way of life of its people. The islands and people of Fiji are a natural fit for tourism, and when tourism blossomed throughout the world in the second half of the 20th century, Fiji was ready. Overseas investment poured in. All kinds of supporting industries were started and, above all, jobs were created for the ever increasing population.

One of the people who played a big part in putting Fiji tourism on the map was Mahendra Patel, known as Mac.

Mac's family owned a small store in the backwater town of Ba. Like so many Indian families, they understood the need for a good education and sent Mac to one of the best schools in Melbourne. He returned with a keen commercial flair and saw the opportunities in tourism and, in particular, duty free trading. His duty free shop at Nadi airport was not only a huge success but won many international awards for its quality. Mac acquired agencies for many of the world's most prestigious products and opened shops not only in Suva but in the best tourist resorts. He helped to shape the growth of the industry by influencing government leaders and became a close confidant of Prime Minister Mara. Mac was a cheerful extrovert who exuded charm, confidence and style in keeping with the luxury products that he sold. He was also hyperactive and writing a profile on him for a magazine was a strange experience. I had arranged to interview him in his office but as I sat before him, he responded to my questions at the same time as he issued a continuous stream of instructions to his staff. He never lost track of our conversation.

One of the ironic twists of fate was that this highly successful, respected and influential entrepreneur who was appointed by the government to chair one of its organisations was charged with corruption, convicted and sent to prison. When he was released he left Fiji, never to return.

Two other Gujarati families also saw opportunities in tourism: Tappoos and the business known as Jack's. They established outlets in the main centres and resorts. Along with Motibhai's, they became the commercial face of tourism in Fiji and were extremely successful.

While working for Dad on Taveuni in the 1950s, he sent me to investigate a possible uranium deposit on Waya Island in the Yasawas. He charted a boat belonging to Trevor Withers who had just set up a tourist operation called Blue Lagoon Cruises. Little did I know that it would grow into the most popular cruise operation in the South Pacific with six ships carrying people on three to eight day cruises. The man who really made it possible was not Trevor Withers but David Wilson, who came to Fiji as manager of a travel agency. Through very astute dealings he acquired ownership, bought new ships, set a standard, identified stops in the beautiful Yasawa islands, established a good relationship with the Fijian people in the islands who provided the local colour, and marketed his product with great skill. David made his fortune and eventually sold cruise operation to a Fijian company.

Many of us who called Fiji home didn't really like going to the big resorts for holidays, as we felt like tourists ourselves. We preferred to go to small island operations where we were known to be locals. Jacque and I and our family favoured Nananu-i-ra, a small island off the Rakiraki coast. Nananu means 'dream' in Fijian. The island is freehold and was owned by a number of families. Two of them, the McDonalds and the Bethams, who were related, had cottage operations on a beautiful beach. You had to take all your own food and beverages and do your own cooking, but it was a haven of peace and loveliness, and it only cost a moderate price. We alternated between staying with each family so as to not cause offence, as they were touchy and rather jealous of each other. Oscar Betham had once managed the Club Hotel in Suva and I was drinking with him the night before my son Richard was born. I bet him a case of whiskey that the child would be a boy, which it was, and to my disgust he never paid his debt despite my frequent reminders over many years.

The cottages were right on the beach so most of our time was spent wallowing in the tepid sea or snorkeling around the reef, which was teeming with an amazing variety of fish. Small boats were available to go ocean fishing or picnicking on beaches on the far side of the island. There were never more than a dozen or so people holidaying there, so it was very close to paradise. Later, part of the island was subdivided and sold to overseas buyers, and by the turn of the century there were about 20 luxury homes on one point of the island. On the highest part, a 40-room hotel was constructed. Isolation had become suburbia. Our refuge from tourists was gone.

But that was the way ahead. Tourism was Fiji's best hope and many backpacker operations sprung up on isolated locations in the Yasawas, Kadavu, Taveuni, Ovalau and Lau. Some locals frowned on the backpackers, believing they came to Fiji and enjoyed our natural beauty but paid nothing for it. While this may have been the case with some who went into Fijian villages and tried to live very cheap, many were simply astute travelers. They scorned the expensive resorts, spent as little as possible on rooms and food, but outlaid huge sums on scuba diving or game fishing. More of these tourists' dollars stayed in Fiji compared to the dollars that were spent in the luxury resorts.

Yet that was where the big money was to be made. I had a taste of this when I was invited to be a director of a company that bought into the huge Denarau development out of Nadi. It was one of the most stimulating periods of my life, as I became part of a team of investment bankers, developers, planners, architects and financiers as they put together plans for villas, hotel, marinas and golf courses. It was fascinating to observe the rivalry between the various interest groups and the intensity with which they applied themselves to the tasks. Lengthy meetings were held in Fiji, Auckland and Wellington. Consultants came and made presentations. Data was analysed and decisions involving many millions of dollars were made. Chairmanship of the group alternated between Brierleys, the New Zealand investment bankers who owned Air New Zealand, and Fay Ridgerite, the international firm of merchant bankers. At one point, the Chairman was the man who built Sky Tower in central Auckland, and who incidentally also built a beautiful home on Nananu-i-ra. Another chairman was a Fiji Indian who had migrated to New Zealand and made his way up the ladder at Brierleys to became one of their top men.

Denarau became the cornerstone of Fiji tourism mainly because of a smart strategy that the developers put in place. The natural state of the area was a number of small islands surrounded by mangrove swamps and fringed by white sandy beaches. These were a mixture of freehold, state owned and native land. The developers reclaimed the mangrove swamps and embarked on a land swap whereby the freehold land was put together in one place and sold as residential blocks to New Zealanders, Australians and locals. The state land was accumulated in the centre for the golf course and other infrastructure, while the land around the coast was made into native land and leased out to hotel developers. The freehold land was quickly sold off and by the latest count there were seven international hotels on this land. The native land owners benefitted tremendously from this arrangement as they collected regular rent payments.

The other part of the development plan involved the creation of Port Denarau, which became the launch pad for cruise operators taking tourists to island resorts in the Malolo, Mamanuca and Yasawa Islands. Many of these were backpacker operations and one cruise ship group operated like a bus, stopping at each place with arriving or departing guests

Many quality shops and restaurants were also set up at Port Denarau and these not only attracted guests from the various hotels but the huge cruise liners from overseas that visited Suva and Lautoka and began calling into Denarau.

Denarau consolidated Nadi as the centre of tourism in Fiji and all kinds of activities blossomed in the area.

The main beneficiaries of this growth were not only the native land owners who received rent but the thousands of men and women who found jobs and set up little businesses. They were a natural fit for tourism activities. For many, this brought about a dramatic change in lifestyle. At last there was opportunity and hope for them and their children.

Many more cruise liners came to not only Suva, Denarau and Lautoka, but called at more remote areas like Kadavu and Savusavu. Resorts sprung up at Savusavu, on Taveuni and in parts of Lau. The tourist dollar began to spread to rural areas.

Fiji also became an attractive place to hold international conferences. There were comfortable venues, hospitable people and efficient technology.

It's debatable as to how much of the tourist dollar stays in Fiji. Certainly the government collects a whole range of taxes and the local airline, Fiji Airways, benefits from bringing people to our shores. Local shopkeepers get their share. Employees get a fair chunk. But the big spend is on accommodation, food and beverages. This all goes to the big hotels that are owned by overseas groups and it is a deep dark secret as to how much of that dollar stays in the country.

By the beginning of the 21st century, tourism was the number one foreign exchange earner for Fiji. It had surpassed sugar, garments, gold and all other industries. It was also the largest employer of labour. Capital was pouring in to finance huge tourism projects at Momi on the Coral Coast and at the beautiful Natadola Bay. The Pacific appeared to be a region of peace and tranquility in an otherwise troubled world. The future for tourism was as bright as the tropical sun.

Yet is was well understood that tourism is a fickle industry and the flow of tourists could quickly dry up if they felt threatened by civil unrest, unpleasant weather, poor service, or high costs. Tourists do not want to see guns in the streets or hear about human rights abuses. Often it is foreign governments that advise their people not to go to places that pose any kind of danger.

So it came as no great surprise that the industry came to a shuddering halt in 2000 when George Speight and his thugs invaded the streets of Suva and in 2006 when Commodore Bainimarama removed the democratically elected Prime Minister Qarase from power. Overseas governments told their nationals not to visit Fiji. Hotels were empty. Staff were laid off. Investment dried up. Projects ground to a halt. The Fiji economy went into free fall.

But optimism remained. Fiji was just too good a visitor destination. Those in the industry waited out the threat and put recovery plans in place. When things did return to normal and foreign governments removed adverse advisory notices, the tourists came back, albeit on very attractive packages. The industry continued to grow and provided jobs and much needed foreign exchange.

12. Commerce and Industry

Like so many other things in Fiji, commerce and industry is defined along racial lines.

Throughout the early part of the 20th century, big business such as retail, manufacturing, sugar and copra, wholesaling, importing and exporting, and construction, were controlled by overseas organisations or local Europeans. The smaller retail shops were owned by Indians and many of the corner shops, bakeries and market gardens were in the hands of Chinese, while Fijians were confined to the produce markets.

A story attributed to the esteemed Fijian leader Ratu Sir Lala Sukuna says it all: A Fijian, a European, an Indian, and a Chinese arrived in Heaven to be met by the gatekeeper. The gatekeeper asked the European why he should be admitted. 'To build an empire,' declared the pompous man. 'Excellent,' said St Peter. 'You may enter.' He then turned to the Indian and asked the same question. 'Why, to build a chain of stores,' the Indian said. 'Of course, we need stores,' responded St Peter. 'Do enter.' The Chinese was next and was asked by St Peter why he should be admitted. 'I will plant market gardens all over Heaven.' 'Why I hadn't thought of that,' mused St Peter. 'In you go.' Then he asked the Fijian, 'What about you, what can you contribute?' 'Oh nothing,' said the Fijian. 'I just want to look around.'

During the 20th century, the three big players in commerce were Burns Philp, Morris Hedstrom and W. R. Carpenter & Co. Burns Philp was an Australian company that had interests in most of the South Pacific countries, selling consumer needs through retail outlets as well as being agents for shipping, motor vehicles and farm equipment. Morris Hedstrom was a local company specialising in retail stores throughout the islands. Carpenters were into shipping and copra milling. Then there were the oil companies, the manufacturer's agents, and other Australian and New Zealand companies and banks that had branches in Fiji.

All these organisations were controlled by Europeans, mostly expatriates. One exception was W. O. Johnson, known as Tui, whose father was known as Tavua Johnson. I never knew their real names. For as long as I can remember, Tui was head of Carpenters and it was he, more than anyone else, who dragged the copra industry, kicking and screaming, into the modern age. Up until the 1950s all copra was exported, but Carpenters set up a copra mill in Suva to crush the copra and export oil, which enabled them to control the industry and demand improvements in quality. Some planters loved Tui for setting up the mill, others hated him for forcing them to spend money on quality control. All were convinced that he was making huge profits for Carpenters at their expense. Tui also established a fleet of inter-island ships to transport copra from the outer islands to the mill in Suva. Whenever he introduced a new ship he would take it round to the copra producing areas and invite the copra producers to a grand booze up on the ship's deck.

In many respects, Tui was a real colonial. He was a short, stocky, balding man with a blubbery, slightly crooked face. He always wore starched, long white trousers and a white shirt with a pith helmet, and he spoke in a very impatient manner.

While he got on well with his staff, he was a hard taskmaster who demanded results. Yet despite the criticisms of him, Tui Johnson was fair and honest with the planters and he eventually won their respect.

Maurice Helsen, a Frenchman, was a long time manager of Burns Philp during the 1950s and 1960s. He was largely responsible for expanding the company's range of merchandise and set up the first Burns Philp store on Taveuni. He was a very serious drinker. I remember him coming to our house on Taveuni on one occasion. As it was drinks time, I brought out our very best crystal glasses and offered him a whisky. He took one look at the fine glass and said, 'Haven't you got anything bigger?'

Earlier, while I was still living with Dad at the old home, he came to stay overnight. As my room was the only one with a spare bed, he slept there. We had been having a lot of rat problems at the time so I had set some big wooden traps in the ceiling. The only access to the ceiling was through the manhole in my room. That night, well after we had all gone to bed, one of the monster rats got himself trapped but not killed. He thumped around in the ceiling making a terrible noise, but Helsen didn't move. I waited for some time, hoping the rat would give up, but eventually I realised I would have to go outside, get a 12-foot ladder, bring it into the room, set it up, climb into the ceiling, find the trapped rat and come down again with the squealing rat and remove the ladder. It was a very noisy business but Helsen didn't move. He had consumed a good deal of Dad's Scotch.

With the growth of the tourist industry and the arrival of more passenger ships in Suva from the 1960s, the duty free industry flourished. Prior to this, Cumming Street was a collection of drab little general stores and tailor shops. It suddenly blossomed with flashing fluorescent lights advertising Sony, JVC, Sanyo, National and Seiko. The shops were filled with a dazzling array of electronic gadgetry.

Gokals was one of the first to recognise the potential from tourism. For the Gokals, trade began in the mid-1950s when the founder, Bob, sold a small

12. Commerce and Industry

transistor radio to a Bank of New Zealand officer. This led to an order of 60 more radios and gave the shrewd Bob an indication of the vast potential of the growing transistor market.

He began importing cameras, binoculars and watches, and supplied these under the draw-back system to tourists visiting Suva on ships. This system provided that the goods were delivered to the ship's purser and handed over to the buyer only when the vessel was beyond territorial limits.

But the drawback system had its own drawbacks and merchants like Bob Gokal suggested to the government that in order to induce more tourists to visit Fiji, a certain range of goods should be declared duty-free.

The government agreed. Customs duty was removed and the tourist industry took off. The Gokals closed down their old tailoring and drapery shop and opened a new shop close to the Garrick Hotel in Pier Street, and it was this proximity to the hotel as much as anything that brought tourists to Gokals. Once inside, they were quickly won over by Bob Gokal's odd lopsided smile and backslapping familiarity. Bob was a short bespectled man whose real name was Bhagwan. Like his brother Magan, he was a Gujarati, who are sometimes called 'the Jews of the East.' They are taught at an early age to shun evil or suffer the wrath of God. They are encouraged to be thrifty, hardworking and make sacrifices in the interest of enhancing family prosperity. In contrast to Bob's rather odd appearance, his brother Magan was a debonair, silver-haired man with a sparkling smile. He, like his wife Sumitra, was an expert at yoga and he exuded the real objectives of yoga: physical well being, self reliance and assurance. Like many others, their business flourished: they acquired many world famous agencies and expanded to Hong Kong and Australia. The little tailor shop had grown beyond all expectations.

Another Gujarati who I grew to respect over the years was Kalyan Hari. He was a diminutive man just over five feet tall, articulate with polished manners. He always dressed immaculately and conveyed a surprising impression of strength. His family came to Fiji in 1918 and his business grew from a little tailor shop to a conglomerate of wholesaling, hardware, garment manufacturing, motion picture exhibition and distribution, and footwear. I worked with Kalyan on a number of Rotary projects and grew to respect his dedication and his integrity. I was sad that he died prematurely from stress, prior to realising his dream, which he told me was to 'make G. B. Hari & Co more powerful than the giants Burns Philp, Carpenters and Morris Hedstroms,' and to spread through Australia, new Zealand and East Asia.

The pre-eminent auctioneer in Suva for many years was a great character whose real name was Mirza Namrud Buksh. But he was known to all as Lulu, meaning owl in Fijian. Apparently his family gave him this name as he slept all day and cried all night when he was a baby. Lulu had a mix of Fijian, Indian, English and American blood in his veins and spoke eight languages. He made his name by conducting 12-hour marathon auctions selling Persian rugs. His auctions were a lot of fun. Lulu thrived on family life and had 17 children, 11 of whom were adopted. His youngest child was named Count, after the Count of Monte Cristo. He stood for every election to parliament so he could express his views publicly, but he never won and said he would hate to do so. 'I would only make enemies and my goal in life is to make friends,' he proclaimed.

Up at the corner, where my street meets the main road was, for many years, Kestor's Store. We would often buy things such as bread, a tin of this or that, or potatoes, if we were desperate and our main supplier had closed. Kestor, who was Chinese, remained open from five am till eight pm, or later if there was a sale to be made. The store was like a large room with every square inch cluttered with an amazing jumble of bags, boxes and miscellaneous merchandise. Only Kestor knew exactly where everything was located. It was a dirty shop that was never cleaned and Kestor himself looked just as grubby. I tried to avoid going in to buy anything for, if I did, Kestor would harangue me with the latest crimes of politicians and bureaucrats in a high-pitched voice that mixed English, Chinese and Fijian. He was very difficult to understand, so I simply said, 'Yes, yes I agree, you are right,' and fled as soon as I could. Kestor's greatest achievement was to get a license to sell alcohol, which is when he started to make a fortune. This was at a time when house-breaking and shop burglaries became prevalent and criminals began to look for ways to sell their ill-gained items. Enter Kestor, the fence. For a while he did very well but when the police caught up with him Kestor went to jail. His family carried on the business and there is no doubt they made a lot of money out of legitimate trading.

When he came out of jail he decided to sell his business. It was a good time, for the Fiji Development Bank was just starting a scheme of buying successful small businesses and setting up Fijians in them. The bank bought Kestor's shop, put in a Fijian owner and lent him money to get started. The keen new man cleaned up the shop, restocked it and set about making his fortune. But he only wanted to operate during normal business hours and take time off for holidays and sporting events. He went broke within a year.

Ambition and politics have been the downfall of many, but not so for one of Fiji's most successful businessmen. Jim Ah Koy came from humble beginnings but was imbued with incredible energy, ambition and business acumen. He began work in an office equipment distribution company, which he eventually bought and expanded into the largest in the country. He realised the potential of the computer age and became one of the biggest players, as well having huge investments in real estate. Ambition took him into politics, where he became an

12. Commerce and Industry

excellent Minister of Finance. But his party lost the election in 1999 and in May 2000 George Speight wrecked the country. Jim continued to flourish in other parts of the Pacific, China and New Zealand. The Papua New Guinea government invited the Queen to bestow a knighthood on Jim for his service to that country. Prime Minister Bainimarama appointed him to be the Fiji Ambassador to China and he was no doubt responsible for bringing a great deal of Chinese business to Fiji. It's an odd twist of irony that Speight began his career in one of Ah Koy's companies and modeled his business style and appearance on Jim. Though he switched churches a few times, Jim remained an extremely devout man and constantly attributed his success to the Almighty.

Fijians have not had a good track record in business and it was for this reason that Fijian Holdings was set up. Its shareholders were not only individuals but Fijian provinces, and the company was run by a board of successful Fijians. Though it was listed on the stock exchange, shares could only be bought by ethnic Fijians. Fijian Holdings invested in blue chip companies like the brewery, cement and concrete manufacturing, successful tourism ventures and computers. The company made huge profits and, despite the fact that these may not have filtered down to ordinary people, it made the Fijian-owned company a big player in national business.

One of the longest serving companies in Fiji was Colonial Insurance, which opened a branch in Fiji in 1876, just six years after my grandfather arrived in the islands. The Chairman of the Colonial NSW Society read the Deed of Cession when it was signed in Levuka in 1874 and was knighted for his part in the event. Colonial Insurance grew with the nation and was to become the dominant finance company, having investments in insurance, real estate, health care, hospitals, banking and unit trusts.

In 1986, the Chairman of the Fiji Branch of Colonial Insurance, Sir John Falvey, invited me to join the board as a director. He said there wouldn't be much to do but they did put on a good lunch from time to time. That was the case for a few years until a new drive for expansion, profits and compliance came from head office in Melbourne and I had to earn my fees. Sir John was the senior partner in one of the oldest legal firms in the country. He had a passion for the law, politics and golf, all laced with a fair share of gin. He played a major part in preparing the 1970 Constitution and was roped in again to draft another one in 1990. In between, he served in Ratu Mara's Alliance Government as Attorney General and was a generous benefactor to the community. Gin, golf, cigars and obesity were to be his downfall. He and his playing partner would take thermos of gin and tonic out on the course whenever they played and I am sure they enjoyed their golf as they drank their way around the course, leaving an odour of cigar smoke in their wake. Sir John was a jovial man with rapier-like repartee. I am sure he died a happy man. Colonial Insurance was eventually taken over by Papua New Guinea's Bank South Pacific.

Through the end of the 20th century and into the 21st century, foreign domination of Fiji's commerce and industry was maintained. The banks and oil companies made huge profits, and companies like W. R. Carpenters and Burns Philp, whose foreign ownership had changed to other foreigners, reaped the benefits of Fiji's economic growth. Carpenters became Malaysian-owned, while Burns Philp joined up with one of Britain's retail giants, Courts.

That is not to say that local businessmen missed out. One of the most colourful local businessmen was James Datta, who became head of Burns Philp and Courts. James grew up in the rural town of Ba. His family was so poor that they could not afford shoes for him when he first went to school. But he had a driving ambition to succeed and rapidly made his way up the Burns Philp ladder. After the coups of 1987 he decided that he'd had enough of Fiji and managed a transfer to Burns Philp Australia. He even became an Australian citizen. But when a new manager was sought for the organisation in Fiji, James agreed to come back in that capacity. He was a super salesman of their homeware products and appeared in every TV advertisement. He was a short, rotund man with a happy, trusting appearance and he became the face of Burns Philp. People loved and hated him, but they certainly went into his stores to buy his products.

Many of the 'old' Chinese families came to Fiji three or four generations ago. They were storekeepers and market gardeners. One of their great contributions was to set up small general stores in villages around Fiji. They provided villagers with their basic needs and bought their copra, which was then sold to millers in Suva. These old Chinese families had little in common with the new breed that are now arriving in Fiji.

Hoy Shang Yee arrived in 1925. He travelled a long roundabout route, via Sydney and Lautoka, before arriving in Suva, where he was met by an 'uncle' who got him a job at Kwong Tiy. That was the company of which his father was co-founder and which means 'venture of potential greatness' in Chinese. The company, incorporated in 1928, began as a small trading post but rapidly expanded its range of goods and established a reputation for importing Chinese groceries for the growing Chinese community in Fiji.

But it became far better known for the trading stores it set up in lonely island communities throughout Fiji. They played a vital role in economic and community life.

12. Commerce and Industry

It was to them that the Fijian copra producer sold his one or two bags of copra, and it was here that he purchased his tea, tinned meat, biscuits and other daily needs. The stores were grocer, draper, hardware store and banker all rolled into one.

By extreme hard work and enterprise, Hoy Shang Yee quickly rose in the hierarchy of the company until he was a key figure in its growth. It was he who held it together during the difficult war years, and with his associate, Kam Chee, directed its diversification into so many other activities.

But Hoy Shang Yee's real legacy was his family. By willing sacrifice he ensured that his eight children all attended tertiary institutions. The who's who of his family makes fascinating reading:

> Tong, A.A.S.A., chartered accountant, Justice of the Peace, Managing Director of Hotel Metropole Ltd.
>
> Chang, B. Comm., A.A.S.A., chartered accountant, Managing Director of Kwong Tiy & Co Ltd.
>
> Lewis, LL.B., solicitor in Sydney, his wife Leonie, B.A., Justice of the Peace, business consultant.
>
> Gregory, A.A.S.A., chartered accountant, Managing Director of Leylands Ltd.
>
> Franklin, M.B.B.S. (Hons), F.R.C.S. Ed., F.R.C.S. Eng., F.R.A.C.S., consulting surgeon in Sydney, his wife Gloria, B.A.
>
> Kevin, M.B.B.S., wife Lesley, M.B.B.S., both doctors in Sydney.
>
> Irene, M.B.B.S., doctor in Sydney, husband Alfred B.E., M. Eng., M.Sc., M.B.A., M.I.E., Australian property developer.
>
> Florence, B.A., Dip. Ed, teacher, husband Erwin, dental surgeon in Sydney.

Little is heard of Chinese wives, but Hoy Shang Yee wrote of his wife: 'She is a person of generous nature, kind and warm hearted, hard working and thrifty, endowed with the traditional Chinese thinking. Our family affairs are well attended to. She is a tower of strength to me, a good wife and an able mother. Her love and care for the children are exemplary.'

Although the sons of Hoy Shang Yee control a range of highly profitable enterprises, like so many Chinese, little is known about them. They are the quiet community, busily going about their activities in an orderly, ethical way, giving due respect to their competitors, other ethnic groups, and the law of the land.

While they say that their roots are firmly planted in Fiji soil and there is no possibility of them leaving Fiji, they admit that there will always be a strong affinity to mainland China, no matter what regime is in power.

That is not to say there is any disloyalty to Fiji. They believe that the government is doing its best in difficult economic circumstances and their rights are being adequately safeguarded.

With the growth of tourism, local companies such as Motibhai's, Tappoo's and Jack's grabbed the lion's share of the tourist dollar. They provided bright, modern retail shops with pleasant, helpful staff to match the best in the world, and they prospered. These were owned and operated by Guajarati families. It is said that when any Gujarati family gathers, the only subject of discussion is business. Otherwise there is silence.

Some Gujarati families saw the opportunity of cashing in on the building boom and set up extensive hardware operations. Family firms such as Vinod Patel and R. C. Manubhai established enormous hardware supermarkets in towns throughout Fiji.

After the 1987 coup, when business went into serious decline, garment manufacturing was encouraged in Fiji. Valuable tax concessions were offered to foreign and local operators and the industry grew at a phenomenal rate. Not only did sales bring in much needed foreign exchange but the industry provided jobs for otherwise unemployed women and men. The main markets were Australia, New Zealand, the USA and Europe. At one point, the value of garment sales was exceeded only by tourism. Garment sales had more value than sugar.

One of the largest and most successful operators was an Australian Lebanese, Mark Halabe. Mark had businesses in Australia but saw the benefit of Fiji tax concessions and so moved his family and his base. Mark and the company flourished, for not only was he committed to commercial success but to the Fiji nation and the benefit of the garment industry to Fiji. He insisted on a high standard of work environment for his staff, which is a lot more than can be said for many smaller operators. He threw himself into social and political activities. When the 2000 coup took place, Mark became an intermediary between those held hostage and the people outside.

He lived in the same street as myself and acquired a block of land at the end of the street, where he built a block of residential units. He later constructed a ten-storey block of units elsewhere. His commitment to Fiji was total.

At one stage, Mark was thinking of listing his company on the South Pacific Stock Exchange.

This exchange had been set up during the later part of the 20th century and there were about 16 companies trading on it. It was not a very active exchange but it did provide an opportunity for investment, and the dividends paid by listed companies were tax-free. Small investors could buy units in a number of unit trusts, which were very popular. The regulator of the exchange and all other capital market activities was the Capital Market Development Authority. When Mahendra Chaudhry was Prime Minister in 1999, he invited me to serve on the Authority. It was an interesting variation from my other activities, so I accepted. A few years later I was asked to take up the position of Chair.

It was no easy task to try and encourage companies to list, as the main constraint was the disclosure requirements. Many successful local companies, particularly the Gujarati family companies, were loathed to reveal their secrets. The other main task for the authority was development. This entailed explaining to middle and low income Fijian and Indian people the benefits of saving by investing their surplus funds in shares and unit trusts. Of course the responsibility for driving the work of the authority was the CEO and I was fortunate to work with two outstanding young people. My first CEO was the daughter of my golfing colleague, Bill Apted. Bill struggled all his life to build up a medium-sized grocery store. His wife Tess worked as a secretary for Burns Philp. They had three girls and two boys. Bill ended up selling the business to Carpenters for many millions of dollars, and Tess ended up Chair of Burns Philp. One daughter became partner in KPMG, another girl topped the NSW law exams, a son became a partner in the top legal firm in Fiji, another son set up and ran the most successful nightclub in Suva. The third daughter, Julie, qualified in law and was CEO of the Capital Markets Development Authority when I joined. She was an outstanding executive, competent, hard working and tough.

When she left, Suren Kumar, a really switched-on young banker who had a passion for the capital markets, took over. He ran a really tight ship and introduced all kinds of innovative ideas to stimulate the market.

A rather ironical twist of fate for Fiji was the way remittances from Fijian people living and working overseas became the second most valuable foreign exchange earner. Many professionals who left after the 1987 and 2000 coups and took up lucrative jobs continued to send money to their relatives in Fiji. Likewise, because of the security problems in many parts of the world, our soldiers were in demand and were recruited to serve by the United Nations and private security firms. They too sent funds back to Fiji. The third group was our sportsmen, particularly rugby players. They were recruited to play in Australia, New Zealand, Japan, and many parts of Europe. Their remittances all helped to boost Fiji's coffers and lift this category to second behind tourism as the main foreign exchange money earner. Sugar dropped from first to third.

Interlude: A Fijian Delicacy—Balolo

'You might have given me some warning,' Jacque said. 'Three couples coming for dinner and these Sydneysiders are used to some pretty heavy gourmet dining.'

I delicately suggested to my loving wife that we search the deep freeze. Which we did. And just when I was about to conclude that there weren't any real treasures, Jacque straightened up with a smile, thrust forward a frozen parcel and said, 'What about this? I'm sure they've never tried worms before.'

I put my arms around her and smiled. 'Worms it is, sweetheart.'

The solid, green-coloured mass was placed in a large bowl on the kitchen bench to thaw. It doesn't take long, and by the evening it had dissolved into something that resembled a tangled, viscous bowl of noodle soup.

The guests were seated at the table, elegantly set with Jacque's best silver cutlery, crystal, and lace placemats. Before each guest, the maid placed a small plate on which was a serving of

the green worm-like entrée and two triangular slices of toast.

Our guests studied the dish politely, then looked up at Jacque inquiringly.

'Balolo,' she said sweetly.

They smiled uneasily and turned to me. 'It's a marine worm,' I added, somewhat mischievously, noticing the lady on my right turn a paler shade of white.

'Oh, how interesting,' someone murmured.

I scooped up a forkful and as the Balolo slipped down my throat leaving a delicate taste of the exotica of the sea on my palate, I nibbled a slice of toast.

They watched, then cautiously followed suit.

'How unusual,' one said.

'You can taste the iodine,' commented another.

'Its rich with iron and riboflavin,' I said helpfully.

I took another mouthful then added, 'Actually, it is a sac of eggs and sperm of the sea annelid which lives in the crevices of the coral.'

They all looked at me a little startled. One of the men took a deep draw on his glass of Moselle as if to disinfect his throat.

I smiled pleasantly, 'it's not as bad as it sounds. It's a Fiji delicacy, known as the caviar of the South Pacific.'

'Tell us more about this—what did you call it?' I was asked.

'Balolo,' I said. 'It's one of the most curious phenomenons of the South Pacific. It's a worm that lives in the deep coral. Twice a year the bottom half, which is laden with sex cells, breaks off from the rest of the body and rises to the surface of the sea to die, phoenix-like, in the propagation of its kind. They swim around on the surface, spilling their sperm cells which sink to the bottom, where life begins all over again. The remarkable thing about it is that it keeps both lunar and solar time, for it comes to the surface only at dawn in the third quarter of the moon in October and November, when the tide is low.'

One of the ladies pursed her lips and asked, 'what does it look like when it's ...,' she paused and, in rather a pained way, added, 'alive?'

'Like a thin green tube about 45 centimetres long. Actually, the female is green while the male is green-brown. Some people eat it fresh as it is taken from the sea,' I said. 'But in its raw state it tastes like a rather potent dose of iodine.'

'Have you ever seen it rise?'

'Oh yes, plenty of times. I used to live on the island of Taveuni where the balolo is noted for its risings. Those two days in October and November are the big events of the year. Of course, there is a natural explanation for the rising of the balolo, but the Fijian people had their own way of reading the signs well before the Europeans researched it, and we depended on them to tell us when it would rise. They were seldom wrong.'

I took a sip of wine before continuing.

'There is a magnificent horseshoe reef circling a deep blue lagoon off the southern end of Taveuni. On the shores of this lagoon is the village of Vuna. Twice a year we would get a message from the Tui Vuna, the chief, that the balolo would rise the next day. We would set the alarm for three am and by four o'clock we would be on our way to the reef in the cool morning gloom. It was quite a hazardous business negotiating the treacherous reef passage into the lagoon in the darkness and the visibility was usually further impaired by a shower of rain. According to the Fijians, this shower of rain was a sure sign that the balolo would rise as predicted.

'Once inside the lagoon we would stop the engine and lie in the still water, waiting for the dawn. As the sky brightened, we would be able to see other launches and punts and canoes scattered about the lagoon. All waiting! No one knowing exactly where it would come up. Then there would be a shout: 'It's rising,' and all the boats would converge on the spot from where the shout had come. Sometimes there would be only a small rising. But on most occasions, there would be a seething mass of wriggling green tendrils spread over a large area of the lagoon.

Nets, buckets and all kinds of receptacles were used to scoop up the prized delicacy and it was stored in drums, tubs and basins in the boats. Then, suddenly the sun would rise above the ridge of the island's hills and the balolo would sink. Its life span was over. The sperm had been spent to sink to the bottom to regenerate new life.'

'How extraordinary,' someone commented. 'Can you see it when you are diving?'

'Not that I know of,' I replied.

'Does it only rise in Taveuni?'

'Oh no. It comes up in many parts of Fiji as well as other parts of Polynesia and Melanesia. The Samoans are particularly partial to it and wrap it in leaves and cook it in ground ovens. There is another interesting side effect. Some species of fish become poisonous at balolo time. This is supposed to be due to them consuming vast amounts of scum that rises with the balolo.'

Our guests exchanged nervous glances. Jacque asked, 'Have some more?'

There was a pause before one of them responded, 'Yes, please. It's delicious.'

13. Diplomacy

A nation's main contact with the outside world is often through diplomatic missions.

Diplomacy is the conduct of relations between one state with another by peaceful means, but the real purpose of having a diplomatic mission in a country is often vague. When the British Empire was at its height, its motivation for establishing relations with foreign countries was strategic, primarily to extend trade. It's debatable whether that has changed. Britain was the first to set up a consulate in Fiji in 1874 and it has had a base here ever since.

Other countries with full diplomatic missions in Fiji include Australia, New Zealand, the United States of America, France, Japan, China, India, Malaysia, Korea, Marshall Islands, Papua New Guinea and Tuvalu. Many other countries, such as Spain, the Netherlands, Denmark, Mexico, Pakistan, Canada, Chile, Nauru, the Philippines, Italy, Belgium and Sri Lanka, have honorary Consuls.

In 1989, I was asked if I would take up the appointment as Honorary Consul for Germany. An increasing number of German tourists were coming to Fiji and getting into one form of trouble or another. I seemed to spend a great deal of my time in my early years as Consul helping those who had their passports stolen or who had been jailed for being in possession of small amounts of marijuana.

But I also administered a small-scale aid scheme. My task was to identify projects costing no more than $15,000 that would in some way improve the quality of life of people, particularly in the rural areas. Such projects included water supply, school libraries, kindergartens, agricultural projects, equipment for training and facilities for the handicapped or underprivileged. I genuinely felt that such schemes, which directly touched the lives of the people, engendered greater good for donor countries than multi-million dollar projects.

People responded to this aid in different ways. An urban school may accept my cheque with gratitude but little ceremony, whereas Fijians in a remote village where I had done a drainage scheme would use the occasion for the completion of the project as an opportunity for a celebration. There would be a full, elaborate ceremony, presentation of gifts and a huge feast. I tried to discourage such extravagance as it all cost money that they did not often have. However, life in a village can often be dull and mundane and they welcomed the chance to celebrate, have a feast and some fun. The least I could do was to redistribute the gifts of food and mats that were presented to me as the honoured guest. This was customary and often expected.

While this type of consular duty was very satisfying, there were others that gave no pleasure.

Fiji law provided that should a person be found to possess any quantity of marijuana, no matter how small, there was a mandatory custodial sentence of 30 days jail. Many young German tourists, unaware of our laws, were apprehended and sentenced. I was often the only contact with their relatives back in Germany and had the unpleasant task of explaining their predicament. It was a stupid law as it costs the Fiji taxpayer money to keep people in jail and it has now been changed. For the young German, often with a good job back home, it was a rude awakening to find himself locked in a cell for 30 days. I visited them and tried to make life easier but was really of little comfort.

There were also deaths. I remember the case of a young German who went for an ocean swim at a resort the first evening he arrived. He got caught in a current, was swept out to sea and never seen again. Telling his parents back in Germany was agonising. It was worse that the father insisted on flying to Fiji to see exactly where his son died. The poor man was completely distraught and I could do little more than sit with him and tell him about Fiji and how dangerous the ocean can be if you do not understand it. The outstanding natural beauty of the resort grounds, the beach and the ocean, at peace at sunset, had no impact on him. All he could see was a black hole as he wallowed in abject misery.

In my role as Consul I saw a great deal more of people in the main diplomatic missions and United Nations agencies. They were of course feted by our own government and local organisations who hoped to get aid from them, and I suppose this tended to give some of them an exaggerated opinion of their own importance. They had all kinds of diplomatic privileges, such as duty-free booze and cars, and this aggravated locals. One that really annoyed me was how the drivers with DC plate cars took advantage of parking in no parking areas.

However, I should not give the wrong impression about diplomats. Some very fine men and women represented their countries with charm and dignity. The Indians always had very suave and dignified high commissioners. Once during my early years in the Sugar Industry, a newly appointed Indian High Commissioner sought to pay respects to my Chairman, Sir Charles Marsack. After the meeting he passed my door on his way out. He stopped and very politely put his leg across the doorway and said, 'I just wanted to say that I had called upon you.' I supposed this would enable him to legitimately say in his report that he had visited the Chairman and the Secretary of the Sugar Board.

The diplomats often reflected the characteristics of their nationalities: the Americans were often brash; the Japanese imperial; the Chinese inscrutable; the New Zealanders parochial; the British aloof; the Australians down to earth; the Koreans difficult to understand; the Malaysians rather carefree.

One of my favourites was a big, heavily built Australian High Commissioner, Colin McDonald. He was a straight talking man who called a spade a spade and to hell with the diplomatic niceties. Because of these characteristics, he got on well with the then Fiji Prime Minister, Ratu Sir Kamisese Mara, who seemed to enjoy the company of big men like himself. Colin typified the Australian persona. I remember once, years after he had left Fiji, my secretary came into my office and said someone was here to see me. She gave me a look that I knew said, 'I don't approve of his appearance.' I was surprised to see that it was Colin, with ruffled hair, a faded floral bula shirt, short pants, and flip flops on his feet. 'Just passing through,' he commented in a jovial manner. 'I have time off from my formal obligations and wanted to say g'day.'

One of the main events in the calendar of all missions is the celebration of the national day, which provides an opportunity to have a large function and in some way reflect the character of the nation they represent. On one occasion, Colin decided to celebrate Australia Day, which is in January, one of the hottest months in Fiji, by holding a function at one of the local cinemas where Crocodile Dundee was showing. Invited guests were served pies and tinnies throughout the evening. The cinema was not air-conditioned and it was one of the hottest nights for many years. This had two effects. Firstly, we all sweltered in the oppressive heat, and secondly, the guests tried to alleviate the heat by drinking more tinnies. It turned into a very boisterous occasion. Colin also arranged for Lulu (the auctioneer mentioned earlier) to raise money for charity. Lulu was a laugh at any time but when he was very full of good Australian beer he was incorrigible. The auction got completely out of hand and Colin had to ask Lulu to leave.

The British celebrated events such as the Queen's Birthday in a more formal way by having the Governor General, Prime Minister and other dignitaries present. You signed the book as you entered and there were appropriate toasts and singing of anthems.

A feature of the Japanese celebrations of the Emperor's Birthday was the magnificent spread of traditional food. There was always a keen expectation of receiving an invitation to this function.

The high commissions and embassies were staffed by a varied collection of people, many of whom made very useful contributions during their term in Fiji. The first woman Australian Trade Commissioner to Fiji was Clare McMahon. Her appointment occurred at the time when women were breaking down the walls of male dominance and one of those organisations to succumb to the pressure was Rotary. Since its establishment in 1905, it had firmly resisted the admittance of women, but the headquarters in Chicago finally buckled and I had the pleasure of proposing Clare to become the first woman Rotarian in Fiji. Despite her heavy schedule she contributed a great deal of service to the community.

Some foreign missions had a rather easy time in Fiji and their staff could spend time at their favourite recreations. Fiji was heaven for Asian diplomats who enjoyed golf. It was a game they could not afford in their home countries, but in Suva the course was only ten minutes from their place of work and the annual subscription fees of only $300 compared favourably to tens of thousands of dollars in Japan.

Another of my favourite high commissioners was Karim Masuki from Malaysia. He loved golf so much that he constructed a pitch, put a course in his garden and invited his friends to lunch parties and golf. His other passion was game fishing and he found time to join the Fiji competitions as well as those in New Zealand and Hawaii. He was a man who loved life and though he was a Muslim, he enjoyed a drink. He did much to foster good relations between Fiji and Malaysia.

An American Ambassador who did more to generate good relations between Fiji and the USA than any before or after was Mrs Evelyn Teegan. She and her husband, Dick, had a real passion for their task. Dick was a retiree who threw himself into a number of activities, while Evie did her job as Ambassador. He resurrected the YMCA, which was virtually defunct, by indentifying funds from overseas, starting training and vocational programmers and personally driving the affairs of the organisation. He was also a dynamic force in Rotary.

Evie exuded charm and bonhomie that won her countless friends. She was a successful businesswoman, hence her selection by the Republican President as an ambassador, and there was a tough side to her. She played her diplomatic cards with great skill, which won her respect.

Jacque and I and our group of friends became close friends of Dick and Evie and had many enjoyable functions together. Just before she departed, the incumbent British High Commissioner was due to end his term in Fiji. He was a rather staid and reserved man, but with whom we had also become friendly. We decided to play a ruse on him. Evie invited him to what was supposed to be a formal function at her embassy to meet a visiting sheikh from Saudi Arabia who was being accompanied by his son and the American Ambassador to Saudi Arabia. This person was, in fact, an official in the US Embassy in Fiji; the son was a friend of ours. I was nominated to be the sheikh. The son and I were dressed in the fine raiment of an Arabian sheikh, with false beards and moustaches. We waited in the lounge of the American Embassy and, in due course, the British Ambassador arrived and Evie presented my son and me. When she said 'British Ambassador,' I angrily turned to my son and castigated him for putting me in a position of having to be polite to an Englishman who he knew I hated. I spoke in very loud and angry Hindi, as I didn't know any Arabic, and the Ambassador didn't know either. The poor Ambassador was flabbergasted at my outburst and simply stood before me not knowing what to do as I ranted and raved and vigorously pointed my finger at him. Evie and Dick tried their best to keep a straight face and only when the Ambassador turned to her, his face ashen, and asked what was going on, did she burst into laughter and explained the ruse. The poor fellow collapsed into a chair and I really through he would have a heart attack. We then took off our makeup and revealed who we were, but it took a long while for him to realise that his diplomatic career had not suddenly floundered on the last day of work

Another woman diplomat who made her mark in Fiji was the Australian High Commissioner, career diplomat Susan Boyd. It would have been a very hard road for any woman to make her way up through the Australian diplomatic service, particularly if you had been born in India to English parents. But Susan, an attractive, effervescent personality, had all the right characteristics. She was extremely smart, committed to her tasks, and could tell a risqué joke better than most men. She worked a cocktail party, the workplace for most diplomats, with great skill, but often shocked 'proper' diplomats when she came out with a bar room story in mixed company. She had served as High Commissioner in Vietnam before coming to Fiji and was on her way back there on 19th May 2000 to open an Australian aid bridge that had been commissioned during her term She was at Sydney Airport when she got word of the coup by Speight and boarded the next plane back to Fiji. Susan worked extremely hard and skillfully during that difficult period to keep her people in the Australian Government informed about developments and advise them on appropriate actions. Her efforts contributed greatly towards maintaining relationships between the two countries.

She was, of course, at risk during this period and the Australian Government sent four burly Australian police officers to Fiji to protect her. Before she ever left the compound in Suva, two officers would go and check out the route of her car and destination to ensure that it would be safe. Only when they were satisfied did Susan and the other two officers venture forth. It was a trying time for her and she often sought to escape from the pressure.

Jacque and I and our daughter Sandra had discovered that we had a lot in common with Susan and we became close friends. She apparently felt she could let her hair down with us and we would not betray any of the confidences that she shared with us. Sometimes Susan would phone and say, 'I have to get out of this bloody place. Can I come up for a drink?' Of course she was always welcome. Two of her bodyguards would accordingly be dispatched to check out the security of our home. When they were satisfied that all was well, they would contact their two colleagues, who would bring Susan to our house. On one occasion the first two came up, checked out everything, and then reversed out of our drive into a drain. When their efforts to get out were in vain, I offered to use my four-wheel drive to pull them out. They were most grateful but swore me to secrecy. 'If our mates find out what happened to us we will never hear the end of it,' they pleaded. I respected their wish but had to tell Susan, who had a great laugh.

The Bainimarama government greatly extended Fiji's diplomatic contacts by establishing missions in many countries. Fiji had been a member of the United Nations for many decades and its peacekeepers have served with distinction in many trouble spots. But during the second decade of the 21st century, Fiji's Representative to the United Nations, Peter Thompson, began to play a more prominent role as chair of various bodies such as United Nations Development Programme. Bainimarama himself was chair of the influential Group of 77 and China, as well as the International Sugar Organisation.

So people in many different parts of the world began taking notice of Fiji and its representatives and decided that perhaps Fiji wasn't just a country of coups.

14. Politics and Leadership

There has never been any shortage of self-proclaimed political leaders in Fiji.

While living in the isolation of Taveuni during my childhood years, the term 'politics' was seldom used, for there was no such thing as party politics. We only knew of the colonial administrators who ran the affairs of the nation. That began to change in the 1960s as Fiji was steered towards independence and local leaders were given more authority and assumed the stance of politicians.

My first experience of such a person was when Freddie Archibald was voted into the Legislative Council. Freddie was a part-European from Savusavu. He was a small copra producer who enjoyed expressing his own opinions and he took little notice of the highbrow attitude of the Taveuni planters who voted him into office on a number of occasions. His only opponent in these elections was Harold Gibson, a lawyer from Labasa. Harold had a high-pitched voice and looked untidy. He was regarded by the Taveuni people as a rather shady kind of fellow who had made a great deal of money out of the cane farmers in the Labasa area. He was certainly the most powerful man in the area, was mayor for many years, and owned the only hotel, the Grand Eastern, which was far from grand.

Just prior to elections, Freddie and Gibo (as Gibson was called) would visit the Taveuni constituency and listen to the complaints about the government and promise to fix everything if they were elected. When one was elected and went into Legislative Council and failed to make good on his promises, he was voted out at the next election. During one of his periods in office, Freddie had a mental breakdown and was seen running down the main street of Suva without his pants on. He spent some time in the mental asylum but was released in due course and went back to his duties in the Council. During a heated debate, Freddie stood up, waved a piece of paper at the Speaker and said, 'Mr Speaker, I am the only one in this House with a certificate to say that I am sane.'

Political maturity came to Fiji in 1970, when the nation was granted independence by Britain. One of the unique features of Fiji's relationship with Britain was that it was never conquered. The chiefs voluntarily ceded the islands to Queen Victoria in 1874. When the winds of change swept across the British Empire, Fiji didn't have to fight for its independence, the people asked for it, and it was granted.

Patriotism is an old emotion that touches some but not others. For me, Independence Day on the 10th October 1970 was one of the most moving days of my life. Albert Park, in the heart of Suva, was the centre of the celebrations. Prince Charles came, on behalf of the Queen, to deliver the instruments of independence to the Prime Minister, Ratu Sir Kamisese Mara. Stands for the public were set up around the park and the dignitaries of all races, dressed in their best, watched the ritual process. There were cultural displays by Fijians, Indians, Chinese, Europeans and other Pacific Islanders who called Fiji home. The police and army bands gave stirring displays. As the sun set, the Union Jack was lowered for the last time. The bugler's solemn notes echoed across a silent crowd, many of whom wondered, 'What happens to Fiji now?' There were, of course, plenty of prophets of doom. But the next morning a huge crowd gathered again to watch the Pacific blue Fiji flag being raised to the masthead in the middle of the park, and the new national anthem was played for the first time. There was an enormous surge of emotional pride and, 45 years after the event, I can still feel my chest heave and remember the tears trickling down my cheeks. It was one of the few moments in our history when all the population, of so many racial groups, thought of themselves in non-racial terms.

Fiji was fortunate that it was not led into independence by a pack of power hungry politicians, but by a distinguished group of Fijian chiefs. Ratu Mara, Ratu Edward Cakobau, Ratu George Cakobau and Ratu Penaia Ganilau had been groomed from birth to lead their people, and the colonial powers wisely decided to mould them into national leaders. They did not take up office for their own personal gain. They did not crave power. They looked upon their political leadership as a responsibility to their people, be they Fijian, Indian or others. They commanded respect by the way they conducted themselves.

This is not to say that Fiji was free of traditional politics. I was thrown into the fray when I began to work in the sugar industry, for it was the cauldron of Indian politics. One quarter of the population of Fiji had direct links to sugar, so winning the cane community vote was a vital stepping stone to national power. Politicians have a habit of promising to fight for whatever they think the voters want, regardless of the merits of the demands. Cane farmers had always been heavily in debt to moneylenders, storekeepers and banks. This was partly due to the fact that they only got four payments a year for their crop and they had a cash flow problem. To alleviate this, the sugar industry leaders decided to initiate a compulsory savings scheme which involved deducting a certain sum from each ton of cane and putting it into a farmers' fund. Initially, there was a lot of support for this but when the political leaders began to feel the pulse of opposition and began speaking out against it, the Sugar Board had to go out and sell the concept.

At this time, my Chairman was away and the Vice Chairman, Faiz Sherani, an Indian lawyer, was acting. Faiz was an urbane, cultured, soft-spoken Muslim who dressed immaculately, smoked cigars, drank and tried to avoid confrontation. Rather reluctantly, he agreed that I arrange a series of meetings in the cane areas so that he could explain the merits of the scheme. Our plan was to fly from

14. Politics and Leadership

Nausori Airport to Nadi, pick up a car and go to the first meeting. Unbeknown to us, the farmers' political leaders had decided to deal with us at Nadi Airport and they arranged buses to bring hundreds of farmers to the airport. When the plane landed and taxied to the terminal, we looked out the window and saw the throng of farmers with banners. We knew from experience what the mood would be and Faiz turned to me and said, 'I am not going in there.' It was only after I had pointed out how bad it would look if we stayed on the plane that he very reluctantly moved. Trying to stand tall and brave, we strode towards the farmers who began chanting when they saw us. In no time, we were swallowed up by the crowd who pressed us on all sides, yelling demands and shaking their fists. Faiz carried himself with great aplomb until they ran out of steam and he was able to address those nearest to him and they let us through. Although it was extremely uncomfortable, there was no malice nor personal threat. It was noticeable, however, that Faiz drank a lot more whisky than usual that evening. Eventually the politicians had their way on this issue and the savings scheme was abandoned.

Politicians didn't just stir up cane farmers. The mill workers were also their target. On one occasion in 1973 the four mills ground to a halt as members of the largest union downed tools. My Chairman, Sir Ian Thompson, who had the responsibility of settling disputes, did his best to resolve the matter, but the strike dragged on. Eventually, Ratu Sir Penaia Ganilau phoned and asked if he could help. This wasn't his area of responsibility but Fiji and its economic well being was his concern. He was that kind of man. Sir Ian welcomed his offer and the three of us decided to go to the mills and meet the workers. At Lautoka, thousands were gathered in an old wooden hall close to the mill. As we approached from a distance we could hear the angry yelling of workers condemning the sugar company and the government. It was quite unnerving. When we entered the hall we found it packed to capacity with angry people and I could feel the hostility and tension. It was like a keg of dynamite with a short fuse that was hissing and crackling towards an explosion. We followed Ratu Sir Penaia as he strode with military precision, scowl on his face, down the centre of the hall where a table and chairs were set. The noise began to subside as the men became aware of Ratu Penaia's commanding presence. We sat, the workers all around us, and waited, not saying a word, until there was a complete hush. Sir Ian rose and introduced Ratu Sir Penaia. He remained seated as he spoke in a slow, well-modulated voice. Then he launched into a pep talk the likes of which I have never heard. The atmosphere in the hall changed as the men wilted before his stinging condemnation. Even the political agitators were fearful of pressing their demands. There was absolute silence. He then handed over to Sir Ian, who gave the mill workers a chance to speak and air their grievances. It was all done in an orderly manner and a way of resolving the matter was agreed. We then went on to the other three mills and the strike ended.

Some years later, I was to write Ratu Sir Penaia's biography and became very close to this man who had been a loyal civil servant, rugby player for Fiji, commander of a battalion in Malaya, District Officer, Minister, Deputy Prime Minister, Governor-General and President. He was the central figure in a huge and devoted family. A big man in every way, he would often put his huge arms around my shoulders and laugh about something. Although he had that common touch and could have fun with just about anyone, the aura of chiefliness and dignity never left him. Even when General Rabuka was at the height of his power as a coup leader in 1987, he paid homage to Ratu Penaia by sitting on the floor before him.

Another of those who led Fiji through the transition from colony to dominion was Ratu Sir George Cakobau. He came up through the same process as Ratu Penaia and was to become the first local Governor-General. Shortly after his appointment I was asked by a magazine to write an article on him. He suggested I go to Government House for the occasion of his accepting the credentials of the new Japanese Ambassador to Fiji. As I stood in the richly decorated reception hall of Government House and observed the ceremony, I mused on how circumstances had changed. The dapper and dignified Japanese Ambassador was in full morning dress and bowed deeply as he presented his documents. Ratu Sir George was in the Fijian version of morning dress. The upper part was traditional, but he wore a striped sulu instead of pants, and had polished black sandals on his feet. He was a fine looking man with a thick crop of silver hair, large sparkling eyes and full lips that carried a rather mischievous smile. What intrigued me was that there, before me, was the epitome of a courtly and dignified gentleman, yet a mere hundred years ago Ratu George's grandfather was engaged in club warfare and ate his enemies with relish.

He suggested rather than have the interview for the magazine at Government House, which I think he felt carried a stigma of colonialism, we should go to his home on the chiefly island of Bau. It was from this tiny speck of land that his grandfather had ruled Fiji. Ratu George had of necessity made many adjustments during his life. He was the Vunivalu, the paramount chief of Fiji, as was his grandfather, which set him apart from others. Yet he had to perform like a good civil servant and as a Minister of the Crown. When he became Governor General he should have been above politics but, as the leader of his people, that was difficult. It was a fine line that he had to walk but he did it with great skill. Obviously he satisfied the Queen, because she bestowed on him a very rare decoration, the Royal Victorian Chain.

The thing that really struck one about Ratu George was his adaptability. Here was a man who believed there was a 'Vu' (a friendly spirit) watching over him, yet he adhered staunchly to the Methodist teachings of Christ. He could wear a sulu or a tuxedo with equal style, drink yaqona or sip brandy from a balloon, or stride through corridors of Buckingham Palace with the same poise and dignity with which he waded across the mud flats to Bau Island.

Ratu Sir Edward Cakobau was the third of the four chiefs who led Fiji into independence. He had a good deal of Tongan blood in him and was groomed in the Royal Tongan court. While he exuded chiefliness and had the biggest following of all the chiefs, he was a man who loved life and often told self-deprecating stories. He was a great raconteur and loved to stand at a bar with a glass in his hand—always a full glass inside an empty one—and regale a loyal audience. One oft repeated story he told was about a sea voyage he made to England. He was seated at the Captain's table and was telling the captive group outrageous stories about Fiji's cannibal past when the steward brought him the menu, which he studied for a while. He then turned to him and said, 'Bring me the passenger list.'

I hesitate to call any of these three 'politicians', in the disparaging sense that the term is often used. They were skilled administrators and outstanding leaders. People of all races and all levels of society loved them. Certainly they had human faults but they were honest men who saw the big picture and always tried to do the greatest good for the greatest number.

Ratu Sir Kamises Mara, on the other hand, while having the attributes of the other three, was a very skilled politician. It was he who forged the Alliance Party after independence, bringing together Fijians, Indians and people of other races in one party. He led with an autocratic style and few questioned his decisions. Unlike the others, he was aloof and sensitive to insult. It was said that if you crossed Ratu Mara he would never forgive you. He had wisdom and knowledge that few others possessed and a toughness that enabled him to win many concessions for the people of Fiji and the Pacific from the international community. While he was held in high esteem and respect by the people of Fiji, he was not loved with the kind of adoration was bestowed on Ratu Edward and Ratu Penaia.

In 1977, Fiji was shocked when many Fijians turned their back on Ratu Mara's Alliance Party and voted for an Indian party. This party captured many Fijian votes, which resulted in Koya's Indian National Federation Party winning the election by a slim margin. Ratu Mara was preparing to clean out his office and go back to his chiefly island of Lakeba when he received a summons from the Governor General, Ratu Sir George, to say he was appointing him a minority Prime Minister. Koya had tried for four days to get his party to agree that he should be Prime Minister, but they wouldn't have it. Finally, in desperation, they did agree and Koya went to Government House only to be told that he was too late. Mara had been sworn in. In many ways, I am sure it was a relief to Koya, for he was at heart a defense lawyer. He would have preferred to be Leader of the Opposition rather than Prime Minister.

Koya was one of the most arrogant men I have ever known. He was full of bluff and bluster. He was an actor and a chest-thumping orator and lacked any social skills. When Timoci Bavadra, who won the elections in 1987 and became Prime Minister, died, his funeral was held at Viseisei. It is customary in Fiji for groups of people to go to the place of the funeral, pay homage and present gifts to the family of the deceased. It was agreed that a joint sugar group should go the village and present what is called a 'reguregu'. As Chairman of the Sugar Cane Growers Council, Koya was asked to lead the group and be at the village at two pm About 50 of us were there on time but when the heralds told us it was our turn we had to say we were not ready as Koya had not yet arrived. It was most disrespectful. We waited for 45 minutes, holding up others. As the next most senior person there, I decided we could wait no longer and we went in to make our presentation. Just as we were leaving the village Koya turned up and appeared shocked that we had proceeded without him. When I told him why, he was furious and he didn't talk to me for a long time after that. It was the nature of the man.

It is strange how life rewards some and punishes others. We all thought Koya had a very successful legal practice, but he died at a relatively young age and his estate was worth very little. A short while after he passed on, his office, which was in an old wooden building in Lautoka, was burnt to the ground, destroying all his files and records. I had known his wife and found her to be a very pleasant person. I was therefore shocked when she was charged with arson and sent to jail.

I was never interested in entering politics but there came a time in the 1990s when Fiji was heading into troubled waters when one could not just stand back and do nothing. We non-Fijians had our own party and elected three people to parliament. We didn't have much influence, but one or more of our elected members usually ended up in cabinet. I began attending constituency meetings of our party to help steer them in what I thought was the right direction and before long I was writing speeches for our member in the House. He was not very articulate and was noted for being the appointed person to second any motion put before the members. He must have stood up hundreds of time to say, 'Mr Speaker Sir, I second the motion.' It was about all he ever did. He wasn't much use to us but he knew how to win votes and get elected. The members of the General Voters Party were a mixed lot. There were high-powered businessmen and women, Chinese market gardeners, part-European tradesmen, Melanesians from the Solomons, and Micronesians from Tuvalu and Ocean Island, all of whom had made Fiji their home. There were only a handful of Europeans like myself. At one time it was suggested that I stand for President of the party, but I declined, saying that as I was still working in the sugar industry I had to be impartial. The trouble with the General Voters Party was that, though they were small in number, there were serious divisions and too many people with personal agendas. The party eventually split into three groups.

In the second half of the 20th century, people of all races played an influential part in the politics of Fiji. But that began to change as Indians and others lost their influence. Politics became dominated by Fijian politics. Throughout their history, Fijians have been accustomed to living within their chiefly system, which has been the mainstay of their society. All customs and traditions revolved around the chief. The focus at any ceremony was the chief. Order was maintained by the chief. Many Fijians drifted into the urban areas and became academics, businesspeople, professionals and became distant from the chiefly domination. Others had been educated to the point that they don't see the need for the chiefly system. For them, the demise of the chiefly system would be no loss. Some may like to see it preserved as part of their tradition and heritage, but they don't want it to dominate their lives. In the long term, the domination of the chiefs as an elite group is bound to end. We live in an era of the common person and their voices cannot be stifled or ignored.

The end of the era of the ruling chiefs came in 1987 when the Labour Party leader Timoci Bavadra became Prime Minister of Fiji. Bavadra was a kindly, decent civil servant of lowly chiefly rank. Some would say that while he was nominally Prime Minister, the real power was vested in the hands of Mahendra Chaudhry, and that the subsequent coup was more against Indian leadership than Bavadra.

The man who removed him from power, Army Colonel Sitiveni Rabuka, had no chiefly standing, but he had a commanding presence and the bearing of a chief. He had a strong, warm personality with a keen sense of humour and he was extremely intelligent. There was no question about his leadership ability and he commanded respect as a soldier and subsequently as a politician. Many would deplore his moral values and at one time he openly confessed to being a 'carnal man.'

Rabuka skillfully transformed himself from a soldier to a political man of the world and he quickly ingratiated himself with both local and overseas leaders. When he staged his military coup he was clearly a champion of Fijian indigenous rights but during the 1990s he and Jai Ram Reddy, the leader of the National Federation Party, worked towards a new constitution that would be a model of multi-racial equity. In fact, he moved so far to the centre that at national elections in 1999 the Fijian electorate dumped him in an unprecedented fashion.

He would never recover from this election failure. Although he was a man of considerable talent, and indeed he had a lot to offer Fiji, he was never again called upon to carry out any national duty. He became a discarded man. Allegations were made that he had something to do with the military uprising in 2000 but he was never charged.

The civilian coup by George Speight in 2000 brought another commoner into the Prime Minister's office. Laisenia Qarase spent his working life in the civil service and at the time of the coup was head of the Fiji Development Bank. Though serving as a senator, he was an unlikely kind of politician, for he was reserved and introspective. When he was invited by the military leader Bainimarama to lead the government, there was considerable surprise and doubt about his ability to lead the nation out of crisis.

Being a technocrat, he skillfully managed the affairs of government, but he never really mastered the art of politics. As a result, he was manipulated by those more adept in the political arena. Politics is not usually the stage for people of integrity, and Qarase found himself surrounded by many unscrupulous opportunists. He was caught up in the multi-party experiment that was an integral provision of the constitution. No one really knew how to apply the arrangements but Qarase was determined to try to comply. He could not afford to alienate his own elected Fijian party cabinet ministers by dropping some, so, in order to accommodate the Labour party nominees, he had to create a cabinet of 36 members. The cost of this was astronomical.

Laisenia Qarase became Prime Minister in a coalition with a nationalist political party following the elections in 2001. This saw the return to overtly racial policies and programs of affirmative action. The rationale for this was that the only way to ensure security and stability was to address (and prioritise) indigenous Fijian grievances over issues to do with land, resources, identity and so on.

This pandering to ethno-nationalism was opposed by the military commander Commodore Voreqe, leading to a deepening tension between the government and army between 2001 and 2006.

Following a return to power by the Qarase government in elections in May 2006, the military mounted a coup in December—labeled a 'clean up campaign'—aimed at eradicating corruption and racial politics. As a result of this coup, Commodore Bainimarama became Interim Prime Minister.

I was saddened by the removal of Qarase for I had served on many Boards and Committees with him over the years. I always considered him to be a man of the highest level of integrity. He was extremely devout and during his time as

Prime Minister I regularly attended a prayer breakfast with him. Leadership was always high on the agenda of our discussions and he was a great supporter of the Leadership Fiji Programme that I helped to run.

One of the most damaging effects of the coups of 1987 and 2000 was the migration of talented people from Fiji. Many of these were our next generation of leaders. This was the prime reason that I joined with a group of concerned people in setting up Leadership Fiji. It is a programme modeled on one that has been running in Victoria, Australia, for many years. The object is not so much skills training but seeks to develop a person's understanding of the real issues facing the nation. It is common among many professional people to be so focused on their careers that they pay little attention to matters outside their offices. This programme sought to prepare people in the 35-year-old age group for the time when they would head their organisations. We sought to take in 28 people for a ten month period and tried to get a racial, gender, vocational and regional balance so the group would be dynamic.

Each year when we completed a programme and a group of people graduated, I felt a tremendous surge of optimism about the future of Fiji for there was clearly a wealth of talented leaders in the community and I felt confident about their ability to lead in all walks of life.

Bainimarama was another commoner and in ousting Qarase he sidelined the paramount chiefs. Qarase had cleverly included chiefs from all the confederacies in his cabinet. In doing so, he united the Fijians, but he had also created a monster that Fiji could not afford. Bainimarama's claim was that many of the chiefs were implicated in the 2000 coup and, while some may have been charged and convicted, they had been let out of jail under compulsory supervision orders. He further claimed that many of the chiefs had abused their power and grown rich at the expense of the taxpayer. One of his first actions was to close down the operations of the Great Council of Chiefs, which since cession, had contained the collective wisdom and been the voice of the Fijian people. Only the Great Council of Chiefs had the constitutional power to appoint the President and Vice President.

Bainimarama's rise to power in the military and as Prime Minister came as a surprise to many people. He had the reputation as a fine sailor. When writing the biography of Ratu Sir Penaia Ganilau I was told that, in 1985, Ratu Penaia travelled by the Royal Naval ship Kikau to the small island of Ceva-i-ra at the extreme edge of Fiji's nautical border, and Bainimarama, who was captain of the vessel, saved his life. The Kikau was an old wooden minesweeper that had been 'given' to Fiji by the United States. Just north of the island they ran into a vicious storm. Huge waves battered the ship, smashing the bridge and putting one of her two engines out of action. A mayday message was sent out and the crew prepared to abandon ship. According to Ratu Penaia, Bainimarama kept his cool, and in a report on the incident Ratu Penaia said, 'The Commanding Officer, Lt. Frank Bainimarama, bore himself in exemplary manner at all times and the behaviour of those under his command was equally praiseworthy.'

The appointment of Bainimarama, a naval person, to head up the military was seen as a slap in the face to senior army colonels, but he consolidated his position and weathered the military uprising in 2000 when he was nearly shot. While he obviously had military skills and was respected as a leader, he was not a chief, indeed he seemed to treat the chiefs with a certain degree of contempt.

But he proved to be a very skilled political leader, albeit one who has never gone out to campaign for votes until the September 2014 elections which his Fiji First party convincingly won. He has surrounded himself with competent people, identified problem issues and took what he regarded to be appropriate actions. Of course none of his new policies had the consent of the people. Few citizens are happy about their inability to object to anything his government has done, nor of the suppression of many human rights. But it cannot be denied that he has produced a favourable balance sheet for Fiji.

While relations with Australia, New Zealand, the United States, European Union and United Kingdom became somewhat strained, he has effectively re-directed Fiji towards China and South East Asia, where he is apparently held in high regard. On the international stage, he has frequently addressed the United Nations and has chaired the Group of 77 and China and the International Sugar Organisation.

On the home front, he has been conducting himself like a natural political leader by giving frequent addresses to organisations all over the country, opening government projects to benefit the community, and has effectively been recognised as the Prime Minister of Fiji.

Interlude: A Conversation of Spirits

You could not see them, nor could you hear the way they communicated, for they were merely vapours. But they were indeed the spirits of Ratu Sir Kamisese Mara and Ratu Sir Penaia Ganilau.

They floated in the breeze above Vanuabalavu and looked down upon Laisenia Qarase sitting on the ground cutting copra. 'This is ridiculous,' exclaimed Mara angrily. 'The man was elected leader of the nation. How long before Bainimarama has elections?'

'He said September 2014,' responded Ratu Penaia, before asking, 'Do you think Qarase made a mess of things?'

'Perhaps. Unfortunately he was a victim of his own willingness to accommodate the multi-party provisions of the constitution. This resulted in a bloated cabinet, a breakdown in administrative control and discipline, and massive costs.'

'But what about the corruption?'

'That started in our time, Ratu Penaia. We can't just blame Qarase,' Mara stated.

'Do you think he should have dismissed Bainimarama?'

'I doubt he could have. Bainimarama was determined to overthrow him and he had the guns,' said Ratu Mara sadly.

There was silence for a while as they floated towards Taveuni. Then Ratu Penaia commented, 'Perhaps we are all to blame. We made mistakes.'

'Yes, starting with you taking us out of the Commonwealth in 1987. If you had given me a bit more time I could have sorted things out. But you had to declare a republic and pardon that man, Rabuka. Now every rebel expects to be pardoned.' Mara's vapour flipped impatiently. 'If you had stood firm and gone up to the barracks and spoken to the men you could have ended the 1987 coup there and then. You had the power.'

Ratu Penaia was a placid man in life and he wasn't offended by Mara's accusation. 'I made a judgement call. I would not have been able to get through to Nabua. They would have stopped me. As to the pardon, that is what I was advised to do.'

'Well it was wrong advice,' snorted Mara.

By this time they had arrived over Taveuni and Ratu Penaia looked down on his island with nostalgia. His vapour swelled with pride and he was emboldened to say to Mara, 'If we are going to point fingers, let me ask, why did you run away from Government House in 2000? If you had stayed there the nation would have rallied around you and the army would have been able to take out Speight and his people. By leaving, you gave him a free hand.'

Ratu Mara ignored the comment for a time before exclaiming, 'I had no choice. The army forced me out.'

'Were you not the President—the Turaga? You could have refused.'

There was no response and they floated along the Taveuni coast. Eventually Ratu Mara said, 'Look at how all this rich coconut land has gone back to bush. Do you realise that we used to produce 40,000 tons of copra a year? Now we are down to 8,000 tons. We should have done more to help the industry. Remember when I started the coir factory in Lakeba?'

'It was a good idea,' commented Ratu Penaia. As they passed over Somosomo, Ratu Penaia asked, 'Why don't we Fijians make better use of our land?'

'Our tradition is to grow subsistence crops, not to engage in intensive agriculture. It may take another generation to change our way of thinking.'

A breeze carried them rapidly over to Labasa. They gazed down upon the vacant cane farms. 'Look at this deplorable situation,' Mara said. 'I once had a cane farm in Seaqaqa. It was a model farm. Now it's gone back to bush.' He mused for a time before asking, 'Whose bright idea was it to tell Fijians not to renew the leases?'

'Our own Fijian leaders,' responded Ratu Penaia. 'You and I allowed this to happen,' he added.

A strong northerly wind suddenly picked up the vapours and carried them across Bligh waters, over to Ovalau and Bau. As they arrived over this small historic island, other vapours rose to greet them. Ratu Sir George Cakobau was his usual cheery self. 'Have you two come again to ask why we have not appointed a new Vunivalu?'

Ratu Penaia chuckled and said, 'Maybe it's because you were too much for your people. One Vunivalu like you was enough for 100 years!'

The other spirit, that of Ratu Sir Edward Cakobau, smirked and said, 'The real reason is that men are afraid to anoint a woman.'

'What the people now want is a strong leader,' said Ratu Mara earnestly. 'If the people of Bau could appoint a strong Vunivalu, he or she may be the one to lead Fiji out of its present misery.'

Interlude: A Conversation of Spirits

'We put Ratu Joni Madraiwiwi in as Vice President and the army got rid of him,' said Ratu George. 'What more can we do?'

Ratu Mara's vapour shuddered violently. 'It's up to the Bose Levu Vakaturaga [Council of Chiefs]. They are the voice of the Fijian people,' he exclaimed.

'But the army got rid of them,'

'Yes, they walked away like sheep when Bainimarama pointed a gun at them,' said Ratu Mara.

'Well what do you expect them to do?' asked Ratu Penaia.

Ratu Mara glared at the spirits around him for a time before saying, 'The wisdom of the Fijian people collected over generations has been inherited by those chiefs who form the Bose Levu Vakaturaga. They have the responsibility to safeguard the interest of all our people, and this included people of other races, for they make up the citizens of our nation. We may have had a form of democracy here since 1970, but governments have come and gone. So have dictators like Rabuka, Speight and Bainimarama. Well, he hasn't gone yet. The one constant has been the Bose. Now, in the hour of real need, they have wilted before a few guns. They must stand up and show courage. Your son was chairman once, Ratu Penaia. He made a good chairman. Why doesn't he mobilise the chiefs instead of siding with the army?'

It was Ratu Edward who intervened. 'The truth is, Ratu Mara, many chiefs have disgraced the Fijian people. There are too few of integrity, wisdom and courage whose motivation is service to the people. The back of the Bose Levu Vakaturaga has been broken.'

'Then what hope is there?' raged Ratu Mara.

The four spirits floated over Suva. They gazed down on the bustling city and observed the traffic jams, the potholed roads, the squatter areas, the unemployed people roaming the streets, the empty parliamentary complex, the crowded schools. They mused about what it was like during their lifetime.

'What would Ratu Sukuna say if he were alive today?' asked Ratu George as they floated over Boron House, where he had once lived.

They thought about it for a few moments. It was Ratu Mara who commented. 'He had the difficult task of dealing with the colonial masters. I am sure that would have been a lot harder than coping with Bainimarama and his guns. One of his great achievements was to ensure that all of us had the proper training as leaders so that we could progress the nation towards independence. I think he would be of a similar mind today. Develop the leadership.'

Just then another vapour joined them and said, 'The trouble with all of you and the leaders who are still living is that you, and they, have stopped thinking like Fijians. Everyone has gone global.'

The four vapours cringed before the dominant face of Ratu Sukuna's spirit. 'Do you understand what I mean?' he asked. The four vapours shook their heads in denial.

'What has made the Fijian people different are their values: vakaturaga—their behaviour; veidokai—their respect for others; vakarokoroko—their deference to others; and yalo malua—humility. It would seem that these characteristics have been abandoned as they seek to copy other people. If they continue to do so they will lose their identity.'

The vapours bowed in respect and were silent before Ratu Mara had the courage to respond. 'Io saka, but the world has changed. You have to behave differently today in order to survive. Fiji is no longer a place for Fijians only. Many others live here and are just as equal.'

Ratu Sukuna's vapour was impassive as he said, 'If we forget who we are and change our way of life we are lost.' With that he floated away.

The four vapours glided along the Viti Levu coast, past the many tourist resorts, until they arrived over Denarau. 'Is this the way of the future?' asked Ratu Mara.

Ratu Edward responded immediately. 'It has to be. It's the only industry that can provide investment, jobs and prosperity for our people. What is more, we have a fantastic product to offer the tourists.'

'Not if we continue to have coups' said Ratu George.

They gazed down on the tourist properties, at the many tourists having fun, at the happy and courteous staff, and the clear blue waters, shimmering beaches and colourful reefs. Ratu Penaia observed, 'There can be few places as lovely as this anywhere else in the world.'

They were all silent as they floated over the Yasawas and continued to soak up the idyllic beauty of the islands. Ratu Mara exclaimed vehemently, 'The army has to go or these coups will never end.'

Ratu Penaia, who was once an army man, said forcefully, 'That will not happen. We will never have a government strong enough to remove the army.'

'You know I have always been an admirer of the American system,' said Ratu Edward. 'A President elected by popular vote who then selects a cabinet from the best people available in the country. He could even select the army commander.'

Just then a thunderous black cloud appeared from the west. 'There is a storm approaching,' said Ratu George. 'I think we had better get back to our bulu.'

'Yes,' said Ratu Mara, 'and continue to exert our influence for the common good of all. You know most Fijians still believe in spirits like us. Don't give up hope.'

15. Sports

Fiji is a sporting nation.

Fijians engaged in traditional spear throwing games in ancient times but these died out after the arrival of the British. Yet it was some years later before sports became a part of regular life. An Irishman introduced rugby in 1916 and it quickly gained popularity among Fijians, who played it in bare feet. But it wasn't until the 1930s that a team went to New Zealand and won every game on tour, a feat never repeated. Chiefs like Ratu George and Ratu Penaia excelled at the game and gave it great impetus. Ratu Penaia would spend a lifetime as player, administrator and president of the union. Once, at an international rugby conference in Cambridge, he addressed the gathering and said, 'I have often thought what a funny lot we rugby folk are, sitting in an ancient hall, tied by a set of rules that no one agrees on, in pursuit of a ball that won't even bounce straight.'

As a 15s team, Fiji has always been at the middle of the international ladder, though individuals have done very well overseas. In 2013, it was stated that over 200 Fijian rugby players were linked to clubs in Australia, New Zealand, Japan, China, Europe and the United States, and many have excelled. But it is in the sevens code that Fiji won international fame. I was attending a national sevens competition in 1989, just before the selection of the team to go to Hong Kong where the most prestigious international competition is held. A diminutive young man, who no one had ever heard of, began showing up the recognised stars by racing all over the ground, scoring try after try. The crowd loved him and began calling out 'Hong Kong, Hong Kong.' He was Waisale Serevi, who was selected that year and every year thereafter that until he retired. He became the world's best player and was known by such sobriquets as Sir-revi, the Magician, and the Maestro. He was a small man, humble, cheeky, and yet lovable, who became a household name throughout Fiji and a role model for the youth of the nation.

The British colonial officers brought cricket to the islands. One who devoted much of his life to cricket was Philip Snow, brother of the famous author C. P. Snow. Philip came to Taveuni as a District Officer when I was a boy and spent a great deal of his time fostering the game on the island. My father was no slouch at it, having been captain of the Geelong Grammar School team, and he and Philip did much to popularise the game. Even after Philip retired from the colonial service, he remained an advocate of Fiji cricket and arranged overseas tours, coaching and financial support. But the game never really became universally popular. Perhaps it was too slow and Fiji was certainly too hot and wet for cricket.

The Indian people took to soccer, perhaps because it was less of a contact sport than rugby, and up until the middle of the 20th century it was almost exclusively Indian. But by the end of the century, nearly all the players were Fijian, while the administrators were Indian. Soccer is played to huge crowds throughout Fiji.

When I came to Suva in 1968 I decided that, as Suva was such a wet place, I would take up squash and I never regretted that decision. The beauty of it was that you could always play at the appointed time regardless of the weather and I played three or four times a week. All levels of people competed and many were very good. One of those was a young Chinese man named Devlin Ah Sam. He was not only a good player but was super fit, so he decided to have a crack at the Guinness Book of Records world record for continuous play. All of the squash players were rostered to take turns with him as he played through day and night for 75 hours. Under the rules he was allowed short breaks to go to the toilet and have meals. Otherwise, he had to keep playing game after game, hour after hour. It was hot and tedious and at times he began to flag. But we cheered him on and he set a new world record.

Golf was another game brought in by the British and Australians. The district administrators made small courses at the main centres, and CSR made other courses at each of their mills for their own staff. During the first half of the 20th century, only Europeans played, but as racial barriers collapsed and the CSR staff was localised, other races took it up. In the 1970s a young man in Nadi, named Vijay Singh, began swinging a club. Despite the lack of expert coaching and competition, he was destined to go on and win the US PGA and the Masters. He became the top ranked player in the world. This was quite an achievement when one considers there are millions of players throughout the world. Although Vijay always carried the Fiji flag and was a great ambassador for the country, he seldom came home. On the one occasion that he did, he played in a fundraiser at the Denarau course in Nadi. Many local golfers went to see him and were quite awed at his expertise. He and another Australian professional, who came with him, offered to give us lessons but I am sure they quickly realised we were hopeless cases.

Prior to the establishment of the Denarau course, the early golf courses in Fiji were rather ordinary, providing little challenge. The first real international 18-hole course was designed by the famed Robert Trent Jones Jr at the Pacific Harbour development at Navua. This was also the first major international standard development, which it was hoped would put Fiji on the map. Indeed it was a wonderful complex and the golf course was the centrepiece, with fairways winding through jungle covered ranges and skirting waterways and luxury villas. Some fairways were so skillfully located between hills and bush that one got the feeling that man had played little part in their construction except to mow the grass.

On one occasion, the Eisenhower Cup, the world's team championship, was held at Pacific Harbour. It was a great event for Fiji to host. The course was in pristine condition. Golfers came from all over the world. For us locals it was a rare opportunity to see the best in action. At one stage I was following a young, up-and-coming American golfer, who hooked his ball into the bush. He went in to find it, and shortly after he came running out with hornets buzzing all round him. These little yellow insects get very angry when their nest is disturbed and can give a painful sting. The poor golfer had quite a few on his arms, neck and face and was in considerable agony until I came to his assistance. The old Fijian cure for a hornet sting is a creeper aptly named mile-a-minute. When this is crushed in your hand and mixed with saliva it is rubbed into the sting and gives instant relief. I think I saved the golfer's day.

Ratu Mara was a very keen golfer and while he was Prime Minister, touring the world, he met and played with many of the world's leaders. I occasionally had a game with him and in 1995, when he was President, I was paired with him. I happened to putt so badly that we lost the game. Shortly after, I went to Government House to receive one of the first Fiji awards, Member of the Order of Fiji, from him. There were 30 other recipients, all formally dressed, seated in the splendor of Government House. When my name was called I had to rise, walk down the red carpet to where the President was standing, bow, and wait stiffly before him as he pinned the medal on my coat. It was a very solemn moment, so I could hardly keep a straight face when he said quietly, out of the corner of his mouth, as he was trying to attach the medal, 'I am only giving you this in the hope you will putt better when we play next.'

While attending Melbourne Grammar I discovered that I was quite a talented boxer and I went through Grammar undefeated. When I went back to Taveuni, I was still interested in the sport and with Dad's agreement we began to stage boxing events. We set up a ring that could seat 500 people and brought in boxers from all over Fiji. The boxing event was a gala occasion. The little bay off our wharf was crowded with a flotilla of small craft that brought people from all surrounding islands, and nearly every taxi, car and lorry and bus on the island was parked outside the ring. At that time there was a lot of corruption in the sport and promoters were more interested in making money than promoting the sport and giving fighters a fair go. Our objective was to cover expenses and give all the proceeds to the fighters. It was a resounding success which helped to give the sport credibility in other parts of Fiji, and in due course a few Commonwealth Champions were to emerge.

While there were many talented boxers in Fiji, corruption and mismanagement continued to plague development and the sport fell into disrepute.

As we lived on islands surrounded by the sea, nautical sports were very popular. Fishing was the prerogative of everyone. Indian farmers with small punts and outboard engines fished for food, or to sell and supplement their income. Fijian villagers went netting or spear fishing for the same reasons. In urban areas many had small boats and went out at night to bottom fish. But no matter what the reason, fishing was fun, fishing was sport. There were, of course, the real sports fishermen who owned large boats that carried tourists after bill fish, tuna and wahu. International game fishermen came from all over the world and many world records were set. Annual competitions were held and the newspapers were splashed with photos of unkempt, salty looking characters, standing beside mighty fish, hanging from scales. It was good for tourism.

When I joined the Sugar Board, my chairman, Sir Charles Marsack, owned a 30-footer and was a very keen fisherman. His preference was for bottom fishing at night. Knowing of my background as a fisherman on Taveuni, I was always included in his weekend expeditions. His fishing crony at the time was the Governor, Sir Robert Foster. The other members were Marsack's son, Ray, who skippered the boat, and a friend of Ray's. We would leave on Saturday morning for a pre-determined destination, arrive there in the afternoon, and begin fishing at dusk. If we were lucky, we would pull up fish all night. Other times, we would get nothing and have to raise the anchor time and time again till we found the right spot. It was either lots of fun or rather tedious. The first chore at daylight was to go ashore at a small sand spit and clean the fish. We stripped down to our underpants and sat on our haunches on the sand gutting and scaling fish, then go into the sea to perform our own ablutions. I have often reflected on the image of the mighty British Governor of Fiji squatting on the sand in his underpants cleaning fish and thought governors were, after all, mere mortals like any of us.

Perhaps the most widely published and popular athletics event in Fiji is the annual Coca Cola games. This brings together students of all ages and those in the senior groups often go on to represent Fiji at international events such as the Olympic, Commonwealth and South Pacific Games. The South Pacific Games began in Suva and have been held every four years in other Pacific nations. Fiji has not been very successful in the Olympic and Commonwealth Games but in 2013 a one-legged high jumper from Fiji won gold at the Paralympics in London.

Hockey and mens' and womens' basketball are immensely popular and in recent times volleyball, which can be played anywhere at little cost, has become a favourite. Another marine sport that has brought Fiji international fame is windsailing. One family, the Philps, have excelled at windsailing. Tony took it up at a young age and for years was among the top ten in the world. He took part in many Olympic and Commonwealth Games and put Fiji on the international circuit. It is, of course, popular at most of the tourist resorts.

Another sport for which Fiji is gaining international prestige is surfing, as there is a venue off Nadi that is now part of the international circuit.

However, rugby and football remain the dominant sports in the country. While a few very talented sportsmen, such as Serevi, Vijay Singh, and a few Fijians who have played rugby for Australia and New Zealand, have done well, it is unlikely that our teams will ever reach the highest rungs in the international sporting arena. In Fiji, as in other Pacific Islands, the people are rather laid back and lack the motivation and discipline to reach the top. For them sport is fun, and perhaps that is the way it should be.

Interlude: China Rose

What, you may ask, do the names Devil's Gold, All Aglow, Mini Skirt, Blooming Blazers, Blue Berry Tart, Brown Bomber and Terry Smith have in common? They are the unlikely names given to some hybridised blooms of the Hibiscus rosa-sinensis, otherwise known as the China Rose, or, more commonly, the Hibiscus.

Developed by the gardeners of Chinese Emperors and Mandarins as something exotically new for their masters, the hibiscus is now more synonymous with the South Pacific Islands of Hawaii and Fiji, and places such as Florida, Australia and Madagascar. It is the state flower of Hawaii, and the most popular carnival in Fiji is the Hibiscus Carnival.

No doubt the plant was brought into the Pacific by the migrations of people from South East Asia, but there are known to be some indigenous varieties in Hawaii and Reunion, and a single one on Fiji's lush garden island of Taveuni.

There are dozens of genus hibiscus, but the queen of them all is the Hibiscus rosa-sinensis.

Hundreds of varieties of this can be found and they all have their own individual charm, but they are poor cousins to the incredibly striking blooms that have been engineered by man.

Men such as Fiji's Ken Perks, who lived all his life in the islands and had a love affair with the hibiscus since boyhood. Following his retirement after 35 years in the public service, his infatuation blossomed as he honed his skills at hybridisation. The results of his efforts are, simply put, spectacular.

Ken Perks had few of the artistic refinements or academic pomp that is normally associated with flower lovers. He was a rugged, private man, who smoked odious home-grown Fiji tobacco and drank over-proof Fiji rum. But he was driven by a researcher's dogged perseverance. His reward was the beauty that results from hybridisation. 'After that,' he said, 'I have no interest.'

It was his wife, Joy, who catalogued the hundreds of new varieties that he created and reaped the pleasure of having a house full of blooms.

'Growing hibiscus is just something to do,' he says matter-of factly.

But make no mistake, hybridisation takes many years of patient dedication.

Thousands of attempts are made to pollinate the flower with the pollen of another hibiscus. The flower then falls off, leaving a seed pod, and the seeds are planted. If the plant grows, it remains constant, with a distinctive new bloom. But it is a hit or miss affair. You can't design a new bloom, and what you get is a surprise.

Out of a thousand trials, he might get only two hibiscuses that are worth keeping. The rest of the creations will be too ordinary to retain. 'Keeping them,' noted Perks, 'would be like collecting the same postage stamp with only the perforation being different.'

In the early years of his interest in hybridisation, he didn't have much success. It wasn't until he managed to procure some of the magnificent Hawaiian varieties, which he crossed with local hibiscus and grafted onto hardy stalks, that he was able to create something special.

Many who have specialised in hybridisation have aimed at producing spectacular blooms with scant attention to the strength of the plant and little chance of reproduction from cuttings. Through grafting, Ken Perks has made it possible for other hibiscus lovers to grow his flowers in their gardens.

The hibiscus is called the 'Senitoa' in Fijian, meaning the flower of the chicken, perhaps because the stamen resembles a cock's comb. Naming new blooms is all part of the fun. The names seem to be more often related to specific people, but they can arise out of other situations. Once Ken saw an exquisite bloom and exclaimed 'Oh!' And that was what it was called: 'Oh.'

Hibiscus growers in Florida, Hawaii and Australia are usually members of a hibiscus society, through which members exchange knowledge and share in each other's successes. Not so Ken Perks. He neither sought nor was given any international recognition for the uniquely marvelous flowers he created, or for the expertise that he demonstrated. It was all for personal satisfaction.

While the hibiscus is a tropical bloom, Ken claims that he has seen better blooms in Auckland and Sydney. 'Perhaps the variable climate is more agreeable. Ours is more constant, rather harsh. We probably get more blooms throughout the year, but they are better in New Zealand.'

While Ken had 400 or so plants in his garden, he advised the home gardener to keep only ten or 12 plants and tender them with care by regular fertilising and pruning.

It is an oddly incongruous fact that while Perks had some of the best hibiscus in the South Pacific, the blooms are produced on plants that are scraggy, stunted and ratty looking.

'At age 74, it has become too much work to look after them all. I don't worry about bugs or diseases, I leave that to Mother Nature.'

It is a risk that he took as hibiscus are threatened by a host of such pests.

But the blooms gave him great pleasure. 'I often just sit and admire them and wonder how my hands managed to work so well with nature.' His success is a contradiction of Rousseau's opinion that 'Everything is good as it leaves the hands of the Author of things; everything degenerates in the hands of man.'

But others have reaped the pleasure as well. Ken's wife Joy was Personal Assistant to former Prime Minister Ratu Sir Kamisese Mara for 25 years. Each day throughout that period, she took a selection of flowers to Ratu Mara's office for him and his visitors to admire.

Fiji artist Liebling Marlowe, who was the first Miss Hibiscus in 1956, comments: 'Looking at hibiscus blooms gives me a feeling of joy, happiness and peace. It makes me feel good to be alive.'

Hibiscus is the favourite choice of exotic island girls, and the flower tucked behind the ear focuses attention on both the face and flora.

Unlike many flowers, hibiscus have no scent. Its appeal lies in a rich blending of colours, the unusual curl of single and double petals, its luster, size and sheer overall beauty.

While most flowers, such as roses and carnations, display beauty in the cluster of folded petals, the China Rose has only five petals which unfold in the morning to reveal its charm. By nightfall, after only a few hours of exotic loveliness, the petals of China Rose wrap around the stamen column and die.

After wandering around Ken's garden in Suva, I was invited into his lounge, where a magnificent pink hibiscus, about ten inches across, stood in solitary splendor on the centre of his table. 'Strike me pink, that's magnificent,' I blurted out. He smiled and said 'I haven't named it yet, but thanks for the idea. I'll call it "Strike me Pink."'

16. Clubs

The Suva community is made up of many races and groups of people. Whenever one gave a public address, it was prefaced with recognition of the chief guest, perhaps the Prime Minister, then members of cabinet, followed by members of the diplomatic corps, and finally ladies and gentlemen. This, then, was the hierarchy of society. But the groupings of the ladies and gentlemen are extremely diverse. There are, of course, the racial groupings: Fijian, Indian, European, part-European, Tongan, Samoan, Solomon Islander, Rotuman, Chinese, and others.

The expatriates comprised a separate group. They came mainly from Australia, New Zealand, Britain, the United States and, more recently, South East Asia. These racial groups were then broken down into sub-groups of those working within church communities, the university, aid organisations and professions.

Even within the racial groups there were sub-groups. Within the Indian community there were Gujaratis, Muslims and South Indians. The old local Chinese felt different to recent immigrants of Chinese origin. There were, of course, countless overlaps within the civil service, in the professions and the business community. But on the whole most of these groups preferred to socialise among themselves. Needless to say, there were the rich and the poor, the middle class and the destitute. What was remarkable about this complex Suva society was that a great many people knew each other, or at least knew who people were, and most of the locals could speak Fijian, Hindi and English.

A great deal of the social and sporting life of Suva, and indeed Fiji, gravitated around clubs. At Savusavu, the copra producing centre on Vanua Levu, there was the Planters Club, a place where copra planters gathered when they went to town to make their purchases or sell their copra. It became a rather boisterous drinking hole for the hard-living Savusavu planters. At Labasa, there was the Vanua Levu Club, which was originally set up by CSR for their own staff. It was mainly a drinking and billiards club. In most of the small towns around the country there were similar clubs for the merchants living in the towns.

The Suva clubs were more diverse. The oldest was the Fiji Club, which had been established at the old capital of Levuka at the end of the 19th century. My great-grandfather was an original member. When the capital moved to Suva, the club was moved. According to its constitution, it was 'for the intercourse of gentlemen,' a term that would certainly not be used in any constitution today. During the colonial days, only British civil servants were eligible for membership. Even successful businessmen were disqualified from membership. They were regarded as 'mere merchants.' As for the 'natives' and Indians, the

British thought that giving them membership was unthinkable. As Fiji changed, so did the clubs. But old traditions die hard, and when Gautam Ram Swarup was proposed as President in the 1980s there was a hard core of whites who saw this as a most retrograde step. But he won and managed to appease the different interest groups. The club offered tennis, swimming, squash and billiards as well as many social events.

Just down the road was the Defence Club, which was patronised mainly by commercial men. As its name suggests, a constitutional requirement was that all members had to respond to defend Fiji if the need arose. Its members were a hard drinking lot and I always wondered about the effectiveness of any defence they may be able to offer.

There was also the Merchants Club, which served the needs of Indian merchants, and the United Club, which had a strong part-European membership.

On the outskirts of Suva was the Golf Club. It was originally a white's only establishment but as golf became more popular with local people it expanded its membership. Saturday was competition day. A draw was posted on the board and you might find yourself drawn with an Australian professor, an Indian fitter and turner from the Public Works Department, and a Fijian salesman. On the golf course, one was judged not by position, race or wealth. What mattered was one's ability to drive or putt. It was always stimulating to spend four hours walking the course with people one had never met before. During the terribly stressful days after the 1987 military coup, it was one of the few places of sanity in the city. Suva was rife with rumours and rocked by tragic events. It was very difficult to concentrate on work. One did not know who to trust or believe. Invariably, golfers of all races and walks of life would find their way out to the course after work to play a round of golf and forget their problems.

The other main club in Suva was the Yacht Club. This was where the yachties and 'stink boat' owners moored their boats and drank vast quantities of beer. In the 20th century, it was more of a white establishment, as few Fijians or Indians had boats. Many expatriates who were on short term contracts bought boats to take advantage of the wonderful opportunities while they were in Suva. In the 1960s and 1970s, sailing was very popular and Suva harbor was a busy place on Saturdays and Sundays when regattas took place.

When we came to Suva, I joined the power boat owners amd acquired a 15-footer. In those days, most of us went to the island of Nukulau for our boating activities and picnics. It was so popular that unless you arrived at the island by eleven o'clock, there would not be a mooring space around the beach.

With the increased cost of fuel in the 1980s and 1990s, power boating became less popular and by the time Nukulau was made into a prison island for George Speight and his treasonous supporters, it was rarely used.

One of the main events in the boating calendar was the Suva to Levuka boat race. This was a time trial that started at the Yacht Club, went across Laucala Bay, through the river system to Bau water on the eastern side of the island, then across to the island of Ovalau and its capital, Levuka. There were normally 40 or 50 boats in the race, which took a full day to complete, depending on the speed you declared. There were secret check points along the way, to ensure that you passed that point at a time calculated by the organisers to be correct based on your declared speed. If you were too fast or too slow you lost points. The team with the least penalties won. There was always a great deal of drinking along the way and the highlight was the prize-giving night. In the beginning, the final night was held at the Levuka Club, but it was later staged at a beautiful, isolated island, back in Bau water. Needless to say, many of the boatees became outrageously drunk and suffered next day on the trip back to Suva.

My first success in the race was with my cousin Spencer. He was the Captain and I was the navigator. We entered at a speed of 26 knots, which was the fastest time, and we crossed the line first with a minimal loss of points. However, another owner had entered at the slowest time of 5 knots and he lost fewer points. We ended up second. I had more luck with Ray Nestor. Ray and his family came to Suva from the heartland of Victoria. He was a dinky-di Aussie, a land surveyor who was contracted to the Fiji Government. His children went to Stella Maris school with our children, but it was our mutual love of the sea that brought us together. Ray decided to build his own boat while he was in Fiji. This proved to be a fine 25-foot craft, which was duly entered in the Suva Levuka race. With Ray as skipper and myself as navigator, we maintained our speed of 18 knots and won.

Service clubs such as Rotary and Lions were well patronised in Fiji. These service organisations were non-racial and did a tremendous amount of good in the community. Rotary had first started when the Suva Club was chartered in 1936. It was followed by clubs in Lautoka, Ba, Sigatoka and Labasa. In 1972, I was invited to join a new club that was chartered in Suva. The Rotary world is divided up into districts that are controlled by District Governors. In Fiji we were part of the then largest district in the world, which included the north of the North Island of New Zealand, Fiji, Tonga, Samoa, New Caledonia, Norfolk, Vanuatu and Cook Islands. The district headquarters were in Auckland and the governors had been New Zealanders until 1974, when Ali Asgar, a Fiji optometrist, was appointed to the position. Ali Asgar was an exceptional man who came from the farming community of Ba. His parents sent him to study optometry overseas and he returned to open a practice in Suva. Ali was an extrovert with a dazzling sense of humour, self-assurance and was always full of optimism. Premature baldness didn't age his baby face with its twinkling eye and constant smile. While Ali had served as a World Vice-President of J. C.'s, to take up the appointment of District Governor meant a big sacrifice, for as Governor he would have to be away visiting all the clubs in the district for at least six months of the year. His practice would certainly suffer. He took great pleasure in pointing this out to me when he asked me to be his District Secretary, which entailed the administration of the district.

I would have to make as many sacrifices as he would, he teased. We had a great year together and staged one of the most successful district conferences ever held. Some 600 Rotarians from all over the district came to Suva for the annual gathering. Our conference organiser was Kalyan Ghose, the manager of Air India in Fiji. Kalyan Ghose was from Goa and spent many years being a good citizen of Fiji. He spoke the English language so beautifully that someone once remarked that 'he made the Queen sound like an Australian ocker.'

I never thought of Ali as vain, so was surprised when one day I saw him with a toupee covering his bald dome. He looked quite different and so artificial that I laughed. But he laughed as well and I eventually got used to it and found it difficult to imagine him without his extra hair. Tragically, Ali died before he was 50 and it was many years before we had another District Governor from outside New Zealand. I have always found the new Zealand Rotarians rather patronising towards the islanders. There seems to be a notion that they are better qualified and that we should conform to their concept of how Rotary should fulfill its objectives. The truth is that islanders are different and many organisations, including business and political organisations, must be moulded to suit their needs. A classic example of this is the application of democracy. Following the coups of 1987, 2000 and 2006, smart sanctions were imposed by New Zealand and other countries 'until Fiji returned to democracy.' Which meant, of course, their brand of democracy, rather than one that could be moulded to suit Fiji.

There were many different sporting clubs, which I refer to elsewhere. There were also clubs such as Charman's All Races. Harry Charman was a Londoner, a real cockney, who loved to wear a pearly suit. He came to Fiji as a physical training specialist and set up his club mainly for boxing. But his main contribution was to encourage young men, who often drifted aimlessly around the streets, to join and discover some focus in life. Harry became a kind of folk hero among people of all races and strata of society.

While there was plenty of opportunity for Fijians and Indians to express their artistic talents of song and dance, the Fiji Arts Club was the only place where Western stage productions could be seen. The club attracted many very talented expatriates who produced Shakespearean plays and the top shows of the day, such as *Fiddler on the Roof* and *Canterbury Tales*. Later, when local playwrights emerged, their productions were successfully put on display.

Nightclubs did not become popular until the 1970s and 1980s. Up until that time entertainment took place in the home. There were few local musicians and young people did not have spare money. One of the first nightclubs was the Golden Dragon. It was started by a very musical Chinese man and soon began to draw crowds. A group of us once decided to try it out. Within our party were Ratu Sir Penaia Ganilau and his lovely wife, Adi Laisa. There were also many other people of all races and social backgrounds dancing and singing with the band. Fijians are a gregarious people, but they are also very respectful of their chiefs. I recall that at one point during the night, a young Fijian man came up to Ratu Penaia, bowed his head and asked very respectfully if he could dance with my wife, Jacque. Ratu Penaia examined him carefully before apparently deciding that the young man wasn't a suitable companion for my wife. He simply pursed his lips and shook his head and the young man thanked him respectfully and walked away. Jacque and I were not consulted.

Interlude: Rotary—Service Above Self

When the 19 members of the Rotary Club of Suva sat down for their charter dinner in July 1936, few of those present could have foreseen the profound changes that would take place in Suva, Fiji, in the South Pacific, and throughout the world.

The world was emerging from the Great Depression, Nazism was raising its ugly head, and the island nations of the South Pacific, as well as Australia and New Zealand, were still regarded as sleepy appendages of the Crown in the antipodes.

Rotary in the region, Fiji Rotary in particular, has also changed. In 1936, the Suva Club's 19 charter members were all Caucasian, predominantly of English descent. The 300-odd Rotarians in the eight Fiji clubs are now Hindus, Muslims, Sikhs, Chinese, Fijians, Japanese, North Americans, Australians, New Zealanders, Rotumans, South Americans, Englishmen, Scotsmen and many others.

As the Fiji economy grew and towns outside Suva expanded during the colonial and post-independent period, Rotary also extended its influence.

In 1958, the Suva Club sponsored the Charter of the Rotary Club of Lautoka, Lautoka in turn sponsored Nadi in 1968, Sigatoka in 1971, and Ba in 1972. The Suva Club later sponsored the Suva North and Labasa Clubs in 1971 and Suva East in 1980.

The expansion took Rotary into the heart of the major towns and cities in Fiji, enabling those citizens imbued with the ideal of 'service above self' to make significant contributions to the communities in which they live.

A brief examination of some of the clubs' main projects is evidence of Rotary's contribution to the nation.

The Suva East club staged an annual bed race. This became a highlight for Suva citizens and raised approximately $6,000 annually. The winners travelled overseas to international bed races, with funds distributed to the Red Cross.

The Labasa Club, with its limited membership, embarked on highly ambitious and successful projects. One was the Annual Queen of the North Contest.

The Nadi Club has always been the 'Gateway Club' and has hosted numerous students coming to, or leaving Fiji after participating in Rotary Youth schemes.

The Lautoka Hospital has been one of the main beneficiaries of the Lautoka Club's efforts which, over the years, have given a variety of equipment and furniture to the hospital, including hypodermic needles, a hydrotherapy pool, wheelchairs, a projector and a camera. The Lautoka Club has joined with Labasa and the three Suva clubs in supporting the magnificent interplast project, through which plastic surgeons are brought to Fiji to carry out surgery on hundreds of needy patients, free of charge. Perhaps the Lautoka Club's most worthy project has been the 'Rota Home,' which provides a simple structure for disaster affected people. Funds have come from Fiji and overseas. This is an excellent example of world community service at work within the Pacific.

The Ba Club's proud efforts over the years were recognised by Rotary International's Meritorious Service Award in 1983. This was in acknowledgement of the Ba Club's presentation of a $10,000 X-ray unit to the Ba Methodist Hospital.

It is said that Rotary Clubs should run projects that can be completed within the Rotary year. However, the needs of Fiji are often so great that this is impossible. The Suva North Club recognised this and embarked on an enormous task of completing an $800,000 school for the intellectually handicapped. The Suva North Club runs an annual casino night and supports needy charitable organisations in Suva.

The Sigatoka Club has played host to many visiting Rotarians staying at the Coral Coast hotels, actively supported town council projects, and helped rural schools and families following natural disasters.

The Suva Club's contributions to the nation are far too numerous to list. When the Club began, even radio was a new invention in the islands. The Suva Club's first project was to install a radio receiving system for patients at the Colonial War Memorial Hospital.

There is no doubt that, in all the areas where Rotary Clubs are established, people are better off. Many organisations, such as the Fiji Society for the Blind, the Fiji Crippled Children Society, and so on, might not exist had it not been for Rotary.

17. Religion

Religion has always been a powerful force in the lives of Fiji people.

The early missionaries converted Fijians from cannibalism and for many years the dominant religions were Methodist, Catholic, Church of England and Presbyterian. Then came the Seventh Day Adventists, Assemblies of God and many others. The indentured Indians brought with them the religions of the subcontinent, Hinduism and Islam. During the 20th century, most of the world's other religions found their way to Fiji and won converts.

While all these religious teachings have been of great benefit to the people, undoubtedly the churches' greatest contribution to the development of the nation has been the establishment of schools throughout the islands. They filled a void that could not have been met by any government. Devoted teachers came from many parts of the world to impart their knowledge, and many of the country's leaders openly admit that they owe their success to their church mentors and teachers. Many Catholic brothers, priests and nuns have been elevated to almost sainthood status by their former students. Methodist church leaders have been revered, and to be ordained is to gain a special place in Fijian society.

While there has been little change in the influences and interpretation of Hinduism and Islam by its devotees, other religions have changed. With the waning of European influence, the Church of England and Presbyterian Church membership shrank before they adopted an evangelistic policy and brought Indians and Fijians into the fold. The Catholics and Methodists retained their strength and there was little racial or political bias. Many of the early Methodist Church Presidents came from Australia or New Zealand. Despite the fact that the Church was predominantly Fijian, there was a time when an Indian was appointed President of the Church. But the myth of a racially harmonious church exploded in 1987 when Methodist Church leaders blatantly sided with the Fijian Taukei movement and drew it into the maelstrom of politics. Many Fijians who abhorred the new direction left the church and joined other new denominations, such as the Assembly of God, Latter Day Saints and the Pentecostals.

The physical presence of a church in Fiji was usually marked by its impressive churches. The Catholic Church built some striking edifices in many parts of Fiji during the 19th and 20th centuries and these remain as evidence of the strength of the church. The Methodists built humble wooden churches in villages and towns throughout the islands and these served a more practical purpose as hurricane shelters and communal meeting places. The Muslims and Hindus built traditional mosques and temples. In the latter part of the 20th century the Church of Latter Day Saints constructed the grandest temple of them all, a massive marble structure costing many millions of dollars that is used only on rare ceremonial occasions. Its opulence, in a poor country like Fiji, is a rather obscene extravagance. As if not to be outdone, another new religion, the World Harvest, constructed the largest indoor auditorium in Fiji.

The men and women who preached the word of God have been as diverse as the religions they represent. Jacque and I were married in Suva in 1957 by Bishop Kempthorne. He was a grand old man who had been in office for so long that many thought the church belonged to him. We had to drag him out of semi-retirement to marry us, and halfway through the ceremony we began to think that it wasn't such a good idea. Standing in front of us in the fine regalia of a bishop, the old man looked magnificent, except that he trembled so violently from Parkinson's' disease that I was sure that it was only God who prevented the Holy Book from falling from his hands.

Another bishop I saw a great deal of was the Catholic Bishop Mataca. A man from very humble circumstances, he became the first Fijian Bishop of the Catholic Church. I have no doubt that he was a very devout man who was much respected by his flock. But I think he loved golf as much as God. Whenever time permitted he was out on the course with a group of friends, and he played to a low handicap, winning many tournaments. On a Saturday after the competition he could often be seen in a corner of the club enjoying a beer and playing cards. He personified the attitude of so many priests who, rather than only appearing at church on Sundays, threw themselves into the life of the community; men like Father Kevin Barr, who set up a haven for homeless street boys and a farm where they could learn a trade, and who wrote constantly to the newspapers condemning corruption and waste, and appealing for understanding of the underprivileged. Few people had the courage to take on the establishment like Father Barr.

One of the most charismatic clerics Fiji has known was George Hemming. He came to Fiji as a school teacher, but this did not offer sufficient challenge, so he became a doctor. Even this wasn't enough, so he took his vows as an Anglican priest. He coerced a number of men to help him build one of the most beautiful little churches at Suva Point. (You did not say no to George Hemming.) He conducted services on Sundays in a most refreshing way. There was neither pomp nor ceremony, and his sermons, which he delivered as he walked around the church, focused on sensible practical matters but were always linked to God in some indisputable way. As a doctor, he conducted a practice at a clinic that was set up by a local philanthropist to help the poor. He was so busy that he couldn't afford to have two consulting rooms. There was just one room with a partition halfway down the centre, with his desk at the end of the partition.

Patients sat on each side of the partition and he dealt with them two at a time. His advice was swift and sure and you didn't argue with him. He was tough and often callous, but people loved him.

Of course the church produced many 'saints.' Just outside Suva city is St Christopher's Anglican Orphanage. For many years this has been the home for children of all races and all walks of life. Even when they matured and left to fend for themselves, the orphans always looked back on this place as home and mother to all of them was Sister Clare Messina. A fat, cheery, Tongan lady who never complained and never seemed to get angry, Sister Clare was the epitome of all that is good in people. The home always got what it wanted from the community because people trusted her and knew she would use their donations wisely. She was always so grateful for what people gave that she made them feel good.

The churches generally kept their distance from the affairs of state, until the coup of 1987, when the Methodist Church began to project itself as the church of the indigenous people. Its ministers became very vocal on Fijian interests and some became ministers in an interim government. Reverend Manasa Lasaro was one of these church leaders who became a household name as he vigorously championed the cause of Fijians. While he was severely criticised in some quarters, he ironically played a significant role in helping to get the beleaguered sugar industry started after the coup of 1987. Indian farmers were refusing to cut their cane, so Lasaro brought in gangs of Methodist Fijians from all over Fiji and it was a result of this action that harvesting commenced.

During the first part of the 21st century, Methodist church leaders were so closely involved with politics that the church seemed like an extension of the Qarase Government. Their ministers served in parliament and on various government committees. When Bainimarama came to power, he clamped down hard on any church involvement in politics.

One impact of the 1987 coup was the way grace became a compulsory first item on the agenda of any meeting or gathering of people. In the past, a few words were uttered at the start of a meal, but after the coup, offence could be caused if a person with some church connections was not invited by a presiding person to say a prayer. No matter that it was a Sugar Commission meeting, a sporting function, or a donation by a foreign government to a charitable organisation. A feature of the grace was also its length. It seemed that God's blessing had to be sought for every aspect of life in Fiji. Grace could go on for five to ten minutes.

People have their own rationale for their faith and each individual gains benefit in a personal way. For many, it's a case of going to church because other people do; it's the right thing. For others, there is a deep and abiding belief in God.

The church often brings hope of a better life and for salvation. The Fijian lady who worked for us as a housemaid was once a Methodist. She had few interests outside her work and life in her village just outside Suva. She and her husband had no children. They seemed content, but had no real focus in life until they discovered one of the new churches set up in Fiji. Life was suddenly transformed as they became totally involved in church activities. They went to meetings nearly every evening and all day on Sunday. She organised women's groups and he purchased a keyboard and learned to play it at the services. He gave up drinking and they never read anything but the Bible.

They conscientiously gave ten per cent of their meager earnings to the church each week. They blossomed in many ways and became better, more mature people. Their life took on a real meaning where previously there was a vacuum. I watched this transformation with interest and gained a better appreciation of how the church can improve the quality of lives.

It caused me to re-examine my own attitude to the church of which I professed to be a member, and to the mystery of God. At boarding school in Melbourne, religion had been drummed into me. There was no room to question the validity of a God. But as I grew older, I became more confused. The harsh reality of life made it hard for me to accept the somewhat unnatural teachings of the Bible and the form of church service. Nevertheless, I had to accept the view of the vast majority of humankind that there must be a God of some kind, and the church was part of the structures of God. So while I stopped going to church, I did accept an invitation from the Bishop to help the church by serving as a trustee of the Anglican Diocese of Polynesia. I supposed it was my way of hedging my bets.

The trustees were responsible for protecting and enhancing the value of church assets throughout Fiji. There were many and some were under-utilised. One of our first tasks was to develop a piece of church property by building a block of home units. When completed the units were the most prestigious in Suva and were eagerly sought after by the growing expatriate community.

Another of the church assets was a large tract of unused land on the island of Vanua Levu. The trustees decided to sell this to the people of Kiribati, whose islands were being inundated by rising sea levels. Perhaps, in times to come, many of the people of Kiribati will be living on this land in Fiji.

Throughout every community and district of Fiji where Hindus and Muslims have settled, there are schools that they have established and funded. Their contribution to the education structure is enormous. The same must be said of Catholics and other denominations. Without these religious schools it is difficult to imagine how the children of Fiji could have been educated.

Both my son and daughter won scholarships to top schools in Australia which resulted from their excellent education at Stella Maris.

While it is significant that the motto in the Fiji coat of arms is 'Fear God and Honour the King,' perhaps it would be more appropriate in an educational context if it was 'Thank God and Honour the King.'

Interlude: The Veli—Fiji's Hairy Myth

We began the ascent of Mount Uluiqalau, Fiji's second highest mountain from sea level. The 1,230 metre peak is the apex of the island of Taveuni. From the coast to the top, the climb is a steady 45-degree slope.

For the first 300 metres, we follow a rough horse track that threads its way through a coconut plantation. With little shade from the mop-headed coconut trees, the fierce tropical sun beats down upon us. It is a relief to reach the cool shade beneath the dense foliage of the giant hardwood trees which we encounter over the next 300 metres.

Wood pigeons coo as they flutter in the berry-laden trees, and parrots screech their warning of our passing. The ground is a mat of leaves quite free from shrubs, except for wild strawberries and delicate pink and white orchids.

There are no snakes, dangerous animals or insects in the forests of Taveuni, so we leisurely make our way up the slopes.

The terrain gradually changes as we climb the ridge that leads to the top. The trees become stunted. Streams flow out of deep gorges. Rocks make climbing difficult.

The higher we ascend the cooler it becomes. Clammy clouds shroud us in a chilly cloak. The tree trunks are slimy with moss.

The sounds of birds gives way to the never-ending dripping of water from leaves and our grunts of effort as we haul ourselves up a network of roots that form a ladder over the last 160 metres.

At the summit, we had hoped for a clear day and a glorious panoramic view of the coconut plantations on the distant flats, with the vivid colours of the surrounding reefs and the blue Pacific. We are to be disappointed, for when we struggle on to the foggy peak, visibility is no more than four metres. The binoculars I've carried with me are useless, so I hang them on a steel post marking the top of the island.

Our first task is to make camp for the night. This takes about half an hour to set up on a small relatively flat spot, some 50 metres along the ridge from the summit. We get a fire going before making our way back to the peak.

'Hey, where are my binoculars?' I ask when we reach the marker post. We search the ground and even check in our gear back at camp, but the binoculars have mysteriously disappeared. One of the Fijian guides says quietly, 'Veli.'

'Veli?' I ask.

'The little people,' he says, indicating with his hand a height of about a metre.

'What are you talking about?'

He hesitates. 'Come back to the camp and I'll tell you all about them,' he suggests.

Bursting with curiosity, we hurry back to the camp and huddle around the fire.

'Now, what's all this nonsense?' I ask, somewhat aggressively.

Laisiasa stares at me for a few seconds as if trying to make up his mind what to tell me, no doubt wondering whether I'll believe him. He then speaks earnestly.

'The Velis are very real people. I've seen one. Many old Fijians have seen them.' He hesitates.

'Tell me about them,' I urge.

'I once went out pig hunting,' he begins. 'I spent the night in the bush and just at dawn the dogs with me started to growl. I woke up and saw that the hackles on their backs were standing up straight. They cowered towards me, teeth bared, growling nervously. I peered out into the gloom and there, standing beside a tree, was a small man. He wasn't wearing any clothes and was almost as hairy as a dog, with the hair on his head hanging to his waist, and eyes that glowed like fire. I was very frightened but knew from stories that my father had told me that this person was a Veli. When he saw me move, he turned and ran away, with the dogs after him. But they didn't go far. They were too frightened.'

He tells me many more Veli stories that have been handed down by generations of Fijians and my interest is aroused to the point that I have to find out more about these fascinating 'people.'

When I return home, I ask my father about the mysterious Veli. He is an old-timer, steeped in Fijian folk lore, and readily confirms: 'Oh yes, they exist alright. I once saw one in the garden. He was sitting in the old frangipani tree when I got up early one morning. He dropped down from the tree and scampered away like a monkey, long red hair trailing behind. The thing that struck me was the dreadful stench. Like a dog that had rolled in excreta. Incidentally, it's said that if you catch a Veli, hold on to his hair, for its apparently sacred, and he will grant you any wish if you release him.'

Over the years I've spoken to many Fijians about these little people who are obviously quite harmless, and I am satisfied that some form of dwarf creature existed, and perhaps still exists in the jungles of Fiji. Stories about them abound throughout the islands from Serua to Cakaudrove, Kadavu to Bua.

Interlude: The Veli—Fiji's Hairy Myth

In 1922, B. Brewster wrote in *Hill Tribes of Fiji*:

> There may have been an Aboriginal population when the Melanesians arrived. The natives of my time used to maintain that the forests and waste spaces were still inhabited by a dwarf or pigmy people, visible only to the faithful. Handsome little folk with large fuzzy mops of hair, miniatures of what their own were like until they were cropped in deference to the sanitary requirements of the Wesleyan missionaries. These little sylvan people creatures were called Veli, and took the place of our own fairies. They loved the woods, the open grasslands and the sparkling brooks, and dwell in hollow trees, caves and dugouts. They had their own bananas, kava and other wild plants from which the varieties now in cultivation have been evolved. There is a beautiful fern called the Iri ni Veli, the fan of the fairies, so called from its resemblance to the fronds of the magnificent Prichardia Pacifica, from which are made the Viu or palm fans, one of the insignia of chiefly rank.
>
> A theory has recently been advanced that our own fairies were the survivors of the cavemen and of the aboriginal race which then populated Britain, and our tales of them a dim recollection of the past. It may be too, that the Veli are also a misty memory of the former inhabitants of Viti. There is superstition always latent in the hill country called Luve ni Wai, which rather prettily means 'The Water babies.' It existed in my time, and in the very last letters I received from my old district, I heard that it was still going on.

Another historian, Thomas Williams, writing in 1931 said:

> A very old Fijian, native of Viti Levu, talks to me of these little gods, with as strong a faith in them as a Highlander has in fairies … 'When residing near the Kauvadra, I often hear them sigh,' said the old man, and his face brightened up as he proceeded: 'They would assemble in troops on the tops of the mountains and dance and sing unwarily. They were little. I have often seen them and heard them sing.'

Then the well known naturalist Berthold Seemann, writing in 1862, commented:

> In Kuruduadua's dominion I could hardly turn without hearing of the doings of the Veli, and the greater part of the evening at this place was again devoted to them. My curiosity had already been so much excited that I determined, come what might, to write their natural history in the very localities most frequented by them.

By enquiry and frequent cross-examination, I found the Veli to be a class of spirits in figure approaching to the German gnome, in habits of life the fairy of England. They have been in the country from time immemorial, and live in hollow Kowrie-pines and Kabea-trees.

They are of diminutive size, and rather disproportionately larger about the upper part of their body. Their hair is thick, and prolonged behind in a pigtail. Some have wings, others have not.

Their complexion rather resembles that of the white race rather than the Fijian. They have great and pretty chiefs; are polygamists, and bear names like the Fijians. They also resemble the latter in wearing native cloth or tapa, which however is much finer and whiter than the ordinary sort.

They are friendly disposed and possess no other bad quality than that of stealing iron tools from the native. They sing sweetly, and occasionally gratify the Fijians by giving them a song.

They feed in the fruit of the Tankua (Ptyshosperma) and Boia (Scitaminearum gen.nov), which they term emphatically their cocoa-bit and their plantain: and men imprudent enough to cut these plants have received a sound beating from the enraged Veli.

They drink Kava made, not of the cultivated Macropiper methysticum, but of a pepper growing wild in the woods, and vernacularly called Yaqoyaqona (Macropiper perbelum, Benth.)

The Fijians have no long stories about them, as they have about their gods. All the accounts of the Veli relate to isolated facts—to their abode, their having been seen, heard to sing, caught in a theft and found to beat destroyers of their peculiar trees; but they are so numerous that it is no wonder the Fijians should consider the evidence sufficient to establish their real existence.

Their reference to the spiritual or god-like qualities is interesting as it has been said that Beqa firewalkers' secret was handed down to them by the Veli. I was told that a party of Beqa firewalkers who were travelling overseas some time ago carried their Veli in a large suitcase, which the group's priest insisted must be carried in the passenger cabin of the aircraft. No amount of persuasion could convince him that the case should go with the luggage or indeed be opened.

Up at Monasavu recently, three girls returning home late at night were astounded to see someone bathing under the village water pipe. A closer inspection revealed that the creature under the tap was a Veli.

Interlude: The Veli—Fiji's Hairy Myth

A bulldozer driver in the same area was startled one evening, as he was completing his task at the edge of some dense jungle, to see a little fairy creature watching him from the concealment of the bush.

As recently as last year, a Suva taxi driver abandoned his taxi in reservoir Road when he saw what he thought was a Veli, sitting on the side of the road.

Last year at Tavua, school children chased what they thought was a Veli into a cane field, where he disappeared into a cave.

Fact or imagination? Myth or reality? Who is to say? But the stories persist and the old time Fijians treat them very seriously. One doesn't mock the Veli story. It's as much a part of Fijian folklore as the gnome of Germany and the fairy of Scotland.

18. The Underprivileged

Back in the 1960s, an author from overseas wrote a book called *Where the Poor are Happy*. He recounted life in Fijian villages and tried to show that while the people had very little wealth or material possessions they were, nevertheless, happy.

While this thesis had some merit at the time, the Fijians have since lost much of their innocence as they have been caught up in the complexities of modern life. To live in a small thatched house in a remote village with your own piece of land and have the support of the community for the duration of your life is no longer enough. Urban life offers more, they believe. But that means getting an education, a job and somewhere to live. Happiness and contentment is replaced by greed, ambition and envy, and the spiral into a life of urban poverty or crime begins.

This proposition also ignores the fact that, at the time, over half of the population of Fiji was Indian. While there were wealthy Indians, the vast majority were extremely poor and far from happy. The motivation of most Indian people is to work hard, live a frugal lifestyle and commit as many resources as possible to the education of their children so that they can aspire to a better life.

A third group of people who are generally poor and far from happy are those caught in the cultural chasm, the so-called 'Part-Europeans.' During the colonial period, the rather disparaging term 'half-caste' was used. At that time, they found it to their advantage to align themselves with the Europeans. But after the coup of 1987, some tended to evoke their Fijian parentage.

In reality, there have never been many rich people in Fiji. While my family was generally regarded as wealthy and influential, the fact is we never had much cash in the bank. In the later part of the 20th century, as the economy grew and businesses flourished, a number of Indian families did become very rich, but they were a minority. Senior civil servants and heads of statutory bodies who commanded relatively high salaries acquired assets, so there has been a growing affluent middle class. But there has also been an ever-increasing number of people who are poor and unhappy.

The government has never had enough money to help the poor. Wages never increased much above the cost of living, which constantly rose, and the growth in the economy was never fast enough to absorb the annual influx of school leavers. It was left to a few charitable organisations and churches to help the needy. One of these was the Bayly Trust. J. P. Bayly was Fiji's first philanthropist. He was born in Levuka in 1882 and after spending his early years in the customs department he began buying land for cattle ventures. While he acquired a great deal of wealth, this was partly due to the fact that he never spent anything on himself. He lived an austere life, with boxes for furniture in his humble house. Before he died he set up a medical centre to benefit the poor, to which was added a welfare section, manned by volunteers and supported by business houses. The clinic provided cheap medical services to the poor and the welfare centre gave out food and clothing.

Church organisations played a vital role in helping the poor. Their motives may not have been entirely altruistic, for those they helped often became members of their flock. I had always visualised the Salvation Army as a low-key group of colourless people with brass bands who provided food kitchen and other means of support for the poor. They came to Fiji in the 1970s and quickly dispelled that image. Theirs was a smartly run, efficient organisation that gave all kinds of practical assistance. As the German Consul in Fiji, I operated the Small Scale Projects Scheme, which gave up to $15,000 to projects aimed at improving the quality of life of the less fortunate. I tried to work through organisations and soon realised that the Salvation Army was good to work with. We undertook a number of projects together, including a refuge for homeless mothers, kindergartens, and small farming and business endeavour aimed at giving poor families an income.

One of the Roman Catholic priests for whom I had a great admiration was Father Barr. He operated a home in Suva for homeless street boys. He would take them off the streets and give them food and a bed. He then set up a small training facility to give the boys some basic skills. I was able to help him with this project. He then organised a farm scheme where boys could learn to plant crops, tend pigs and learn basic mechanics. He was a man with a strong social conscience who wrote often to the newspapers, fearlessly criticising those who failed to fulfill their responsibilities to society. He worked with so many NGOs that I often wondered how he had time to attend to his pastoral duties. But I am sure that the work he did for the poor was far worthier than time spent before the altar.

I always had a great respect for the Red Cross, but it wasn't until I became President of the Fiji Red Cross that I came to fully appreciate their vital role in the community. When I took over, I quickly realised that this was a lot more than a humble NGO. It was a moderate-sized organisation that needed to be run like a business. It needed a person with a strong commercial background to serve as director. We accordingly recruited John Scott, an executive with Shell Fiji. John's father, Sir Maurice, was a distinguished lawyer and former Speaker of the House of Representatives. His grandfather, Sir Henry, was also a leading lawyer of his time. John's credentials were impeccable. But he was gay, and some of my board thought that it would be inappropriate to have such a person as head of the Fiji Red Cross. Fortunately, the majority view prevailed and John was to become a dynamic and progressive director. The Red Cross targeted social welfare, poverty alleviation in many forms, and assistance in times of disasters, such as floods and hurricanes. It taught children how to swim, attended sports meetings to help the injured, and gave traditional instructions in first aid.

In May 2000, when George Speight took over parliament and confined the parliamentarians within the complex, John Scott, as head of the Red Cross, became the only person allowed inside to visit and carry mail to the MPs. He was their only link with the outside world and as such was the target of the media and every other person wanting information about conditions inside. John realised that if he was to maintain Speight's confidence and trust and continue to be allowed to go inside, he had to be extremely discreet. To his great credit, and at extreme personal risk and sacrifice, he continued his vital role until the hostages were released. John brought tremendous kudos to the Red Cross and was showered with greatly deserved local and international acclaim.

Tragically, his personal lifestyle was to be his undoing. A year, later John and his partner were brutally murdered at his home.

One of the groups in society that is severely disadvantaged is people with physical or mental disabilities. They would be a lot worse off if it wasn't for one of the most outstanding men who has ever served Fiji. Frank Hilton came to Fiji from Australia in the 1960s. He was a frail, unassuming man with no manifestations of greatness. But as his commitment, dedication, boundless energy and love for the crippled children in Fiji became glaringly apparent, he grew in stature and won the respect of the nation. He has been honoured by the Government of Fiji and by Her Majesty the Queen for the establishment and management of a school for the deaf, a school for the blind, 'a self supporting sheltered workshop,' a physiotherapy department, and a hostel, which bears his name. It was my honour to read his citation when, in the presence of the President of Rotary International, the Governor General, the Prime Minister of Fiji and the Lord Mayor of Suva, he was awarded Rotary's highest honour for his work.

It's not easy running these kinds of operations in a poor country like Fiji. The government can provide few funds and much has to be raised from the community and donor countries. Not everyone likes working with physically handicapped people, so there is a shortage of trained people. Furthermore, there is often a cultural resistance among Fijians and Indians to admitting they have crippled children. Many children are kept confined in homes and not allowed to go to special schools. Even the children themselves often do not admit to having sight or hearing deficiencies. If they sat at the back of the class and couldn't see the blackboard clearly or were a little deaf and didn't hear what the teacher said, they were chastised and sometimes sent home. I became involved with an organisation called Project Heaven, which aimed at testing the hearing and sight of school children. If they were found to have problems they were given glasses or hearing aids. Sometimes all that was needed was to clear the wax out of their ears. Needless to say, Frank Hilton was one of the organisers of this very successful endeavour. We tested and helped over 150,000 children.

During the colonial era, the hospitals in Fiji were called the vale ni mate, which means 'the house of death' in Fijian. Local people only went to hospital when there was nothing more that the traditional healers could do and they were so close to death that the end was inevitable. Hospitals were only found in the main centres and it wasn't until the latter part of the 20th century that the government set up health and nursing centres throughout the islands so that there was widespread medical care available. Even so, there was a great deal of criticism about the quality of treatment and care.

Medical treatment was virtually free. Our house lady, Litia, a Fijian of 40, was once crossing the main road near our home at night and was hit by a car. Her leg was seriously injured and there was some debate as to whether it should be amputated. Fortunately for her, the doctors decided to try and save it, and she was in hospital for over three months. The treatment was a success and she was able to walk out on both legs. It cost her nothing. One of the features of local hospitals is that relatives are allowed to visit and care for patients and even bring food. It may not be good medical policy, but it has the benefit of comfort for the patient and saves on food. I am sure that Litia's family was a big help in seeing her through that ordeal.

There is very little cardiac treatment or plastic surgery done in Fiji. The worst cases have to be sent overseas at great cost, and, if the family can't afford this, the patient dies or remains disfigured for life. Fortunately, the disadvantaged in Fiji have benefitted for many years from the incredibly generous work of volunteer surgeons who visit Fiji from Australia, New Zealand, India and the United States to carry out free treatment. It's not hard to imagine the joy that a destitute family experiences when their child's disfigurement is miraculously repaired for free by some of the world's best doctors, when sight is restored, or when a malfunctioning heart is repaired.

For most of the 1990s, I worked with a group trying to set up a private hospital in Suva. Our aim was to have a facility that was on par with any hospital in Australia or new Zealand. What was required was not only money, but also a link with a reputable private hospital operator overseas. We had many false starts, but finally in 2000 I had the great pleasure, as Chairman of the group, to invite Prime Minister Chaudhry to lay the foundation stone. Our investors were the giant insurance firm of Colonial, the large Fijian investment company

Fijian Holdings, Unit Trust, an investment organisation for the people of Fiji, and Maine Health, the largest operator of private hospitals in Australia. While this facility was not much help to the poor, it did give a choice for those with insurance or funds to get treatment in Fiji.

As the standards of public hospitals deteriorated throughout the 20th century, more and more people turned to traditional healers. Fijians have a bark or leaf or juice for just about any complaint known to man. In a publication, *The Secrets of Fijian Medicine*, 240 medicinal plants are identified. Chinese acupuncture is also widely practiced and there is little doubt about its healing capabilities, though today, with the fear of AIDS, fewer people want to take the risk of contaminated needles.

For most of the 20th century, the aged were cared for by their family. This was natural in a Fijian village communal environment. The old helped out with village chores or in the food gardens till they were too feeble to do anything. Their family fed and housed them till they died. Indian people also had a strong family culture that provided for loving care and attention for the aged. But as economic pressures mounted in the last quarter of the century, the burden of feeding an extra mouth or two often became too great for a family who earned only a few dollars a week. Beggars started to appear on the streets of the towns and cities. A number of old people's homes were established, but they were sad places that were under-resourced and under-staffed.

One of the most positive developments was the establishment of the Fiji National Provident Fund in 1967. Under the scheme, each employee contributed seven cents in the dollar from his pay, while the employer contributed the same. At the age of 55, the employee could retire and either draw out all of the funds or take an annual pension, set at 25 per cent of the sum in the account. In other words, if a person ended his working life with $100,000 in his account, he could take that as a lump sum, or receive an annual pension of $25,000. It was one of the most generous schemes in the world. Indeed, it proved to be too generous and 40 years later it was reviewed and the pension rate reduced to 10 per cent.

One weakness of the fund was that it benefitted only employed people. The self-employed, including farmers and shopkeepers had to provide for their own old age or depend upon their family. Another fault was that, as the fund grew and finding suitable investment opportunities became difficult, the Board decided to make it easier for members to withdraw funds for school fees, housing loans, sickness and other humanitarian reasons. This resulted in member's pension entitlements being depleted. When a member reached the age of 55, he or she had the option of withdrawing all their funds or converting to a pension. Most people decided to take their money and, of course, in a few years it was gone and there was nothing left for old age.

According to reliable data, a great many Fiji people are living below the poverty line. However, most of those do have a reasonable roof over their heads and few are starving to the same extent as millions in other parts of the world.

19. Media: The Voice of the People

The media has always had a tremendous influence on the economic, social and political life of Fiji. Newspapers are, after all, 'the nation talking to itself.'

The age of the media began with the establishment of the *Fiji Times & Herald* in Levuka in 1869 by a man named George Griffiths. The business moved to Suva when it became the capital in 1881, and passed through various owners until it was acquired by Murdoch's News Corporation.

For many years it has been published not only in English but in Hindi and Fijian. It has, by far, the widest circulation and the greatest influence on the people. It courageously tried to remain independent during the various coups and in 2006 suspended publication rather than bow to government censorship. But in 2009 it was up against a greater force and had to accept censors in the newsroom. This was too much for Mr Murdoch and in 2010 he sold his interest to local entrepreneur, Motibhai Patel.

Other newspapers have come and gone and today the only real opposition to the *Fiji Times* is *The Sun*, which is locally owned. Following the 2006 coup, the owners of *The Sun* decided to toe the government line. The government now gives no news reports or advertising to the *Fiji Times*; it all goes to *The Sun*, which has resulted in a significant increase in their circulation. If one wants to know what is going on in government, one needs to read *The Sun*.

While accepting the notion that the newspapers are the nation talking to itself, in Fiji, it has always been radio that has reached out to the greatest number of people in urban areas, rural villages and distant islands. Everyone has a radio. But it wasn't until 1935 that the first government, English language radio station, was set up. Its call sign was ZJV.

In 1985, the first private radio station was established. A young cadet in the Fiji Broadcasting Commission, William Parkinson, decided to buck the system and go it alone. Most people thought he was crazy and would quickly go broke. But he had a dream, and he gathered around him a team of people who made that dream become a reality, and eventually Communications Fiji grew to become a public listed company that dominated the airwaves, broadcasting in three languages and in many different formats.

The other main player in the media business is television. Fiji TV, a public company, went out to viewers in 1994 and had its own way until a private station, Mai TV, was started. In 2010, the Fiji Broadcasting Corporation also moved into television.

The media scene also includes many magazines. Fiji is well served.

When I was growing up on Taveuni in the 1930s, radio was our main contact with the outside world. Not only did it bring us the Australian news but also the BBC news. Sometimes the reception was quite good but usually the static was so appalling that Dad or Mother had to sit with ears glued to the speaker as they strained to separate words from the static. Besides the overseas news, they also listened to the local radio station, ZJV, which broadcast from Suva at certain times of the day. But the radio's most important purpose was to bring us the new of the weather, particularly between the months of October and March. This was hurricane season and it was vital to receive as much forewarning as possible of a 'blow.'

Every Friday night, ZJV broadcast in Fijian and Hindi, and Dad would invite the labour to come and sit on the back lawn where he rigged up a loudspeaker from the radio so that they could listen to the news and other programmes in their own language.

The radio was contained in a varnished cabinet on one corner of our lounge. In front of it was Dad's chair, where he could sit and fiddle with the knobs. A wire ran from its innards to a bayonet switch in the wall, which served as a link to the aerial, which was strung between two 30-foot poles in our back garden. God help anyone who left the aerial switch on when the radio was not in use. We were all sternly warned that if lightning struck while the switch was on, it would blow up the wireless.

We live in a small island nation blessed with natural beauty, remote from many of the pressures of the developed world. But we are not free from the social and economic complexities of race, religion, poverty and limited natural resources. The media is an integral part of our lives. Press, radio and TV keeps us in touch with each other, and with government, commerce and industry. The media is our eyes and ears. In a nation as small as ours, people read the press, listen to the radio, or watch TV with avid interest. The printed word is regarded as sacred. People believe what they read or hear. Often the slightest error or omission is taken very personally by politicians.

In Fiji today we are bombarded with news and entertainment by 18 radio stations broadcasting in various languages, two daily English language newspapers and other newspapers in various languages, countless magazines, local television in various languages, and, if you have a dish, there is international television, radio and press, and, of course, the internet with blogs and social media.

19. Media: The Voice of the People

In all its various manifestations, this is the media. It has a huge impact and power over our daily lives. Without it we would live in an information vacuum. With it we know what is going on in every corner of the world every minute of the day.

The media also has a role in nation building. But if it is to influence public opinion, it must be free of statutory regulations. It must be free to communicate ideas, opinions and information without government restraint. There must be editorial autonomy. The media must be free to criticise the government without fear of being shut down, and without journalists being taken in for questioning.

A primary purpose of a free media in a democratic system is to keep the public informed about government activities. There can be no compromise on this but it often leads to adversarial relationships. There is nothing wrong with that, provided that comment is correct and balanced. It is a characteristic of most governments to manipulate information in order to cast them in the best light. It is up to the media to probe, analyse and fearlessly report on government activities.

So how free and responsible is the media in Fiji? What goes on between the media and the government? Who decides what is news and who interprets it? Is there such a thing as journalist ethics? What rights do the general public have? What is their right to know?

In 1995, I was invited to help set up and chair a Media Council, whose objectives were to promote high journalistic standards, enhance the media's image, safeguard its freedom and independence, uphold freedom of speech and expression, uphold the public's right to be informed accurately and fairly, and promote a code of ethics and practice. Its members represented media organisations as well as the public and the government. It drew up a code of ethics, set up an independent complaints committee and functioned very effectively for over 15 years.

Of course, there are many in the political arena who would like to see a far greater degree of control over the media. There are those who have advocated that penalties be imposed on the media for any breach of the code. This is unheard of in any free democratic society. Naturally, governments would prefer that the media highlight only their achievements and not be critical or negative. That is certainly the type of media that exists in many developing countries where there are authoritarian governments.

The media in Fiji is not perfect. There will always be room for improvement. But the people of Fiji are fortunate to have such a diversity of options from a free press, radio and television. It is a difficult environment in which to operate. Not many media organisations are commercially successful. The last thing they and

I believe the people of Fiji want is for some form of government regulation and control which will make it even more difficult to satisfy public needs. Once any legislation concerning the media is enacted, it is there forever and can be used constructively or abused. The media must regulate itself or be sanctioned by public opinion.

But there is another question. If the media is the watchdog of government, who watches the media? The answer to this dilemma is that the media must regulate itself through a code of practice with enforceable sanctions. If the media does not effectively do this, then it should not be surprised if the government steps in and imposes its own rules and regulations or assumes ownership of the media.

In Fiji's case, it was the Bainimarama government that clamped down on media freedom by imposing censorship and reacting strongly to any negative reporting of government strategies and actions. The Media Council was dissolved. Many senior journalists left Fiji and the quality of the media suffered drastically. People turned to blog sites for their news and many of these were biased and often grossly inaccurate.

Of course the media also has the additional role of educating and entertaining, and in this respect it is fulfilling a useful role. The people of Fiji need free, independent and responsible media. It has a tremendous impact on their lives. But—and this is a big but—with the massive growth of social media and the internet as a source of news, information and communication, how much longer can newspapers and radio remain commercially viable? The lives of more and more people now gravitate around iPods and iPads and other technical devices. It seems inevitable that the age of traditional media will come to an end.

20. Rumblings of Discontent

Together we can prosper and achieve unity. Fiji is home to us all. Here, with compassion, understanding and goodwill, we can live together in happiness.

Ratu Sir Penaia Ganilau

During the first half of the 20th century, Fiji was relatively free of serious crime. There were rare cases of murder or assault. Car theft was unheard of. Breaking and entry was a rare event. Rape was seldom mentioned. Official corruption and white-collar crime just didn't happen. There are some good reasons for this happy state of affairs. The colonial government had very strict ethical standards and these were enforced on the local people. They had strong disciplinary procedures and no hesitation about applying them. The police force was small but very efficient. The chiefly system dominated within Fijian society and maintained order and discipline within the Fijian structure. Indian communities were committed to work and improvement in the quality of their lives. Crime was not a consideration. Fortunately, most people lived in rural areas and the urban population was fully employed and reasonably housed. Another factor was that Fiji remained isolated from the outside world. There was no TV and few cinemas. Radio broadcast only informative programmes. Not many local people travelled overseas or read about crime.

All this began to change in the third quarter of the century. Significantly, it coincided with independence, although it would no doubt have occurred even if Fiji had remained a dominion. Pressures were mounting as the Fijian communal system began to collapse. Respect for their chiefs began to wane and young people drifted into the cities seeking a more glamorous life. They became exposed to Hollywood crime movies. They saw how the more affluent lived and they wanted the same, but didn't have enough money. Jobs were hard to get without proper training. The police force was localised and short of resources. The gap between the rich and the poor widened. People lost trust and respect for leaders in civil society, parliament, business, and the professions. Racism reared its ugly head.

When we lived on Taveuni, nothing was locked up. The doors and windows of our house were left open whenever we went out. Nothing was ever stolen. When I brought my family to live in Suva in 1968, we moved into the exclusive Tamavua area. There was no fence around the compound nor bars on the doors and windows. I thought we would be just as secure. I was wrong. Within two years we had ten burglaries. We lost jewelry, money, cameras and radios and, of course, liquor. Once I caught a young man in the act and grappled with him.

But he was too tough and slippery for me to hold and he got away. On another occasion, much later, we were having dinner with guests and heard someone trying to force one of the doors in our bedroom. Quietly, I crept to the window beside the door, pointed my .22 rifle out of the window and fired a round into the ground. The man got such a fright that he yelled and ran. I fired another round at his heels and think he ran on for a long time. We then got a vicious dog and constructed a 10-foot fence around the compound. Someone poisoned the dog. Later I was forced by the insurance company to put iron bars on all my doors and windows. It was a horrible way to have to live and I later replaced these bars with heavy armour glass.

In the same street as us lived former District Officer Dennis Williams. He retired from the Colonial Service and set himself up as a real estate agent and property developer. The thieves must have taken a particular dislike to Dennis, because he had over 30 break-ins over a 24-month period. At that time he was building one of the first multi-storied office buildings in Suva and he modified it to provide for a penthouse on the 12th floor. When it was finished, he moved into the penthouse and hoped that would be the end of burglaries. He was right, but they occurred in ever increasing numbers elsewhere.

Fijian people are traditionally rural and seaside dwellers. Living in cities and big towns away from the customary communal life style is not natural, and those unemployed youth who left their villages found adjustment difficult. It didn't help that the authorities decided to provide a form of low cost housing that simply copied what was done in urban areas in other parts of the world. They put up high-rise tenements in suburbs instead of utilising the vast areas of unused land on the fringes of the urban areas to build modest homes surrounded by small areas of land that could be cultivated. These low cost urban areas became the breeding ground for crime.

One of the targets of criminals was the small corner store owned by Chinese or Indians. At one time, a buyer could walk into the store, select an item, pay at the counter and leave. But with the rise in shop break-ins, owners had to put up iron grills across the front of the store and the buyer had to stand outside, look in through the grill and identify an item, which the shopkeeper would get for him. Needless to say, thieves found other ways to break into shops.

Going to jail was no real deterrent. In fact, for some, jail meant a place to sleep with food and clothing. One of the ironies of prison life in Fiji was that many of the prison gangs worked outside, clearing land or planting crops. It was a common sight to see a jail warden leading a group of prisoners out to work. He would be holding a wooden baton while ten or 12 prisoners would each have razor sharp cane knives and digging forks. I never heard of a warden being attacked. Often prisoners tried to escape if they wanted to spend some time with their family.

One of the most notorious criminals of the 20th century was Sairusi Nabogibogi. In the 1960s he was convicted of burglary and it was suspected that he had shot the Commissioner Western. The greatest manhunt Fiji has ever known was mounted, but Nabogibogi remained at large for 12 months. The Governor eventually asked Ratu Sir Penaia Ganilau to take charge of the matter. I recorded Ratu Penaia's account of this incident in my biography of him and it says a great deal about the Fijian way of doing things. At Lautoka, Ratu Penaia was met by Apisai Tora, who that said Nabogibogi wanted to see him. Arrangements were made to transport Ratu Penaia to Nabogibogi's hideout in a lorry at the dead of night. At the end of the road, they walked for some time through cane fields and bush before they came to a lonely hut. There in the dark hut, illuminated by a benzene light, sat Nabogibogi. Ratu Penaia said he quickly realised that this was not to be a meeting between a hardened escaped criminal and an officer of government, but between a Fijian and his Chief. Permission was sought to prepare yaqona and present whales tooth. This was done and Ratu Penaia asked why Nabogibogi wanted to see him. Nabogibogi claimed that his trial was unfair and that if the judiciary agreed to a re-trial he would come out of hiding. Ratu Penaia said he could not give such an undertaking, but asked Nabogibogi to go with him so that he would take the matter up with the authorities. Nabogibogi thanked him for the suggestion, but said he would prefer to remain in the bush until he heard what the authorities had to say. They had a meal, drank some more yaqona, and Ratu Penaia returned to Lautoka. It was six months before Nabogibogi was seen again.

The kind of leadership that Ratu Penaia and a number of other chiefs provided ensured stability in Fiji for most of the century. But when they died, chiefly authority began to decline and the influences of the common man became stronger. This was apparent when Dr Bavadra was elected the first non-chief Prime Minister, and when Sitiveni Rabuka mounted his coup and took control of the islands. As leader of the army, Rabuka imposed a different kind of authority and was still able to control the rumblings among Fijians who felt that they were beginning to lose control of Fiji. But the genie was out of the bottle and 12 years later Speight gave it complete freedom.

But it wasn't just the need for political control that had agitated the Fijian genie. It was the fact that the economy, the real wealth, was in the hands of others. Fijians owned most of the land, but they made no money out of it. They believed, quite wrongly, that Indians had become rich on Fijian cane land, and as soon as the cane leases expired they wanted the land back. Most of the successful business enterprises were owned by Indians or expatriate companies. The large tourism plant was owned by foreigners, though it was on Fijian land. There was the threat of roadblocks and demands for payments by tourists going diving on reefs. The hydro plant was on Fijian land and even though Ratu Penaia had negotiated a lease agreement for the catchment area, there were further demands for huge sums of compensation.

Throughout my years in the sugar industry, I had been impressed by the way in which rural Fijians and Indians had lived and worked together in apparent harmony. I felt sure that there was a great depth of good will between them and that they would go on helping each other. But when I saw the brutal way Indian farmers were treated when their leases expired, I realised that I was wrong. The underlying feelings of envy and animosity were more dominant than brotherly love. Tragically, those who tried to force out the Indian farmer triggered the demise of the sugar industry. Production of cane fell dramatically. Indian farmers, feeling insecure, stopped working the land efficiently and refused to agree to changes to the industry that would make it more efficient and able to survive into the 21st century.

The surge of Fijian nationalism that the events of May 2000 triggered had massive implications for the economy. At that stage, Fiji was poised to take significant strides forward. The garment industry was booming, providing thousands of jobs. A number of huge new tourism developments were about to start. Small businesses throughout the country were growing. But overseas investors are fickle people, and at the first hint of instability they re-think their plans. Garment manufacturers moved to China, Thailand or Vietnam. Developers put their plans on hold. As confidence waned, spending ceased and small businesses stuttered to a halt. Aid donors stopped their grants and building contractors closed down. A massive cloud of doom descended upon the islands of Fiji. People of all races, even Fijians, began to re-examine their future. Should they stay in Fiji in the hope that things would get better? Should they apply for visas to Australia, New Zealand, Canada or the United States, and move their families to a safer place with greater opportunity? Should they hedge their bets and keep a foot in both places? Many of my friends and business associates, particularly Indians and Europeans, decided to go.

'Fiji—the way the world should be.' That was the offical tourist slogan of Fiji before May 1987. It wasn't an idle boast, for Fiji is one of nature's loveliest creations and its people appeared to have come up with a political formula that took adequate account of racial diversity. There was peace, progress and harmony. The economy was growing steadily. Inflation was being contained. Unemployment was at acceptable levels. There was a free and outspoken press. The judiciary was quite independent. A rather unique political system was working. Political leaders were respected throughout the world.

Visiting tourists, businessmen, foreign diplomats, and World Bank advisers saw Fiji as one of the few successful third world countries. But there was a dormant malignancy.

Few foreigners would have been aware of the deep rooted frustration and resentment that was simmering in many Fijian hearts, for the Fijian conceals such feelings. Fijians placidly accepted the changes that had taken place in their islands over 150 years, for that was apparently what their chiefs desired. But that didn't mean they were satisfied. For over a century, foreigners, particularly British, Indians and Australians, had provided political, economic and social leadership. These people had imposed their customs and traditions, some of which were deeply offensive to Fijians.

Some foreigners are often brash, pushy and insensitive, and when there was no voice of opposition, they assumed they were doing the right thing. But they failed to take into account the excessive politeness of the Fijian. Fijians have an inherent reluctance to speak out unless invited to, a characteristic that represents a respect for their chiefs.

Although the Fiji formula appeared to be working, for a long time there had been a simmering undercurrent of Fijian resentment and a desire to re-assert Fijian influence. Rabuka gave the Fijians the opportunity to voice their feelings, and reassert themselves.

While many Fijians welcomed this move, opposition politicians and foreign governments voiced their condemnation of the demise of democracy. Fiji was ostracised. The Western world expected, indeed demanded, that Fiji conform to the Western brand of democracy.

Few people really approve of military regimes, yet the world abounds with such governments. The West condemns communism in China but deals with the regime. Islam terrifies most Westerners, yet its people are the most devout. Right thinking people are sad at the treatment of North American Indians, Hawaiians, and Maoris. Yet Fiji is condemned when its indigenous people try to re-assert themselves in their own country and search for a system that will provide adequate safeguards for people of other races.

The orderly and rather simple world of the mid-20th century was rapidly giving way to instability, anarchy, terrorism and immense technological change. While Fiji was once considered remote from the rest of the world, able to dictate its own pace of change and development, that is no longer the case. Today, when Bainimarama blinks, the Secretary General of the United Nations phones him. The people of this little nation are inevitably caught up in the complexities and changes of the modern world. They can no longer steer their own course.

All they can hope to do is fine tune the direction and try to adhere to some fundamental principles, such as the rule of law, independence of the judiciary, and basic human rights and freedoms.

Despite these many pressures, Fijians and Indians share gifts and sympathy at weddings and funerals, chat together in each others' tongue around a bowl of grog and help each other on cane farms. Children of all races learn and play together at school. Indian and Fijian trade union leaders work together to improve the lot of employees. At festivals all races have fun together. One could go on and on. The fundamentals are already in place. They are deeply imbedded in all levels of society, in business, NGOs, government and community organisations.

There are those who will say that unacceptable disparities have arisen between the races; that in trying to keep pace with the globalisation we have lost our way; that in trying to impose Western brands of democracy we have sacrificed traditional values; that Fijians have been in danger of losing control in the land of their ancestors. These claims contain elements of truth.

There is no doubt the coups have done a great deal of damage to our nation.

Many were hurt grievously. A great deal of harm was done to the economy. But we came through it all. In many other parts of the world the kind of trauma we experienced would have destroyed the nation. One reason why we have survived that misery is the enormous reservoir of good will that does exist between people of all races in Fiji. After the 1987 coups, Ratu Mara said, 'the people of Fiji looked at themselves and found that there existed a store of goodwill and basic humanity.'

A question to consider is whether there is indeed a shared vision in Fiji for these diverse cultures. A man for whom I have the greatest respect, the late President Ratu Sir Penaia Ganilau, said, 'Together we can prosper and achieve unity in diversity. Fiji is home to us all. Here with compassion, understanding and goodwill, we can live together in happiness.' I am absolutely certain that the vast majority of people share that belief and that vision.

One of the most divisive issues in Fiji has been that the Fijians have always considered non-Fijians like myself or Indians or Chinese to be vulagis: visitors. For electoral or administrative purposes I have been labeled a 'general,' an 'other,' or 'European.'

One of the boldest actions the Bainimarama government has taken has been to decree that henceforth there will be no ethnic labels, all citizens of Fiji will now be called Fijians.

It is natural for an ethnic group to want to preserve its culture, particularly a race such as the Fijians. There are but a few hundred-thousand in existence.

Fijian culture is extremely rich and old and complex. It has some wonderful characteristics and values. Ratu Sir Penaia Ganilau said, 'It is the bedrock of our being.' It is no less important to humankind than ancient Indian and Chinese cultures.

One can justifiably argue that all cultures must be nurtured and preserved. But there is no reason why various cultures—the ways of life of people living in Fiji—cannot be adapted to suit the times in which we live without causing offence.

We must take account of the different groups of people who want to co-exist and provide an environment that is compatible with their expectations. What we must keep uppermost in our minds is that this generation is responsible to future generations to forge a nation of a united people. If we do not, then we will have failed in our trusteeship role. We need to develop a national ethos, call it a culture if you like, which characterises us as one people living in one nation.

Perhaps we should look to nature for a model. We have plants and trees from many parts of the world growing in our forests and gardens, as well as many native species. They all have their botanic names and individual characteristics. But they all derive the same nutrients from the same soil. They thrive on the same rainfall and temperature range. They live in harmony and give Fiji its own special, natural, exotic character.

It is too early to assess the full implications of the Bainimarama coup and his government's actions. But what he has done is to give himself a space in which reforms can take place. Many of these could not have been implemented during a multi-party type of government. While multi-party democracy is the accepted norm in many parts of the world, it has its disadvantages. Party politics can be a destructive force. It is a costly process in which parties strive to introduce policies that win public favour and ensure re-election at a later date through one-upmanship.

A Bainimarama-type regime has the advantage of identifying changes that need to be made and implementing them without reference to party ideologies or popular opinion. Fortunately, Bainimarama is a benign type of leader and many of the changes that he has introduced needed to be made. These included public service reform, land laws, anti-corruption, and eliminating ethnicity. The list is extensive. We could all see that these changes were needed, but no party in previous governments had the courage to act. The down side is that we, the people, have had no influence in those decisions. Perhaps they could have been done more effectively if there had been a wider input of opinion.

Interlude: Reflections on Coups

On 14th May 1987, I was working in my office when my secretary came in to say something had happened in parliament. It did not take long to discover from the radio that the military had stormed parliament and removed the members of the House. Accurate details were scarce but rumors abounded. Shock turned into dismay as the full implication of this unprecedented assault on our democratic system gripped us and the nation began to fall apart.

It was fortunate that full executive power was assumed by the Governor General, Ratu Sir Penaia Ganilau, who followed a pragmatic path in returning the country to civilian rule. Ratu Penaia, one of the most respected men in the country, became a one-man government. Raised in the chiefly tradition, trained by the British as a civil servant, a rugby player for the national team, soldier and commander of the Fiji battalion in Malaya during the insurrection, politician, Cabinet Minister; Deputy Prime Minister, and then Governor General, Ratu Penaia, more than any other, was responsible for steering the country back from the brink of chaos.

Fiji was also fortunate that coup leader Rabuka was not a power-hungry autocrat. Instead, he was an intelligent, personable man with a keen sense of humour. While ostracised by foreign governments when he first took power, he was to win their support as he began to lead Fiji back to democracy. The patriotism shown by many at that time enabled Fiji to recover.

In May 2000, all hell broke loose in Fiji again. I had been addressing a Rotary Youth Leadership Award seminar at Lautoka. My theme was the changing world in which we live and the adjustments we needed to make in order to keep pace. I ended by stressing how fortunate we were to be living in Fiji in such a free and orderly society, where we were blessed with an unpolluted environment, natural beauty and a mixed population that coexisted in peace and harmony. No one could mistake my patriotism.

As I left the seminar to return to Suva, a colleague told me that there had been a takeover in parliament. I was shocked to my very core and a deep sense of foreboding gripped me, for I sensed that this time round it would be far worse.

Speight's coup was ugly and bloody. He surrounded himself with a dangerous bunch of heavily-armed ignorant thugs. During the two months that he held the democratically elected government hostage in the parliament buildings, he succeeded in bringing Fiji to its knees: politically, socially and economically.

Fiji became an international pariah. Aid and all kinds of assistance were cut off. Sporting contacts were severed. Thousands lost their jobs as businesses closed down and tourism collapsed.

During the height of the riots, looting and burning in Suva, I sat on the balcony of my home, which overlooked beautiful Suva harbor and the city, and watched the flames and smoke billow up into the sky. It was difficult to believe that this madness had erupted in our midst. What was worse was the frustration of watching it all happen, of seeing life as I knew it disintegrate before my eyes, and knowing that I could do nothing about it.

As I looked down on the smoke hanging ominously over the city, I tried to analyse my muddled emotions. My overpowering emotion was anger that a small group of armed men should have the arrogance to proclaim that they knew what was best for our people and our country. They apparently had neither care nor consideration for the disastrous consequences of their actions.

The other dominant emotion was one of sadness. Sadness that the hopes and aspirations of so many people, and a nation collectively, should be shattered so abruptly. Sadness about the fear and suffering that the people of Fiji would have to endure and the terrible hardships that clearly lay ahead. Sadness that law and order had given way to anarchy.

The Pacific blue flag meant a great deal to me. I remembered with poignancy that day in 1970 when it had to be unfurled for the first time in Suva's Albert Park. The hearts of every Fiji citizen had swelled with hope and pride. I recalled that Prime Minister Ratu sir Kamisese Mara reminded us that we were not celebrating the end of British rule but the beginning of self-rule.

The flag has remained a symbol of our freedom and to me it has always represented all that is good about Fiji: the lovely islands of Lau and the Yasawas; the rich delta flats of Nadi and Ba; the lush jungles of Taveuni; the clear air that we breathe; freedom from persecution and the right to vote and speak our minds; the brotherhood of Fijians and Indians, Europeans and Chinese, Rotumans and Melanesians, Muslims and Hindus, Catholics and Protestants; hard work and thrift; freedom of assembly; tolerance, honesty, trust and understanding. That is what the flag means to me. That is what I call being patriotic.

Perhaps our very success had been the cause of our downfall, I thought. Perhaps we had been so concerned with economic growth that we had become insensitive of the rumblings of discontent that had been simmering malignantly in our bowels.

We had allowed the flag to become faded and tattered. No one cared so long as there was money in the bank and time for leisure. Patriotism was something we need not waste time on. We treated Independence Day as a holiday rather than an opportunity to rededicate ourselves to Fiji. People only thought of Fiji collectively when we won the Hong Kong sevens.

Now, it appeared that the malignant growth that we could have treated had erupted into a suppurating sore that was poisoning the whole Fiji body. There was no pride in being a Fiji citizen, only sadness as the fabric of life crumbled and the world mocked us and wrote us off as a basket case.

I was reminded of Ratu Seru Cakobau's statements to Sir Hercules Robinson at the signing of the Deed of Cession at Levuka in 1874. 'What of the future?' he asked rhetorically. 'If things remain as they are, Fiji will become like a piece of driftwood on the sea and picked up by the first passerby.'

My other emotion was therefore fear. Fear at the way we are drifting into a sea of intrigue and turmoil. Anxiety about who would pick up the pieces and put Fiji together.

21. Women: The Real Mother Lode

There is an enormous talent in Fiji that is grossly underutilised: women. Considering the fact that Fijian culture is very male dominated, this is perhaps not surprising. The male is considered to be the protector and provider. Traditional parents are overjoyed to have sons. To have daughters is of concern and is sometimes a stigma. A woman who produces male children considers herself far more secure than one who produces girls. They often feel ashamed.

At least that was the attitude, and may still be in the more isolated rural Fijian villages. But times have changed, particularly for those who have moved to urban areas. To a large extent, the welfare of the urban family now depends on the support and resourcefulness of female members. Though not always in the forefront of decision making, they are influential behind the scenes.

There is much less male dominance in Indian culture where women seem to play a more influential role in decision making and in business.

So why are women not more influential? It is not because of a lack of talent but rather a macho attitude that still dominates in government and business. Very few women are ever appointed to the boards of statutory bodies or higher positions in the civil service. Women are not appointed to the boards of commercial organisations or given executive positions.

Yet, in the professions, they excel. In accounting firms, legal bodies, academia, medicine and teaching, women are at the top. They are the drivers. They also have a very strong presence in activist NGOs.

Two such women are Imrana Jalal and Shamima Ali. I was co-editor of the publication *20th Century Fiji: The People Who Shaped the Nation*, where it was stated, 'Imrana Jalal and Shamima Ali are now virtually synonymous with womens' rights in Fiji. Through their consistent and skillful use of the media over the last 20 years, each woman has contributed profoundly to reshaping the consciousness of the nation about womens' issues. Their organisations have become important resources for women across the spectrum of race, class, religion and generation in Fiji.'

Because Imrana was so outspoken about women's issues during the early years of the Bainimarama government, her life was made very difficult and she was forced to leave Fiji and work overseas. But Shamima, still a powerful activist, has stayed on and plays a dominant role in women's affairs.

Another woman to be included in the above mentioned publication was Taufa Vakatale, who, as a teacher, was the first Fijian principal of Adi Cakobau School, a prestigious Fijian girls' school. But that was only the beginning. She was also the first Fijian woman to be Deputy High Commissioner in an overseas mission; first to be Permanent Secretary; first Fijian woman Cabinet minister; first Deputy Prime Minister, and first Acting Prime Minister. She was a real trailblazer.

An Indian woman who made a significant impact on politics in Fiji was Irene Jai Narayan. She began life as a teacher but switched to politics and, as a member of the National Federation Party, she was the only Indian woman elected to parliament in 1963, 1969, 1972, 1977 and 1982. After the 1987 coup, she joined the Transitional Government of Sitiveni Rabuka, which lasted until 1992, and then served as a Senator till 1999. She was a very dynamic and admired woman.

Another of the strong Fijian women of the 20th century was the wife of the late Prime Minister, Ratu Mara. Adi Lala was in fact a higher chief than her husband. She ruled as the Roko Tui Dreketi. But despite this high chiefly rank, with which she exercised considerable influence, and the fact that she was the Prime Minister's wife, she always conducted herself in a Vakaturaga way, that is to say, with dignity, respect and humility. Despite being a large woman, she had impressive grace and style.

When she died she was succeeded as Roko Tui Dreketi by her sister, Adi Teimumu Kepa, who after the 2014 general elections became the Leader of the Opposition in Parliament.

Though married to a prominent High Court judge, Adi Teimumu was respected in her own right. She became an outspoken critic of the Bainimarama government, and, I am sure, would have been arrested but for her status and the fact that she had right on her side. She became a strong leader for her province and is surely destined for greater things.

Throughout my 30 years in the sugar industry, Fiji's largest employer, no woman was ever appointed to a senior position. They were only secretaries. On the 22,000 cane farms, only men were registered as owners. It was a sad indictment of the attitude of the time. However, there was Mrs Bhanmati Lekhram. Farmers' wives usually took care of the house and the children and helped out on the farm when extra hands were needed. Bhanmati did all these things. But she also ran the farm, as her husband had given her power of attorney to control its affairs. It was not that he was subservient to her. Rather, he recognised that the family affairs were safer in her hands. 'We have the Queen and Mrs Gandhi, why not Mrs Lekhram,' she once said to me. She was a very strong and vivacious person who joked and teased and expressed her opinions without fear. Although she helped out on the farm, she was always well groomed. Being such an extrovert, it was natural that she should stand for parliament (when she was 8 months pregnant, no less) and win. She also served on many sugar industry committees and was a constant thorn in the side of the milling company officials.

Although women were not prominent in executive and management positions, as far as the tourist industry was concerned, they were the face of Fiji. Tourists first met the warm, smiling and polite Fiji women on Air Pacific flights. In the many hotels, women were out front, at reception desks, in dining rooms, caring for children and performing traditional dances. When the tourists went home, they remembered the wonderful women of Fiji.

One of the premium events of the Suva calendar is the Hibiscus Festival, part of which involves choosing a Miss Hibiscus. This is a most sought after crown and it brings the young women of Fiji to the forefront. Those selected often progress rapidly in their chosen careers. The selection is not just about physical beauty, but also about poise, personality and intelligence.

One of the most iconic photographs ever taken in Fiji shows a tiny but supremely confident three-year-old Fijian girl in full traditional dress presenting a bouquet of flowers to a young, smiling Queen Elizabeth at the Suva wharf on a bright sunny day in 1953. Despite the passage of time, this picture has never faded from my memory, nor, I am sure, from the minds of the thousands of others who remember that occasion of Her Majesty's first visit to Fiji.

That little girl was Adi Mei Kainona, eldest daughter of Adi Laisa and one of Fiji's most distinguished Turagas—Ratu Sir Penaia Ganilau, who was Tui Cakau, Governor General, and the first President of Fiji.

Adi Mei was born while Ratu Penaia was serving as District Officer Labasa. But Adi Laisa went to Taveuni for the birth so that Ratu Penaia's people could care for his first born.

Because Ratu Penaia was on regular postings around Fiji, Adi Mei was sent to live with relatives at Navua. This veivakamenemenei custom was not unusual, for it allowed for the pampering of the first born—a means of instilling an independent nature into the child. Indeed, throughout her life Adi Mei was to display a strong and independent spirit.

This was detected early in her life by another of Fiji's great Turagas, Ratu Sir Lala Sukuna, when he took her into his household and tutored her for presentation to the Queen. Adi Mei told me, and I quote her words, 'In all our rehearsals he took the part of the Queen and to me he was no less a personage than a king. He was chief just like Ratu but he had a different aura about him that is hard to explain.'

She never referred to Ratu Penaia as dad or father. To her it was always Ratu.

Ratu Sukuna's influence on her was profound and one aspect of his teaching stayed with her all her life. This was vakakusakusavakamalua: being patient and tolerant. This helped her in all her dealings with rural women, for she had the patience to sit with them and guide them quietly in a right direction, while at the same time listening to their points of view.

Adi Mei went to Adi Cakobau School and then Epsom Grammar School in Auckland.

She had a great respect for the Vanua and the associated protocols. She was a traditional and decisive leader who had a passion for community work and particularly for the welfare of rural Fijian women. She was a stickler for high standards and the quality of the handicrafts that were produced by the rural women.

Adi Mei spent much of her working life at the Fiji Broadcasting Commission for she believed that through the radio she could reach out and touch the hearts of rural women. She attended Committee on the Elimination of Discrimination Against Women meetings in Nairobi and Beijing, and many Associated Country Women of the World gatherings all over the world. She was a fantastic Ambassador for Fiji and Fijian women.

In 1993, I was given the honour and privilege of writing Ratu Sir Penaia's biography. By then, sadly, Adi Laisa had passed on. Ratu Penaia was then the President. One of my main sources of information was Adi Mei. She was Ratu Penaia's constant companion—his confidante. She took Adi Laisa's place at Government House and was a most gracious hostess.

She told me a great deal about Ratu Penaia and his life. When he was serving as Deputy Secretary for Fijian Affairs, he went on a visit to Vatulele and while going ashore in a dinghy at night a huge wave capsized the boat. Ratu Penaia managed to cling to the keel of the boat for some hours before he was washed ashore. That same night, a lady of Cakaudrove gave birth to a son and she was so relieved to know that no misfortune had befallen Ratu Penaia that she gave her son a long Fijian name, which, when translated, means 'The Deputy Secretary for Fijian Affairs swam ashore safely after a wave capsized his boat at Vatulele.' That was the boy's name. I remember Adi Mei laughing her head off when she told me that story.

Adi Mei had three children and was a kind and generous person who always had time for the bubus (grandmothers) and others in need. She was a Marama of high standing, yet one with the common touch. Throughout her life she epitomised the chiefly characteristics of Vakarogorogo.

During the 1960s and 1970s, Lavinia Ah Koy was the Clerk to Parliament. This may not sound like a very important position, but it was equivalent to being the CEO. The Speaker may have been the President, but it was Lavinia who was the real boss. She was a complete authority on all aspects of parliamentary procedure, and even though she was a quietly spoken, extremely polite person, she ruled the parliamentary precincts with a rod of iron. No member of parliament, no matter how large his or her ego, argued with Lavinia. She was the respected public face of parliament.

Within the medical profession, a number of women have made their mark. But it is the nurses who have won the hearts of so many patients. Always gentle, caring and efficient, it is as though nursing is their natural role in life.

One very unusual nurse is Mere Samisoni. After serving in her chosen profession for many years, Mere saw an opportunity in business. Breadmaking was traditionally in the hands of small Chinese bakers, until Mere introduced the Hot Bread Kitchen. She set up bakeries and retail shops all over Fiji making quality bread. The business was a huge success and she became quite a force in commerce. But Mere had greater ambitions. She aimed to be a political leader and was elected to parliament, where she served with distinction. She had very strong views and naturally came into conflict with the Bainimarama Government.

Few women have excelled in sports. Indeed, there have never been many opportunities. Rugby and football are so dominant that women's sports such as basketball, hockey and softball do not attract much attention.

The church is also a male-dominated arena. While the women may do most of the hard work in organising church activities, and their choir singing is outstanding, very few women became preachers, or pastors or leaders in any church denomination.

When the YWCA was set up in Fiji in 1962, one of the founders was Amelia Rokotuivuna, a woman who was destined to significantly change attitudes about women in Fiji. Born in very humble circumstances at the Vatukoula Gold Mines, it did not take her long to make her mark. She became Head Girl at the prestigious Adi Cakobau School, before taking on the role of pioneer feminist. As Executive Director of the YWCA, she brought together like-minded people of all races, and fearlessly addressed women's rights, workers rights and political justice with great passion. Her activities brought her into conflict with political leaders of the time but her moral conviction about the need for change never wavered. She also fought vigorously against nuclear testing in the Pacific and must be given some credit for the cessation of tests.

So, to the question—to what extent do women, the other half of the population, impact on Fiji?

They are without doubt an extremely valuable natural resource. Like a gold mine which has been only partially worked, where the real lode is yet to be exposed. In time, the golden resources of women will be brought to the surface and they will make Fiji a very rich country.

22. Islands

While my fascination with my homeland has always been about its great diversity of people and the pragmatic manner in which they have adapted to the changes that have enveloped the nation over the past 80 years or so, one can't ignore the charm and allure of the many islands where history has been indelibly written.

Not the least of these is the island of Bau. While only 20 acres in extent, it has maintained a central place in Fijian influence and culture since the days of Ratu Seru Cakobau in the 19th century. At that time, four thousand people lived on the island and there were more than 20 high temples. A flotilla of 20 or so huge war-going canoes, 100 feet in length, could be seen around the island. From this tiny speck of land Ratu Seru Cakobau ruled Fiji and with other chiefs he ceded Fiji to Queen Victoria. It is an island situated at the mouth of a river where there is nothing but mangroves. There is little of beauty about it. Yet the Bauan people are immensely proud of their heritage and influence over the affairs of Fiji. I have written elsewhere about one of their greatest sons, Ratu Sir George Cakobau. Many other sons and daughters of the island have risen to prominence in Fiji but, regrettably, since the death of Ratu Sir George, bickering within the family circles have prevented the people of Bau from appointing a successor Vunivalu, that is, paramount Chief of Fiji. Possibly because it is so steeped in history, I have always experienced a powerful feeling of mystique whenever I have been at Bau. I felt uneasy about walking on its sacred soil. There is a dignity and charm about the way people from Bau behave, yet I can't ignore the barbaric rites that were conducted there a mere 150 years ago. In many ways, Bau and its people symbolise the way that the world and Fiji has changed and how difficult it to adjust.

Another tiny, round island, even smaller than Bau, is Nukulau. Located in Laucala Bay, just a few miles off Suva, it was bought by an American in 1846 for 36 pounds. John Brown Williams built a two storey house on the island and became the American Consul. While celebrating American Independence Day on the 4th July in 1849, the house was burnt to the ground when an American fired off a cannon. Its sparks set the house alight. According to Williams, Fijians then looted the house, and his claim for compensation from the Cakobau Government overshadowed the affairs of the nation for the next 20 years. Williams claimed $5,001.38 and a visiting American Naval Commander carried out an investigation and ordered the 'natives' to pay the amount in pigs, guns and fish, and to build him a new house. Commander Boutwll assessed other losses of Americans in Fiji at $43,531. It was Cakobau's inability to pay this sum that eventually led him to invite the British Government to assume dominion over Fiji. It took many more years to reach agreement but finally the islands were ceded to Queen Victoria. The people of Fiji have often speculated on what the islands would be like today if the Americans had gained control.

Nukulau was to be thrust into the limelight again in 1884 after the Indian immigrant ship Syria was wrecked off Naselai Reef. The survivors were transported by the CSR sugar boat, Ratu Epeli, to Nukulau, and this was the Indians' first real contact with Fiji. From there, they and many who followed, for Nukulau became a quarantine depot, dispersed to many parts of the group and helped to build their fortunes and fortunes for Fiji.

Both Fiji and Nukulau gained unwanted international notoriety in 2000 after George Speight mounted his parliamentary coup. When Speight was arrested, the authorities sought a safe place to incarcerate him. It was felt that the jail facilities around Suva were unsuitable as his supporters could easily break in and free him if they so desired. They sought somewhere more isolated and Nukulau, which could be patrolled by the navy and wasaccessible enough to be serviced, was considered the right place for him and his followers. So George Speight and some of his followers had the beautiful island of Nukulau all to themselves, though I have no doubt that the glamour of imprisonment on an island paradise soon wore off. Perhaps he also meditated on the irony of his fate. His coup was aimed at reinstating the absolute paramouncy of the Fijians. Yet, there he was, a prisoner on the island where Indians first landed.

Another island steeped in history is Ovalau, with its town of Levuka. This was Fiji's first capital, though it was hardly a capital to be proud of. In its early years, the town was populated by many dregs of humanity and was a den of iniquity. Yet is was where commerce, industry, government, justice, politics, education and law and order began. Its main attraction then was the deep, sheltered harbor, and for those with an eye for natural beauty, the jagged mountain peaks that stood like sentinels directly above the town. Commerce and government was conducted on the tiny coastal strip while colonial-style houses were built on the hillsides. Many of these houses and stores remain today to remind us of the way that people lived and Levuka has now been listed as a World Heritage Site. Levuka will always be an integral part of Fiji's heritage as it was there that the Deed of Cession was signed. A deed that stated, inter alia, 'That possession of and full sovereignty and dominion over the whole group of islands … known as Fiji … and over the inhabitants thereof … are hereby ceded to … Her said Majesty the Queen of Great Britain and Ireland and her heirs and successors.' Seldom in history has there been such an act of faith and trust by one people in a foreign monarch.

22. Islands

Levuka today is a kind of quaint backwater curiosity where there is clearly a great deal of poverty. It is kept alive by a tuna canning plant and by backpacker tourists who find its laid-back style appealing. But it remains the emotional soul of Fiji.

The Island of Rabi was sold in the early part of the 20th century to Unilever, which is today one of the giant multinational companies. Unilever developed coconuts and copra, as they were one of the world's largest buyers of coconut oil. The island off the northern tip of Vanua Levu is rugged and the hills are covered in verdant forests, as it is the wet zone of Fiji. The coastal strips are rich and fertile.

After the Second World War, the British Government sought a place to relocate the Banaban people of Ocean Island. The British Phosphate Company had been mining phosphate on the island for many years and had laid waste most of the arable land. The Japanese had also occupied it during the war and had all but wiped out the Banabans. They were a dejected and demoralised people and had been persuaded to try living on Rabi. But it was a difficult adjustment for them. They had been used to a dry warm climate on Banaba while Rabi had over 100 inches of rain a year and was comparatively cold in winter. While there was sufficient land to cultivate and the sea around Rabi had abundant fish, it was not their homeland, where their ancestors had lived and died for centuries. The older generation fretted and longed to return and some did go back each year for short spells to re-establish their ownership. However, Banaba could not sustain them and gradually the younger people adjusted to life on their new island and the people became an integral part of Fiji. Yet they retained their culture and their identity and Rabi is always regarded as different to the rest of Fiji.

Only a few miles away from Rabi is the lovely island of Kioa with its idyllic white beaches. This island was sold to the people from Tuvalu, which was part of the former Gilbert and Ellice Group. Like the Banabans, they were moved because their small atoll could not sustain them. They too retained their culture and identity. I recall visiting the island when we were out on a fishing trip. It was soon after the people had settled there in 1950 and little was known about their customs. It was a Saturday and we had planned to anchor off the island for the night. The people received us warmly and invited us to join in a feast and celebration. Exotically prepared food from the sea and root crops were spread out in vast quantities on coconut leaves on the floor. When everyone had eaten, the music and dancing began. Music was made by singing and beating the floor vigorously with hands. The building we were in was an old wooden structure and it shook to its foundations as 100 men and women beat the floor and began leaping around in dance. It was the first time I had witnessed the exuberance of the Tuvalu dance and 50 years later I can still hear the full-throated singing and thumping of feet and hands on that old floor and picture the joy and happiness of the people that evening. Like the Banabans, many of the Tuvalu people have now integrated with their Fijian hosts, but when it comes to election time they were bracketed with Europeans, Chinese and others.

Another island that became off limits for the people of Fiji was Makogai. When Europeans sailed into the Pacific they brought with them many diseases, and isolated communities had little resistance to them. Measles killed off more than a third of the Fijian population in the 19th century. Another common disease was leprosy. It was then thought that the only way to deal with leprosy was complete isolation from the rest of the community. Accordingly, the colonial government set up a leper station on Makogai, an island not far off the old capital of Levuka. Anyone found to have the disease was transported to the island and remained there for life or until they were considered cured. The patients were cared for by Roman Catholic sisters. One of many who gained enormous respect was Sister Mary Agnes. She came to Fiji from France and took charge at Makogai in 1916. She was feared, loved and respected, and ruled the island with a rod of iron. Yet, despite her tough exterior, the patients said she was a devoted 'mother' to every person on the island. She lived there till she died at 85 and was awarded France's highest decoration, the Legion of Honour.

While no unauthorised person was allowed to land on Makogai, I travelled on an inter-island ship that called there many times. My family, with their large herds of cattle, were contracted to supply beef to the community. The inter-island ship that commuted between Taveuni and Suva during the 1940s and 1950s would load our cattle at Taveuni and offload them at the island two days later. While this process was taking place, with the ship lying half a mile off the coast, we would stand on deck and watch the lepers go about their business, fearful that somehow the wind might blow germs out to us. Leprosy then had a horrible image and we dreaded the thought of catching it. My Mother and Father had the very unpleasant experience of discovering that one of our 'house boys' had the disease and he was hastily shipped off to Makogai.

Eventually, new ways were discovered for treating leprosy and the facility was closed. The island was unused for many years until the Agricultural Department took it over and began breeding and raising sheep, which were then not found in Fiji. A distinct breed was developed that was suited to Fiji's climate and conditions. The Department also began cultivating sea clams in the shallow waters around the island and these were distributed to other island communities where clams had been denuded.

My cousins Adrian and Spencer and I were avid fisherman and travelled to many remote islands of Fiji seeking the 'big one' and simply basking in the untouched beauty of tiny atolls and marine life.

East of Taveuni are three little islands aptly called Nukutolu, meaning three sands. We had spent the 22nd November 1963 fishing around the reef and had a good haul of trevally and Spanish mackerel. That evening, we anchored the boat in the lagoon and made camp on the sandy beach. The island was crawling with coconut crabs, those unusual creatures with a single huge claw that is capable of shredding the husk from a coconut and breaking it open so as to eat the flesh. We caught a couple and cooked the big claws, which were full of meat and delicately flavoured with coconut. We sat on the beach with a bottle of whiskey and watched the sun burst into scarlet hues as it descended over the distant hills of Taveuni. It was a glorious evening and we sat on the sand, gently fanned by a cool evening breeze, talking about our day on the sea and how fortunate we were to be living in this corner of paradise. We had a short wave radio which was hung on the branches of a nearby, scrubby tree, and at six pm, we listened to the news. We didn't expect anything startling, as the world seemed to be at relative peace, and we certainly did not expect the announcer to say that President John F. Kennedy had been assassinated in Dallas. Like thousands of other people around the world, the moment of receiving that news has lived with me forever. For us, sitting on a small, deserted tropical island in the mid-Pacific, the thought of such an act of violence was hard to imagine. It was too remote to believe, and the three of us drank a great of whisky that night as we discussed and analysed the ramifications of this dastardly deed.

Another island that I went to only once is the most northern of the Fiji group and is located at the very bottom of a huge oblong lagoon. The only entrance to that lagoon is 20 miles to the west. As you sail through the narrow passage there is no land mass in sight at any point of the compass. You must simply trust the chart that somewhere to the east, between the two great arms of reef, there is a small island where people live. Paradoxically, that island is called Naqelelevu, meaning big soil. It is a very rocky island with hardly enough good soil to sustain a village community. Yet it is home to a few hundred people, many of whom would never leave it, or see a big city, car, supermarket or movie theatre. Theirs is a life that revolved around the pulses of nature and was largely sustained by the resources of the vast, abundant reef. One link to the outside world is the lighthouse on the island, which is the first indication to mariners travelling to Fiji from the north that they had entered Fiji waters.

On the occasion that we visited the island, the people had just had a foreign link of a different kind. The fishing ships of Japan and Korea had just discovered the vast fish resources of the southern Pacific and were making incursions into Fiji and other island groups. Perhaps their charts were outdated or their skippers were simply not up to the task, but from 1960 onwards many fishing ships hit the reefs of Fiji. We found one on the reef not far from the village. Getting to it was rather hazardous. We had to wade across the reef from the lagoon side and counter the seas that were crashing in from the east. The boat itself had been abandoned by its crew, so we had the run of it after we had clambered up is slippery side. It was our first experience of what life would be like on a Japanese fishing vessel, and we were not impressed. The crew's quarters were in the focasle. They were no more than dog boxes with straw to sleep on. There was one pot belly stove at the stern for cooking and absolutely no place to relax. It must have been a case of fish and sleep. The holds were half full of rotten fish and many of the lines and glass balls for keeping the lines on the surfaces were still there. The villagers had done a pretty good job of looting the ship. And why not? If they hadn't taken the stuff the ocean would have claimed it in the course of time.

The closest I have come to a treasure island is Vatu Vara, which lies some 60 miles off the eastern side of Taveuni. We could see its misty 1,000-foot peak from the hills at the back of our plantation. According to legend, an American ship loaded with gold hit the reef around the island en route to Australia in the 19th century, but before it sank into the depths some of the crew managed to remove the gold and hide it on the island. Unfortunately, all but one of the crew died before another ship called, and he never revealed the hiding place. Over the years, a number of Europeans bought the island, obviously to search for the treasure. Strangely, many went mad, perhaps out of frustration, or perhaps they found the loot and didn't know what to do with it. In any event, the island developed a kind of mysterious aura and some said that it was haunted.

My cousins and I called there many times, as it is one of the most beautiful islands one could ever experience. The huge lagoon on the northern and western sides had a rare beauty. Most lagoons, protected by a perimeter of reef, have huge castles of coral growing within them, while at Vatu Vara, the bottom is a carpet of pristine white sand. All that mars its perfection are the hundreds of giant clams that grow peacefully in its bosom. The way into the lagoon is a shallow passage that small boats can enter only at high tide. Facing the lagoon is a tongue of fertile land. The island then rises precipitously to its peak of 1,000 feet. This falls away on the eastern and southern side to deep water. The mountain itself is made of what Fijians call culai rock. Translated into English, this means needle rock. It's as though the island was once below the ocean surface and the peak we now see is a dead wall of coral. Climbing that mountain is extremely treacherous, as one has to crawl over the tangled roots of trees that have miraculously established themselves on that inhospitable face. There is also an abundance of bird life there, the most prolific species being the wood pigeon. Wherever we went to Vatu Vara, we took our .22 rifles and had a feast of this delicacy.

On one trip to the island we took with us the Taveuni doctor, an Englishman who we had befriended. It was on this trip that we came to suspect that maybe the island was haunted. We were anchored in the lagoon after entering at midday. After lunch the four of us went off at different directions to shoot pigeons and a couple of hours later we returned to the boat; everyone but the doctor. We waited till about five pm, and when there was still no sign of him we decided to go and search. We found him at the bottom of the cliff looking as though he had been through a mincing machine. He explained that he had been walking along a plateau about 50 feet above when he had inexplicably lost his footing and tumbled down the cliff. His whole body had been lacerated by the razor sharp rock. His most serious injury was to his left leg where the calf muscle was cut through to the bone. We carried him back to the boat and patched him up as best we could with our medical kit. It was imperative that we get back to his hospital on Taveuni and there was only just enough water in the passage to allow us through. Even so, we hit the reef many times. Throughout the journey home, he tried to fathom what had made him fall but he really had no logical explanation. It became another episode in the mystery of the haunted island.

In 1860, William Hennings, a German from Bremen, arrived in Fiji. He married a niece of King Cakobau and introduced cotton growing to many parts of Lau. He befriended both Cakobau and the High Chief of Lau, Ma'afu, a Tongan who was the main threat to Cakobau's absolute control of Fiji. Hennings more than any other person was responsible for establishing peaceful relations between the two high chiefs and the third most powerful leader, the Tui Cakau. His son, Gustav, was to become one of the leading merchants, establishing branches in many of the islands and cornering the copra, bêche-de-mer, pearl shell and tortoiseshell markets. In the course of their lives, the Hennings acquired a number of islands in Lau, including Naitauba. Many years later it was sold to the Hollywood movie star Raymond Burr, who subsequently sold it to an American religious group.

While it was still owned by the daughter of Gus Hennings, we visited it a number of times, as it was only about a four-hour run from Taveuni and was in the centre of some great fishing grounds. Just south of it is the perfectly round atoll of Mailima, whose outside walls drop sheer into the clearest blue sea it is possible to imagine. It was an absolute joy to dive around that reef and gaze upon the wondrous growths of coral and other marine life. Unfortunately, it was also a haven for sharks. I have never seen so many in one place. They cruised around in packs and we dared not spear fish for we quickly found out that to do so was to send them in a frenzy and invite them to shred the fish from our spears.

The spacious old colonial home on Naitauba was unique for one particular reason. It seemed to me that it had been built around the toilet, which was located in a large room in the centre of the building. To sit on the seat, which itself was in the centre of the room, was like being on a throne. The justification for the toilet's position was that it was sited right over a subterranean stream, albeit a stream that was some 30 feet below. The reader can, I am sure, imagine the curiosity of the person emptying his or her bowels, as they waited to hear how long it took for excrement to hit the water far below.

Koro Island was described thus in the rather quaint prose of the early-20th century:

> Nature has been lavish of her charms here. The domain recalls the primitive ages of the world when the earth was fresh from the creator's hands, and its face unchanged by the utilitarian devices of man. The beach is skirted by a gorgeous fringe of trees, through the centre of which the natives have made a shady walk, extending several miles. The avenue is arched by overhanging boughs, which sometimes leave a narrow strip of blue sky in view, while on one side the dense foliage allows occasional glimpses of the sea rising on the reefs or sparkling in the sunlight, falling in spray upon the broken shore. Ascending a thickly grassed eminence, we gained a prospect of woods, water and mountains which would have moved the most callous to admiration.

On arriving at the island one evening in January 1945, my mother, sister and I were not in the least interested in nature's hand. We were returning to school in Suva after the Christmas holidays and had just completed a very rough passage across the capricious Koro Sea from Taveuni on the small cutter, Tui Valavala. She was one of the many 100-foot inter-island trading ships that carried copra and, if necessary, passengers, from the outer islands to Suva. At the stern was a box-like cabin that served as the bridge and accommodation for the captain and passengers like us. The hold, where the copra was stored, was in the centre, and the ten crew were housed on the focasle. She was powered by a stinking, poorly maintained engine that often broke down, leaving progress to the more reliable, yet faded and patched sails on the single mast. The smell of copra and sweaty bodies was all pervading and to escape it we would climb on top of the cabin where we lashed ourselves safely with ropes. On a fine day it was quite pleasant on the cabin top, but when the seas were breaking over the beam and bows it was miserable, though still better than the smells and cockroaches and other insects below.

One this particular day it had been far too rough for safety on the cabin top so we had spent the time rolling around on the poor excuse for bunks and trying to ignore the odours and insects. No doubt it was just as unpleasant for the crew, or perhaps something else had happened during the voyage, for shortly after we entered the sanctuary of the reef a vicious fight broke out. We had just moved out onto the cabin roof.

22. Islands

At first the fight was confined to the hatch area, but when someone produced a cane knife and started swinging, it spread to the cabin and then the cabin top, where the three of us were huddled together in terror. A body crashed against us and we screamed. I really thought that we were about to be carved up. But the captain emerged from the cabin with a long heavy club. He was a rather timid, middle-aged man who had shown great courtesy to us, but he was suddenly transformed into a raging bull. Swinging his club and yelling at the men he rather surprisingly subdued them. He apologised profusely to my mother as we chugged our way to anchorage just off a village and suggested that we go ashore and have a bath. If we could have found some other way to get to Suva from Koro island we would not have gone back on board the Tui Vala Vala. But we did so, and the rest of the trip was uneventful, through the crew remained sullen.

Due north of Taveuni, encircled by a protective reef, there is a cluster of five islands known as the Ringolds. They are dominated by the islet of Thombia. This is a perfect cone rising out of the sea, except for the fact that its tip and central core have been blown away by an ancient volcano. Inside, there are precipitous jungle-covered walls that descend into a bottomless pit. It is a truly beautiful place that evokes strong images of its explosive birth. On another of the islets is the concrete grave of Apolosi Nawai, a self-styled Fijian prophet who, in the early part of the 20th century, opposed the Europeans control and promised to return all lands to the Fijians and founded the Viti Kabani, an all-Fijian cooperative. He went from village to village collecting subscriptions, winning a huge following and gaining control of the lucrative banana export industry. The colonial government saw Nawai as a serious threat and tried to counter his influence by arresting him for what they claimed was embezzlement. He was jailed for 18 months, but when he got out of jail, the government found that their strategy had backfired. He was treated like a king by the people of central Viti Levu and with this support he proclaimed that he would mint his own money, run the towns and schools, manage ships, industry and wharves, have his own police, magistrates and tax system, and his own flag—a sun, moon and star. It was too much for the government and he was arrested again in 1917 and exiled for seven years to the distant island of Rotuma. By the time he returned, Viti Kabani had collapsed, so he projected himself as the leader of a new church: the Church of the Era. He professed to perform miracles and claimed to hold a document, signed by Queen Victoria, giving him supreme powers over Fiji. The government sent him back to Rotuma for another ten years. By the time he was freed, the Second World War had started and the Japanese were threatening Fiji. It was rumored that he was in contact with the Japanese, so he was shipped off to New Zealand for the duration of the war. After he returned, he was again exiled, this time to the tiny islet in the Ringolds, where he died.

Was he a fraud, or a genuine nationalist who wanted to re-establish Fijian pride and dominance in a place that had been taken over by foreigners? Strangely enough, he once blessed the earth at Nadi and prophesied that people from the far corners of the world would one day come there. This spot is now Nadi International Airport.

I shall never forget my first visit to the island of Wakaya over 50 years ago. The voyage, in an old cutter, had begun in Suva, thence to the old capital of Levuka. When we left Levuka at daylight to make the 15-mile crossing to Wakaya, a howling south easterly was blasting through the narrow channel and an early morning drizzle of rain obscured our destination. But slowly, ever so slowly, the full profile of the island emerged from the mist, rising out of the sea at one end to sheer 200-foot black rocky cliffs at the other. It resembled a giant whale butting its way into the seas. This profile and the misty haze gave it a somewhat sinister appearance.

Suddenly, the rain clouds passed and brilliant sunlight blazed down. The lush greenery of the jungle, the starkness of the cliffs, and the sparkling gold of the beaches came to life. The island's character seemed to change to one of beauty and fascinating allure. I had the eeriest feeling that here was an island with a soul. Indeed, as I came better acquainted with Wakaya, I came to believe that it did have a unique character and a certain mystique.

Perhaps this is because Wakaya has not been allowed to lie sublimely in its lonely Pacific haven. Its peace has been shattered by disputed ownership and violent cannibal battles. It gained international fame when an elusive German raider, Count von Luckner, was captured off its shores during the First World War. For many years it operated as a copra plantation. It has now become a private haven for Hollywood and international celebrities like Tom Cruise and Bill Gates. An American doctor's wife who had searched the world for the right place to build a holiday home told me, 'We have found the most beautiful place on Earth.'

It has rich archaeological remains of Pacific Island cultures dating back to 700 B.C. and many stone fortifications. There is some evidence that it may have been settled by people from Samoa. Many bloody cannibal battles took place on Wakaya, the last recorded one being in 1838 when the Tui Levuka crossed the island with 800 men in 40 war canoes. The Wakaya people had constructed strong fortifications, so a lengthy siege took place. They were eventually forced back towards the high cliffs and, rather than surrender and be clubbed to death and eaten, the men leaped to their deaths onto the black rocks far below. Not far from these cliffs is now a colony of flying foxes. Old Fijians say that the screeching of the creatures are the echoes of the warriors cries as they plunged to their deaths.

22. Islands

The first European sighting of Wakaya was by William Bligh as he passed through Fiji in his open boat during the epic voyage after the mutiny. It was reputed to be one of the first tracts of land sold to a foreigner when it was purchased in 1849 by a sea captain. One of the early owners was the American David Whippy who grew cane and made the first crystallised sugar in Fiji. It is the only island in Fiji where deer roam freely.

When I recently returned to the island I was captivated by the uniquely beautiful homes that were built on many exquisite sites. Yet, as I walked through the silent bush hearing only the call of wood pigeons, the bleat of goats and the scampering retreat of wild deer, I got the impression that nothing had changed. Clambering over the ruins of ancient Fijian villages and forts, picking up pieces of old pottery and stone tools, I felt the ghosts of the ancients still inhabited the gnarled twisted banyan trees that are as old as the ruins.

Someone once described the Pacific Islands thus: 'Pacific Islands are like their women. They are beautiful, warm, alluring. But one can never be sure what is hidden in their bosom.'

I have made no mention of the two main islands, Viti Levu and Vanua Levu, for they are somewhat different. They are more like land masses with their towns and cities and industry and urban problems. Viti Levu has the highest mountain in Fiji, Mount Victoria. I have climbed it twice with my family simply because it is there. The view from the top is unspectacular and disappointing, but there is something satisfying about standing on a nation's highest peak, holding your arms above your head and shouting, 'I made it.' There are other more interesting mountains. One is a plug of rock just outside of Suva known as Joske's Thumb, so named because it looks like a thumb. Long before he conquered Mount Everest, Sir Edmund Hilary tried and failed to reach the summit. But he did come back many years later and scaled its rocky face. Looking down on the Nadi plains is a range known as the Mountains of the Sleeping Giant. Need I say that the range resembles the body of a great giant. In the shadows of the range are some of Fiji's most spectacular gardens. Started by the Hollywood star, Raymond Burr, there is an enchanting collection of orchids and other tropical plants.

Fiji's second highest mountain, Mount Uluiqalau, is on the island of Taveuni. From its lofty peak, on a fine day when it's not shrouded in cloud, there is an uninterrupted view across to the rugged hills of Vanua Levu to the west, north to the beautiful Ringolds, east to the remote islands of Lau, and south to Koro Island and beyond. Looking down on the coconut plantations on the fertile flats and the surrounding lush jungle covered hills, it is easy to understand why Taveuni has always been known as the Garden Island of Fiji.

23. In Search of a Soul

What do we mean when we talk about an ethos, or a soul of a nation? Ethos is defined as 'the distinctive character, spirit and attitudes of people, culture, era.'

Soul is defined as 'the spirit or immaterial part of man, the seal of human personality, intellect, will and emotions.'

Why is it important that we try to identify a soul or ethos? The fact is all nations of people do have a soul or an ethos by which they are identified. It is describing, understanding and living by it that is sometimes difficult. In Australia, any new citizen must first be able to talk about and understand mateship. This does exemplify the Australian character, although Australia is a nation of many diverse people. The British, Scots, Irish and Welsh exemplify particular characteristics which they never lose. Their ethos is their core. The Americans seem to honour their founding fathers and have a very strong belief in their constitution. I can't define it, but I sense the Tongans and Samoans have a soul. France certainly has one. I supposed it would be fair to say that, as far as many of the Muslim countries are concerned, their soul resides in Islamic belief. This brings up the question as to whether belief in God should constitute the soul of a nation. However, in the Western world, God means different things to different people.

So, what about Fiji?

In a national sense I think respected academic, Professor Asesela Ravuvu came close to describing the Fijian soul meaningfully. He said, 'The Fijian term Vanua, has physical, social and cultural dimensions which are interrelated. It does not mean only the land area one is identified with, and the vegetation, animal life and other objects on it, but it also includes the social and cultural system — the people, their traditions and customs, beliefs and values, and the various other institutions established for the sake of achieving harmony, solidarity and prosperity within a particular coastal context. It provides a sense of identity and belonging.'

While I accept that there are many races of people living in Fiji, I believe that the fundamental soul of the nation resides in the nature of the culture of the indigenous people. That is where the search for a soul must begin. But to ascribe Vanua as the appropriate soul or ethos for all diverse people who live in Fiji would be wrong. Many do not own any land.

We must search for another characteristic and I believe one that does or should fit all the people of Fiji is the concept of vakaturaga. Vakaturaga embraces concepts such as respect, humility, love and kindness. It includes someone who listens to others. It embraces tolerance and understanding. It is generally ascribed to a leader and the way he or she leads. It is a concept that transcends all racial and religious divisions.

Could this be the elusive factor we are searching for? Doesn't this fit the definitions stated above? Vakaturaga behaviour also embraces many values, such as justice, dignity, morality, hope, trust and political correctness. It is also a concept that is well understood by most people in Fiji. If we were all to manifest vakaturaga behaviour, we could indeed be an example to the world.

24. Conclusion

Fiji and its people are very special to me. In this book I have tried to capture the beauty and charm of some of the islands. In previous chapters, I have given sketches of its diverse people: Fijian, Indian, Chinese, European, other Pacific islanders, and people of mixed race. One of the unique pleasures of life is walking down the main street of Suva. It's a busy little metropolis with an incredible diversity of people going about their daily business. Yet they always have time to stop and exchange a few words or simply smile and be courteous. What makes it really special is to have a very large lady sail towards you like a square rigger, open her arms, wrap them around you, give you a hug and a kiss and exclaim, 'How lovely to see you,' when you may have seen her only a few days before.

I am not so naive as to believe that everything is perfect in our island home. There is a dark side to all people and much that must be done if we are to fulfill our real potential. But one of the main strengths of Fiji people is willingness to forgive. If a tabua is presented in the proper way, murder, incest or coups can be forgiven. This is surely a rare quality that should be built upon.

I will never forget a photograph that was on the front page of the *Fiji Times* many years ago. Fiji had been ravaged by a devastating hurricane and the Yasawa islands had felt the full brunt of violent winds. The newspaper story reported the effects. The photograph in the centre of the page was of an old man dressed in a sulu and a torn singlet. He was surrounded by the flattened remains of his house, his village and his crops. He had nothing left. Most likely he had no financial resources with which to rebuild, but he was smiling happily at the camera as if he had not a care in the world.

Another image that lingers in my mind is of a group of Fijian children playing happily in a river in the interior of Viti Levu, screeching in delight as I drove my Land Cruiser over the flooded crossing. They were naked, playing simple games, totally unconcerned with events outside their immediate locale. These images characterised the fatalism of the Fijian people and their close attachment to their natural environment.

For me, Fiji is home. I don't mean my house, my shelter, or the place where I live. I mean Fiji where I went fishing as a small boy; where I learnt to ride a horse; where I discovered that I was a man and that my penis had a special purpose. The place where my great grandfather was nearly eaten by cannibals; where my grandmother entertained German seamen; where my father discovered gold and copper; the place where I dug the rich soil of Taveuni and planted crops. The place where I walked in the shade of trees planted by my great grandfather. I mean Fiji where there is such a rich interaction of people with diverse ethnic origins and religions. The place where I can play golf with a Chief Justice or a mechanic; where I can drink yaqona with a cane cutter or a managing director; where I can enjoy the warmth and companionship of a Fijian chief or an Indian lawyer or a Chinese accountant; where a high chief will stop his car and change a tyre for my wife. And yes, a place where coups are staged; where there are inept, greedy politicians; where there are horrible crimes and petty jealousies; where there are extremes of wealth and poverty. I mean Fiji, that group of islands of unparalleled natural beauty. From the rain soaked forests of Taveuni to the dry grassland of western Viti Levu; from the sandy atolls of exquisite loveliness to the coral reefs with their swarms of tiny colourful fish and dangerous predators; from the raging tropical storms to the pastel sunsets that fill the evening sky. This is the place where I have lived all my life; where I was married and discovered sublime love; where my children were born and began their lives. All this, and so much more, is the place I call home.

www.ingramcontent.com/pod-product-compliance
Lightning Source LLC
Chambersburg PA
CBHW060929170426
43192CB00031B/2878